The
Future
of
Energy
Use

Robert Hill, Phil O'Keefe and Colin Snape

First published in 1995 by
Earthscan Publications Limited
120 Pentonville Road, London N1 9JN

A catalogue record for this book is available from the British Library

ISBN: 1 85383 107 7

Typesetting and figures by PCS Mapping & DTP, Newcastle upon Tyne
Printed and bound in Great Britain by
Biddles Limited, Guildford and King's Lynn

Earthscan Publications Limited is an editorially independent subsidary of Kogan Page
Limited and publishes in association with the International Institute for Environment and
Development and the World Wide Fund for Nature.

CONTENTS

PREFACE

Energy debates have somewhat slackened as the real price of oil has declined over the last decade. These debates, however, still inform the global environmental future. Decisions made now for power plant investment will live in the landscape in 2050. Care and consideration are needed in the energy decision making process now to build a more sustainable future. We hope that this volume will contribute to the debate.

We could not have written this book without the support of many people. In particular we wish to acknowledge the continuing interaction with our graduate and undergraduate students at the University of Northumbria at Newcastle, who continue to openly criticise our views of energy planning and energy futures. We have learnt more from them than they have from us.

Special thanks go to three Dutchmen, namely Arjan Hamburger, Peter Lammers and Paul Hassing, who together and individually have established a an international framework for consideration of energy, particularly in developing countries, over the last 15 years. Other institutions with which we work, such as the Beijer Institute – now the Stockholm Environment Institute, the Tellus Institute in the US, and IT Power, have at times relied on this Dutch support. We are particularly grateful to be allowed to use background material that was prepared for the energy policy document of the Dutch Foreign Ministry.

Specific thanks for help in the production of this volume go to Peter Middlebrook and Neil Middleton, without whom it would have taken even longer to complete, and to Gary Haley for the typesetting and producing the figures from our rough sketches. Boas Cuamba was initially responsible for drafting Appendix II. Thanks are also due to the University of Northumbria where it is increasingly understood that research informs teaching as much as teaching informs research.

Robert Hill, Phil O'Keefe and Colin Snape,   Newcastle upon Tyne, December 1994

GLOSSARY OF ACRONYMS AND ABBREVIATIONS

AGR	advanced gas cooled reactor	LPG	liquefied petroleum gas
ALARA	as low as reasonably achievable	NEICs	newly emerging industrial countries
APS	advanced photovoltaic systems	NICs	newly industrialized countries
ASTRA	Centre for Application of Science and Technology to Rural Areas	NNI	noise and number index
		NPV	net present value
BNFL	British Nuclear Fuels Limited	NRPB	National Radiological Protection Board
BNA	Bonneville Power Administration		
CAP	Common Agricultural Policy	OECD	Organisation for Economic Cooperation and Development
CBA	cost–benefit analysis		
CEGB	Central Electricity Generating Board	PPP	polluter pays principle
		PSV	public service vehicle
CFCs	chloroflourocarbons	PV	photovoltaic
CHP	combined heat and power	PWR	pressurized water reactor
COP	coefficient of performance	RBE	relative biological efficiency
CV	contingent valuation	REC	regional electricity company
EFTA	European Free Trade Area	RRR	real rate of return
EIA	environmental impact assessment	SEC	specific energy consumption
ETSU	Energy Technology Support Unit	SI	Systeme Internationale
FAO	Food and Agricultural Organisation	TDR	test discount rate
GDP	gross domestic product	UNCED	United Nations Conference on Environment and Development
GEF	Global Environmental Facility		
GER	gross energy requirement	UNDP	United Nations Development Programme
GHG	greenhouse gas		
GIC	gross inland consumption	UNEP	United Nations Environment Programme
GNP	gross national product		
ICPR	International Committee on Radiation Protection	VOC	volatile organic compound
		VSL	value of a statistical life
IIASA	International Institute of Applied Systems Analysis	WEC	wind energy converter/World energy Conference
IPCC	International Panel on Climate Change	WHO	World Health Organisation
		WTA	willingness to accept
IRR	internal rate of return	WTP	willingness to pay
JET	Joint European Torus		
KWDP	Kenyan Woodfuel Development Programme		

LIST OF ILLUSTRATIONS AND TABLES

FIGURES

TABLES

1

INTRODUCTION

Evidence for our use of energy in the course of development may be seen almost everywhere. In the UK, tracks, scored by bulldozers across remote Scottish mountains, lead to new forests of conifers; six-lane motorways carry traffic across the country; derelict, or newly gentrified, windmills abound and on Orkney, among other places, a new generation of wind machines is being built. Spoil heaps from mines of all kinds, coal, shale oil, lead and tin among them, are witness to the consumption of raw materials. Scrap yards and rubbish tips mark the final destination of much that was produced from them. Crofts and mining villages lie deserted and ruinous, while new designer apartments in Thames warehouses in London illustrate changes in living arrangements.

All this activity depends on energy. In the home energy is needed for warmth and cooking. Outside it, activities from housebuilding to farming, from industrial production to hobbies and sport all call for energy. Each of us can see this simply by looking at our way of life and by trying to imagine it without gas, coal, oil or electricity. We may also see this obvious phenomenon all over the world and in all other cultures, for example, those first Australians still following their ancient ways cook over open fires; Thais powering their gondola-like taxis with V-8 engines; the Inuit now using ski-doos, rifles and outboard motors.

These examples are not of energy use for its own sake, but of its use as a means to many ends. We all want goods and services, the most basic of which are appropriate and adequate food and shelter. For this, sources of heat for cooking, for making utensils and construction materials, and, frequently, for warmth and light, are required. After food and shelter the list of desired goods and services extends almost indefinitely; for example, clothing, health care, education, transport, entertainment, sport and so on. All of these need energy both for the creation of their materials and for their continued employment.

The purpose of this book is to show that energy is vital to the provision of goods and services. It will consider where the sources of energy (fuels) are to be found, the history of their use and the future of their supply. It will look also at the ways in which less fuel can be used in the production of the same level of services and at the consequences, commonly undesirable, of consuming large quantities of various fuels.

ENERGY DEPENDENCY

The way in which we live our lives is largely determined by the energy resources at our personal disposal. Every household in the developed world contains a number of appliances which consume fuels of various sorts. They help to free their owners from time-consuming and routine domestic chores, and allow more time for work, hobbies or other pursuits. We have only to consider the appliances found in our own homes, the uses to which they are put, the fuels that they consume, their power rating and the time that they save compared with carrying out their functions by hand to see the point.

Table 1.1 is an inventory of energy-using appliances which might be found in a typical house with a large garden. Four items in it are probably crucial to living comfortably in such a house.

1   An automatically controlled central heating boiler means that the heating looks after itself and the house is warmed when its inhabitants need it to be. Timing controls and thermostats ensure that this end is achieved as economically as possible.
2   An automatic washing machine will do the washing while the inhabitants get on with the tasks that need supervision (for example, cooking) or relaxing.
3   A power driven lawnmower will be used to keep the garden tidy with a minimum of effort, and a substantial saving of time which can then be used for more pleasurable tasks like growing vegetables and tending flower borders.
4   A car, preferably small and economical, makes it possible to get to work, to visit family and friends, to get to social events at any time of the day or of the year. Public transport may, of course, be available for work but is often limited in the evenings and at weekends.

In addition to these four there are many other items in the table, but they all have one thing in common – they are used either, as in the case of the automatic systems, to replace human supervision and decision, or, as in the case of the powered lawnmower, to increase the speed at which the operator can perform the task at issue. The price to be paid for these conveniences includes not only capital and running costs, but also the depletion of natural resources. Users may also become locked into a lifestyle in which the gadgets play an essential part and from which it would be painful to withdraw.

THE POWER OF MACHINES

A person working steadily can sustain an output of power of about 100 watts, while a horse might manage about 750 watts. Table 1.1 also gives the amount of power supplied to the machines it lists. In all but one or two instances this is greater than that which a person can produce and, in the case of the more powerful appliances, greater than that which a horse can produce. In many cases the fuel costs are quite small, particularly as many of the machines are used only for short periods. Detailed consideration of these values reveals just how much power there is at the command of a modern householder or gardener. For instance, a lawnmower with a small petrol engine has power approximately equivalent to that of a team of four horses. It can mow half an acre of lawn in about three hours at a fuel cost of about 50 pence and its maintenance costs are very low. Similarly the motor which drives the automatic washer exerts more power than is possible by hand, and this allows the wash to be done more quickly. The fuel cost for a typical load of washing is about 5 pence and the maintenance costs for the machine are well below £1 a week.

In both these examples the cost of using machinery is very low, compared with the cost of using human or animal labour, and in the domestic and other environments of the developed world, this is invariably the case. So it is that the trend towards machinery and away from human or animal labour in order to save costs continues. This is as true in industry, agriculture and transport as it is in the home. So far the service sectors of the economy have not been affected to the same extent, but it is not difficult to imagine that much of the routine work in such professions as medicine and the law will, in the near future, be undertaken by computer-based systems. The 'brains' of these machines will need much less power than, say, a lawnmower, but the overall effect of replacing human labour with power derived from fuels will be the same.

Item	Power rating (Watts)	Running costs/hour at 5.5p/kwh
Electric drill	400	2.2
Electric saw	1250	6.9
Paint stripper	1600	8.8
Lawn mower (150 cc)	3000	16.5
Strimmer (20 cc)	500	2.3
Hedge trimmer	250	1.4
Washing machine motor at 700 w water heater at 2.5 kw	total 3200	Depends on programme
Drier	2000	11.0
Car (1000 cc)	37000	204.0
Cooker rings at 2 kw grill at 2 kw oven at 2.9 kw	total 12900	Depends on use
Fridge-freezer	195	1.1
Mixer	110	0.6
Blender-grinder	330	1.8
Kettle	2500	13.8
Electric frying pan	750	4.1
Radio	25	0.1
Yoghurt maker	15	0.1
Iron	1000	5.5
Vacuum cleaner	225	1.2
Sewing machine	75	0.4
Hi-fi	160	0.9
Television	50	0.3
Slide projector	50	0.3
Fan heater	2000	11.0
Radiant electric fire	1000	5.5
Electric blanket	75	0.4
Table lamp	60	0.3
Hair drier	300	1.7
Immersion heater	3000	16.5
Central heating boiler	18000	99.0
For comparison:		
Person working hard	100	
Horse working steadily	750	

Table 1.1 *Some domestic appliances and their power consumption*

ENERGY USE AT DIFFERENT STAGES OF DEVELOPMENT

A brief historical consideration of development shows that as civilizations take on more complex physical forms, their consumption of fuels of various sorts increases. A line of development from the harnessing of fire, through settled agricultural practices, to increasing levels of industrialization involves greater and greater per capita use of fuels. This development also increases the number of people that a particular area of land will support.

Early humans lived in warm climates, and where wild fruits and vegetables would provide sustenance for the year round. It was the least energy intensive of societies in which the minimum daily intake of metabolic energy, about 2000 kilocalories (8.2 MJ), was provided by the food which they gathered.

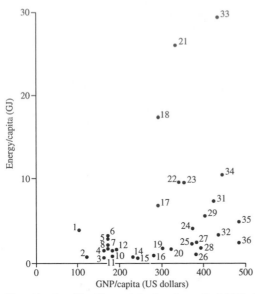

Note: Numbers identify countries (see Appendix I, Table I.1

Source: World Bank, 1990

Figure 1.1 *Energy/capita v GNP/capita for low income economies in 1988*

A million or so years ago the controlled use of fire, and the development of hunting methods allowed a more varied diet and made possible the colonization of less hospitable regions. People still lived off the land, but could now make use of animal products. The use of fire for cooking, heating, lighting and as a focus for social activity, probably entailed a doubling of individual energy use to a daily average of 4000 kilocalories (16.4 MJ).

When semi-settled (slash and burn) and settled agricultural practices were adopted, a greater investment in materials was required in the home and on the farm. By then, as much as three times the daily energy use of the hunter-gatherers was probably entailed, ie 12,000 kilocalories (49.2 MJ). These practices were used in the Middle East around 4000BC, but, in many parts of the world communities are still to be found living in this fashion. But most of the world's peoples developed more advanced agricultural societies where settlement was permanent, where there was a sizeable investment in premises, animals and machinery, and goods were widely traded and transported. Occupations became more specialized, a significant service sector emerged and the use of materials such as metals, glass, spices etc became widespread. The daily per capita

energy use in this way of life, familiar to the Romans and, by AD1500, common throughout Europe and, indeed, still continuing in many countries, was very much higher than that of previous civilizations, reaching about 21,000 kilocalories (88.2 MJ).

In Europe, after many centuries of this development, a rapid transition, largely beginning in the eighteenth century, to an urban, industrial existence took place. Many parts of the world are now experiencing a similar change. This new society is much more energy dependent than its predecessors. Its particular characteristics include city living, better housing, a wider variety of food, and much more transportation of people and goods. In it, daily per capita energy consumption is estimated to be 90,000 kilocalories (378 MJ).

Some parts of the world, for example Europe, USA, Canada, Australia, have now entered a stage of development which differs yet again from early industrial civilizations. Its characteristics include very comfortable housing, personal transport, international air travel, access to a wide variety of goods and services, a high standard of education and health care, a concern for pollution control and a population chiefly working in the service industries. To

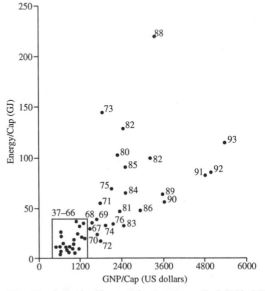

Note: Numbers identify countries (see Appendix I, Table I.1)

Source: World Bank, 1990

Figure 1.2 *Energy/capita v GNP/capita for middle income economies in 1988*

4

maintain this lifestyle a daily per capita energy consumption of 250,000 kilocalories (1 GJ) is needed.

The estimates of early populations and their consumption of energy on which these comments are based are subject to wide error, and, to some extent, are derived from studies of similar societies which exist today. For the more settled farming communities, industrial and post-industrial societies, there are numerous examples available, and, often, fairly reliable historical records.

The next section investigates some of the sources available and discusses some of the information that they give us.

ENERGY AND GROSS NATIONAL PRODUCT (GNP)

The discussion in the previous section suggests a relationship between a particular type of society and its energy consumption. Certainly it seems as if undeveloped economies use less energy than those which are developed. In most cases comparisons of national energy use and GNP broadly bear this out, and it also appears roughly to be the case when the past pattern of energy use and the present economic development of individual countries is considered.

Figures 1.1, 1.2 and 1.3 are derived from data in the World Development Report for 1990 of the World Bank. They show the annual energy consumption per capita against the GNP per capita of 105 of the larger World Bank member countries.

Although there is a very wide scatter in the data points the countries with the largest GNP tend to use the most energy and vice versa. In particular Figure 1.3 shows the very large difference between the low income economies and the high income economies.

It must be emphasized that the energy use and GNP shown relate only to the commodities appearing in official statistics. This means, for instance, that fuel which is not traded, eg cattle dung and foraged wood, is not recorded, nor are goods which are bartered. The records kept by different countries and institutions are not all of equal accuracy, nor are they necessarily recorded in the same way. Both of these points indicate that the diagrams should be used with caution and taken only as illustrating broad trends.

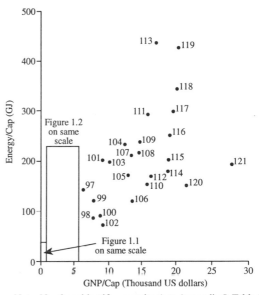

Note: Numbers identify countries (see Appendix I, Table

Source: World Bank, 1990

Figure 1.3 *Energy/capita v GNP/capita for high income economies in 1988*

Figure 1.4 shows the way in which energy use and gross domestic product (GDP) have varied in the UK from 1700 to the present day. The values have been approximately normalized to that for 1800, but again changes in the way the data have been recorded at different times make exact correlation problematical. This graph shows that the relationship between energy use and GDP changes over time. For 50 years from 1830 to 1880 the graph is quite linear, with a steep slope. From 1910 to 1938 it is almost horizontal, from 1938 to 1973 it again rises linearly, but less steeply than in the middle 1800s. Since 1973 it has see-sawed with changing political and economic developments. Again a word of caution is necessary, as lack of detail for the early part of the graph may conceal similar fluctuations. Plotting only the decade and half-decade values for recent years would produce a much smoother graph. This would probably be interpreted as showing that, for the advanced economy of the UK, energy use and GDP were unrelated, with GDP apparently growing steadily while energy use remained constant.

We can extract from the World Bank data some figures for per capita energy use for different countries and these are recorded, with some other data for comparison, in Table 1.2.

5

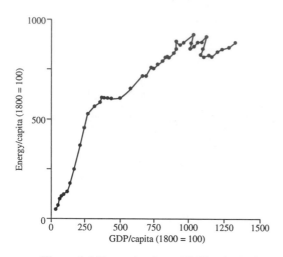

Figure 1.4 *Energy/capita v GDP/capita in the UK, 1700–1988*

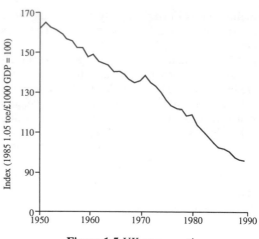

Figure 1.5 *UK energy ratio*

For many countries since about 1975 an increase in GDP has not been accompanied by a pro rata increase in energy consumption. This is a result of more economical energy use by existing processes, and because newer high added value but less energy intensive industries like computers are replacing older industries like iron and steel making. This has sometimes been referred to as a 'post-industrial' society, which is seen as the next stage in development from industrialization. It opens up the possibility of goods, services and acceptable living standards being available at much lower rates of consumption of energy. Some caution is necessary in using this argument, because the heavy industry is now located in other countries like India and Taiwan, and this steel is being imported into more industrially advanced countries. Just as some countries once had 'ghost acreage' overseas from which food was imported, they now have 'ghost heavy industry' from which they import and where they leave pollution.

The average well-fed Westerner eats each day	3 kWh
The average manual worker produces each day	0.5 Kwh
The average Ethiopian uses each year	280 kWh
The average Pakistani uses each year	2800 kWh
The average Briton uses each year	47000 kWh
The average American uses each year	128000 kWh
The average domestic hot water unit in the UK uses each year	2000–5000 kWh
The share of the fuel used in a return flight to Majorca for a couple is	2500 kWh
The average house in the UK uses in space heating each year	4000–15000 kWh
A one-way flight from London to Melbourne for one person consumes in aviation fuel	10000 kWh
The UK consumes each year	2 570 000 000 000 kWh
The UK receives in solar radiation each year	232 500 000 000 000 kWh

Source: After D Oppenheim, 1981

Table 1.2 *Some comparative energy consumption rates, 1988*

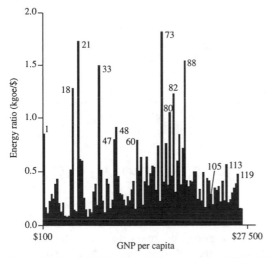

Note: Numbers identify countries (see Appendix I, Table I.1)

Source: World Bank, 1988

Figure 1.6 *Energy ratio of 105 countries in 1988*

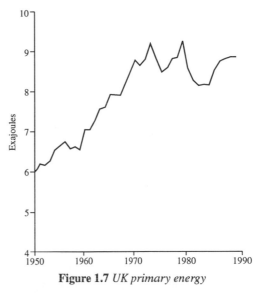

Figure 1.7 *UK primary energy*

The ratio of the energy used to produce a particular amount of GDP, eg MJ/$1000 of GDP, is known as the energy intensity of an economy and is an indication of the efficiency with which energy is used. Figure 1.5 shows how this quantity has steadily fallen for the UK over the last 40 years and Figure 1.6 shows the range of values for different countries revealed by the World Bank figures for 1988. The factors contributing to changes in energy intensity may be short term and reversible or long term and structural. Examples of the former are rapid consumer responses to changes in fuel price (by using alternatives or reducing use); stockpiling when prices are low and using stocks when prices are high; changing fuel priorities and fuel mixes; and temporary substitution of different fuels. The long term structural changes in the developed countries might include the reduction of energy intensity in industrial processes by restructuring industry; the introduction of technical improvements; the permanent change to a different fuel; and the change from manufacturing to services in the industrial base. In the developing countries changes in cooking methods, at present very inefficient, could have a big effect.

Energy use in the UK

The amounts of fuels and the ways in which they have been used can often be traced using national collections of statistics. The completeness, accuracy and amount of detail varies from country to country. Figures 1.7 and 1.8 show the total amount of primary energy used in the UK since 1950, and the different fuels that have been used to provide it at different times. Figure 1.9 shows the amount of energy that has been provided to customers over a similar period. (Note that the total amount of energy supplied to customers is less than the total amount of primary energy used because of losses incurred in the conversion of fuel raw materials to commercial fuels. This will be considered in more detailed later in this chapter.) Energy flow diagrams are often used to summarize data on primary energy supply and its relationship to the final amount of energy supplied to consumers. Energy conversions and the losses they involve are usually included. These diagrams may refer to a small geographical region, eg the north-east, a country, a continent or any other area of interest. They can also cover energy use for different periods of time, although they are typically produced annually. Figure 1.10 shows a simplified energy flow diagram for the UK in 1990.

MEASURING ENERGY AND POWER

Another way in which the ubiquity of energy use may be appreciated is illustrated in Figure 1.11.

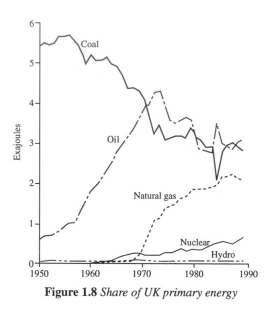

Figure 1.8 *Share of UK primary energy*

All the quantities shown are either measures of energy or measures of power. When a householder buys a 50 kg sack of coal the purchase represents a certain quantity of energy, which will be gradually used to warm the house as the coal is burned. A purchase of a gallon of petrol is again, in effect, a purchase of energy which is used to move the car from home to its destination. The 350 Calories in a 100 g helping of breakfast cereal help provide the energy for the metabolism of the person eating it. Oil wells produce energy supplies at the rate of thousands of barrels a day and coal mines at the rate of a million tonnes or so of coal each year. Electric-ity bills demand payment for so many units a quarter. Chemists measure the number of joules released in chemical reactions and nuclear physicists the number of mega-electron-volts (MeV) necessary to bring two deuterium nuclei close enough to fuse together. Every group, industry or profession appears to have its own individual way of measuring energy.

In most of the world the units used for measuring energy are joules, and those for power, the rate of energy production or use, are watts, but many find it convenient for their own particular purposes to use other units. This variety of units attests to the use of energy in every part of the economy.

The joule and watt are part of the SI (Systéme Internationale) system of units. This internationally agreed system is based on the metre (unit of length), kilogramme (unit of mass), second (unit of time), kelvin (unit of temperature) and ampere (unit of electric current). All other thermal, mechanical and electrical quantities can be described in units which are combinations of this basic set of five. Ways in which other commonly used units of energy and power are related to the joule and watt, together with conversion factors, are set out in Appendix I.

ENERGY'S ROLE IN THE ECONOMY

So far the discussion has been about the progression of societies towards more 'advanced' technological development. Along with this development has been a growth in the population of these societies and, by and large, services have kept pace with population. We know that energy is used in transport, blast furnaces, home heating, tractor fuel and a thousand other individual ways. Is it possible to discern any fundamental reason why energy use is so essential to the economy?

Energy is not used for its own sake. Mention has been made earlier that consumers require goods and services, not energy supplies, and that the use of energy allows the provision of these goods and services. Malcolm Slesser has pointed out that the key to understanding the

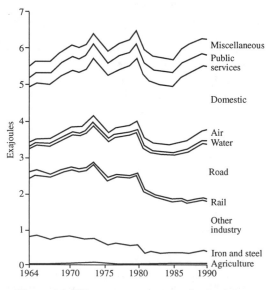

Figure 1.9 *UK energy consumption by final users*

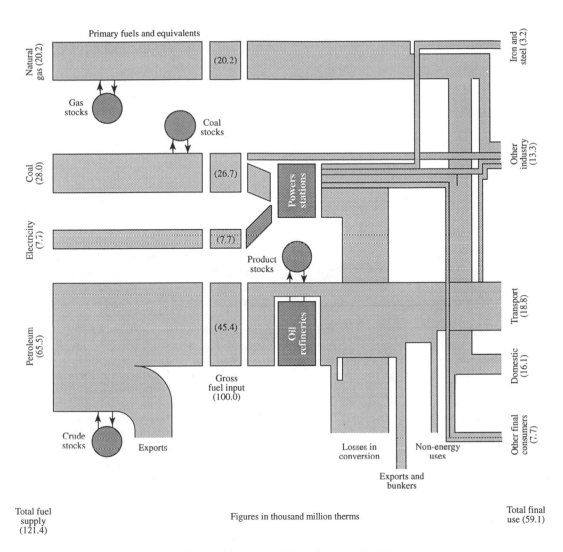

Figure 1.10 *Major UK energy flows in 1989*

dominant role of energy in the economy is that its use allows various substitutions or trade-offs to take place.

Capital–energy substitutions

As larger populations are catered for and as standards of living increase there is an accumulation of capital assets, with more houses, more schools, more hospitals, more cars, more roads, more garden gnomes and so on. These have been provided by the prevailing economic and production system, and have resulted from the conversion of raw materials into the final goods.

This procedure is made possible by using fuels to power the processes of conversion of raw materials to useful materials and to power the machinery used to fashion the final objects from the processed materials. Some of these goods could be provided for a small population using manual methods, but their mass production requires large amounts of energy. We have utilized energy from fossil fuels to increase our capital stock.

Conversely we can also use capital goods to reduce energy use. For example, the one-off investment of energy in the production of insulating materials for buildings can reduce the fuel required to maintain their internal temperatures

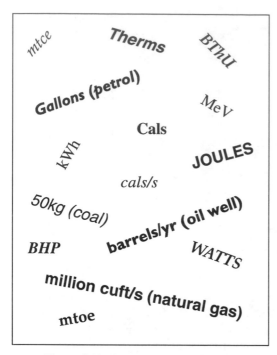

Figure 1.11 *Units of energy and power*

these special requirements and to separate the product from the so far non-reacting constituents. In manufacturing processes increased speed of machining or assembly involves a larger investment in plant and, frequently, in more powerful plant to produce the increased output.

Space–energy substitutions

There are various ways in which space, or land area, and energy are substituted. In agriculture more food may be grown on the same area by increasing inputs of fertilizer and by giving greater attention to the crop (for example, irrigation, pesticides and chemical weed control). All these things use energy.

Large amounts of land can also be taken up in the provision of power supplies. However, a change from the large, fossil fuelled power stations of today to power stations based on sources of renewable energy will call for changes in land use, but not necessarily for more land.

Compared with their more compact counterparts, life in sprawling cities like Los Angeles entails more travel over more roads and more widely distributed services. As populations grow so the amounts of land needed for housing and other services grow too. Agricultural land decreases simply because the same sort of land is preferred for both purposes. All this means that, again, energy use increases.

at satisfactory levels and thus over the lifetime of the insulated building less energy is consumed. Poor insulation is cheaper to provide initially and requires less energy to produce, but in the longer term involves greater expense and higher energy use.

Labour–energy substitutions

One of the most obvious substitutions of energy is of machine work for that of humans and animals. We have discussed this earlier and have seen that machine power is so far in excess of the power of either people or animals that it is now used almost exclusively for tasks once the province of physical labour. Human operators largely act as directors of this power in the form of digger drivers, crane operators, machinists, computer programmers and so on.

Time–energy substitutions

One of the major uses of energy is to ensure that tasks are carried out quickly. This is easily seen in the case of transport. For example, we may compare the time taken to travel 1000 miles by bicycle (perhaps 10 days) with the time taken by a car or train (say 1 day), or with that taken by a fighter plane (1 hour). The quicker the journey, the greater is the expenditure of energy.

However, it is not so obvious that chemical and mechanical manufacturing processes follow the same rule. Chemical reactions proceed most efficiently towards a maximum yield of their products at a very slow pace. If they are to produce a useful yield in a reasonable time they need greater temperatures or pressures, or other special conditions, and the yield is always less than the maximum possible. Energy is used to provide

WHAT IS ENERGY?

In the preceding sections the word 'energy' has been used many times, occasionally with slightly different meanings. In particular, 'energy' and 'fuel' have been used almost synonymously. But what, exactly, is 'energy'?

The concept arose in the nineteenth century from experiments which established that mechanical work and heat are equivalent. It was found that a given amount of work will produce a fixed amount of heat. Reversing this process, to convert heat into mechanical work, is, however, a bit more complicated. One of the most familiar examples of work converted into heat may be seen when two rough surfaces are rubbed together. The work in overcoming the friction between them is manifested as heat.

It was later found possible to incorporate heat generation by electric current and heating by the absorption of the radiation emitted by hot objects into the general scheme of things by proposing that all these processes were examples of changes in a property called energy. This followed from the realization that a closed system has something that remains fixed in quantity when the conditions of the system do not change. If heat or work are put into or removed from a system, it will be left in a different set of conditions. The difference between its initial and final state is said to be a change in its energy. By 'system' is meant a device or process which has well-defined boundaries, for example, an internal combustion engine, an elastic band, a saucepan of food or a planet.

This concept is embodied in the law of conservation of energy, which states that energy may be converted from one form to another (eg from work done against friction to heat or from mechanical energy to electrical energy), but it can neither be created nor destroyed. The possibility of energy changing to a form where it is no longer available for use in performing work is not ruled out, but the energy has not 'disappeared' from the world.

Energy, then, is an abstract idea or concept, not an object, or a fluid, nor anything else which can be isolated and separately identified. The concept was invented to provide a means of unifying the scientific approach to various related phenomena involving work, heat and temperature.

To visualize this concept in a more concrete way it is probably easiest to think of energy as the potential a system has for doing mechanical work. Of course this means that we now have to say what we mean by work and a precise scientific definition is given in Appendix I. To

perform useful work it is necessary to take a process which effects the conversion of energy from one form to another. The process may convert all or some of the initial energy to work.

For example, the potential energy of a large mass of water in an elevated dam can be converted by leading the water to a lower level via a turbine. The kinetic energy of the moving stream turns the turbine and this mechanical energy (of rotation) can be used to perform work. Or again, the aerobic conversion of foodstuffs in metabolic processes allows muscles to contract or relax, so allowing a person to run for long periods at a steady rate. At the end of each of these processes, and all others, when the work has been done the eventual outcome is that heat has been dissipated into the atmosphere. That is to say that real processes are not completely reversible.

All the substitutions above involve the performance of work, indeed the whole relevance of the use of fossil, and other fuels and machinery such as wind and water mills, is that they allow the performance of work to counteract other shortages of one sort or another.

There is one further point to consider, which is that not all sources that can deliver work are of equal usefulness. Some, perhaps most, of our requirements involve only very small departures from normal conditions, eg to keep warm we need only to raise the temperature of our homes by a few °C. Others, for example, motor car engines or steel production, call for high temperatures at some point to achieve the desired result. There are many ways of providing small temperature increases, but comparatively few sources for high temperature heat. The latter are known as sources of energy of high quality and include the fossil fuels.

THE LAWS OF
THERMODYNAMICS

There are two scientific laws which are fundamental to the consideration of any processes involving energy. These are the first and second laws of thermodynamics. Both are empirical, and are based on experiments which measure common variables such as pressure, temperature, length and voltage; they do not rely on making any assumptions about the way in which the world works and this is their strength. It is also the reason why scientists are confident that the laws will not be jettisoned in the future in favour of some newer ideas.

The first law of thermodynamics

The first law of thermodynamics is also known as the law of conservation of energy. When it is stated in terms of the conservation of energy some deductions can be made from it, but very few.

For example, it follows straightforwardly that it is impossible to devise perpetual motion machines, because if the machine's motion is to go on for ever none of its original kinetic energy must be dissipated. However, some heat will always be produced by friction between the components of the machine and lost from it. This will reduce its energy of motion, which, in turn, will cause it to slow down and eventually to stop.

Stating the first law in this broad way is not very helpful when a wider range of applications is being considered. Restricted formulations are often more useful and are frequently called 'operational' definitions, because they are stated in such a way as to allow experiments to be constructed and deductions to be drawn. Comparison of the results of the experiments with those deduced from the law allows the law to be tested. If the results from a variety of experiments and applications agree with the inferences made using the law, confidence is increased in the law's relevance and universal applicability.

The most common operational definition of the first law may be expressed in words as 'When heat energy is added to a system, the energy appears either as increased internal energy or as external work done by the system' or in mathematical symbols as:

$$dQ = dU + dW,$$

where dU is the change in internal energy of the system when an amount of heat, dQ, is added to it and an amount of work, dW, is done by the system.

The second of these two statements is just a mathematical formulation of the first. A system's internal energy resides in the potential and kinetic energy of its atoms, and the system's temperature provides a measure of it.

(NB If the system under consideration is very large, the whole earth for example, the quantity dW is usually very small compared with dQ and dU. In this case, changes in the heat content are the same as changes in the internal energy, and if we imagine that under some particular conditions the heat content of the system (technically known as its enthalpy) has a reference value, we can talk either of changes in heat content, or of changes in energy, from this reference state, the quantities involved being equivalent. In general conversation, the tendency is to refer to the energy of a system, when, more correctly, its heat content or internal energy is meant. We shall do the same, bearing in mind the above qualification.)

Using the first law the efficiency of an energy transformation or conversion system can be defined as

Efficiency $= (W/Q) \times 100$ per cent

where W is the work (or energy) provided by the system and Q is the energy supplied to the system.

For example, if, of the 90 therms of energy supplied to a gas boiler, only 70 therms eventually appears as heat in the water to be circulated to the radiators the boiler is $(70/90) \times 100 = 78$ per cent efficient.

The second law of thermodynamics

The first law does not specify a direction in which energy changes happen, but it is the common observation that some processes have a directional property, for example that heat flows from hot objects to cold ones and not vice versa. The second law of thermodynamics addresses these processes.

It is also a matter of our experience that some material changes have a natural direction, eg the sugar in our tea dissolves and spreads throughout the liquid rather than the sugar in sweet tea spontaneously crystallizing in the bottom of the cup; and iron rusts, rather than rust becoming pure iron. Neither of the 'unnatural' effects necessarily offends against the first law and a realization that it did not tell the complete story led to the introduction of the second law. The second law of thermodynamics qualifies the first law to restrict its application to the sort of changes which do occur in nature.

There are various statements of this law which refer to specific applications. The following two are probably the most useful.

1   'It is not possible to produce a machine which can convert all of a given amount of heat into useful work'. One important consequence of this is that heat engines, eg internal combustion engines or turbines, must produce waste heat, which means that they have a limiting efficiency which is less than 100 per cent.
2   'All processes go in the direction which increases the amount of disorder, or chaos, in the universe'. For instance, iron rusts, rock becomes sand and so on. It is possible to produce iron from widely dispersed iron ore, but this involves large amounts of energy and if the whole process of mining of ore, extraction, refining and of fuel production is taken into account the overall result is an increase in disorder. Disorder may be quantified and entropy gives a measure of it.

Engines and refrigerators

To see what effects the second law might have, we can consider the efficiencies of two ideal machines, a heat engine and a heat pump (or refrigerator). Idealized, simplified versions of these machines are set out in Figure 1.12.

Engines

For the heat engine, which in practice might be an internal combustion engine, or a gas or steam

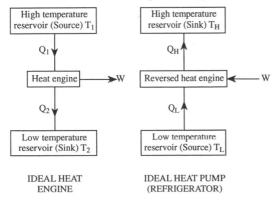

| IDEAL HEAT ENGINE | IDEAL HEAT PUMP (REFRIGERATOR) |

Figure 1.12 *Idealized heat engines*

turbine, we are interested in how much of the heat energy that it absorbs from the high temperature reservoir can be delivered as external work. In a power station this would involve considering how much of the energy released when the coal is burned is eventually available as electrical energy. If the work delivered is W and the heat absorbed from its high temperature source is Q_1 then the efficiency is W/Q_1. In one cycle of operation of the engine Q_1 units of heat are absorbed from the high temperature reservoir, Q_2 units rejected to the low temperature reservoir and W units of work are carried out.

The second law tells us that it is inevitable that some heat is rejected in this way, but the first law allows us to write down the energy balance for the process which is:

$$W = Q_1 - Q_2$$

Therefore,

$$\text{Efficiency} = W/Q_1 = (Q_1 - Q_2)/Q_1 = 1 - Q_2/Q_1$$

and if the absolute temperatures of the high and low temperature reservoirs are T_1 and T_2 respectively this becomes:

$$\text{Efficiency} = 1 - T_2/T_1,$$

because the heat flows are proportional to the absolute temperatures. Expressed as a percentage:

$$\text{Efficiency} = (1 - T_2/T_1) \times 100 \text{ per cent.}$$

A more extensive theoretical investigation would demonstrate that Q and T are related as stated, and that the expression obtained for efficiency is the maximum theoretical efficiency that such an engine can attain. It is usually referred to as the efficiency of a Carnot engine (the name given to this idealized perfect engine) or the Carnot efficiency. A real engine working between the same temperatures would not be able to achieve this level of efficiency because of practical constraints, for example, energy losses due to friction between moving parts, temperature differences within the engine, imperfect heat transfer and so on.

As an example of the implication of this limiting efficiency on the output of electrical power stations, we can apply it to an advanced gas-cooled reactor (AGR). The temperature of the carbon dioxide cooling gas leaving the core of an AGR nuclear reactor is 634°C. This is used to produce high temperature steam for the turbine of the generator. The temperature of the steam leaving the turbines is cooled to 100°C by water circulated through the cooling towers. Its maximum possible efficiency is the Carnot efficiency, ie:

$(1 - 273 + 100/273 + 634) \times 100$ per cent

$= (1 - 373/907) \times 100$ per cent

$= (1 - 0.41) \times 100$ per cent

$= 59$ per cent

If the station can achieve 60 per cent of the Carnot efficiency, its actual efficiency is 60 per cent of 59 per cent which is 35 per cent.

Refrigerators

The action of a refrigerator is the reverse of that of an engine. Its purpose is to use external work to extract heat from a low temperature reservoir and reject it to a high temperature sink, it is therefore moving heat up from a lower to a higher temperature and for this reason is often known as a heat pump. The first law again allows us to write down the energy balance for this process, which is:

$Q_H = W + Q_L$

(see Figure 1.12).

The amount of heat delivered at the higher temperature is obviously greater than the work supplied and the ratio (Q_H/W) is known as the coefficient of performance of the system when it acts as a heat pump, ie when we are interested in using it to provide heat. However, if we are interested in the way the system performs in cooling a low temperature source the coefficient of performance will be (Q_L/W), because the amount of heat extracted for a given amount of work done by the engine is what will determine running costs. These two coefficients may be written as follows.

Coefficient of performance of the heat pump

$(COP) = Q_H/W$

$= Q_H/(Q_H - Q_L)$

$= T_H/(T_H - T_L)$

Heat pumps have considerable potential for providing heating. They offer the possibility of removing heat from the outdoors and using the heat extracted to warm the indoors. The amount of heat deposited indoors will be larger by three or four times (for a COP of three or four) than the amount of gas or electricity bought from the supply company. At present heat pumps are more expensive than conventional heating appliances.

Coefficient of performance of the refrigerator

$(COP) = Q_L/W$

$= Q_L/(Q_H - Q_L)$

$= T_L/(T_H - T_L)$

If the temperature inside a refrigerator is 2°C when the room temperature is 20°C, its Carnot COP is:

$= T_L/(T_H - T_L) = 275/(295 - 275)$

$= 275/20 = 13.8.$

And if the refrigerator can achieve can efficiency of 50 per cent of this, its actual COP is $0.5 \times 13.8 = 6.9$. This means that 6.9 joules can be transferred from the refrigerator cabinet to the room for every joule of electrical energy supplied to the refrigerator from the mains.

SUPPLY, DEMAND AND END-USE: TRENDS AND DEVELOPMENTS

In addition to the technical assessment of energy resources no introduction would be complete without an overview of the changing make-up of energy supply, demand and end-use for the UK, Europe and the world. This section will highlight the major variations over the last 20 years, as well as providing one possible short term energy outlook.

The debate over energy futures has become a central theme in resource management, embracing socio-economic, political and environmental concerns. Energy is a foundation stone of the modern industrial economy, as well as a 'basic need' in subsistence economies. For this reason, an understanding of its supply, demand and end-use is important for energy planning. The patterns of energy flow in any economy broadly reflect the flow of energy from production to consumption, from primary productivity and imports through to end-use. Tracing these energy flows allows the calculation of energy need for everything from individual households up to the whole world. Present debates concerned with energy futures reflect a change in analysis from supply to demand side with an emphasis on end-use.

The debate over energy futures has recently been widened to include, of course, environmental futures, particularly the impact of global warming.

The UK

A look at the history of UK energy supplies shows that resource exploitation is dependent on technical development. The availability of coal in the 1700s, and oil in the 1970s, was directly linked to developments in extraction and process technology, as well as to improvements in surveying. The availability of specific fuel mixes at different historical stages once again determined the development options open to society. For example, the oil price crisis of the 1970s provided impetus for research and development into renewable energy resources that would lessen import dependence, just as perhaps today the need for reductions in CO_2 levels are influencing governmental decisions on solid fuel generation. Energy supply and consumption is therefore bound up with the political economy of technological development.

Coal production in the UK achieved its peak in 1913 and has been steadily declining ever since. Output from the UK is almost entirely of deep mined coal. Its higher costs have left the industry open to competition from open-cast production and from imports. The decision by British Coal in 1992 to close down a number of less profitable mines was not the result of market forces but of the privatization of the electricity sector by the British government. This privatization had many consequences – including the continued subsidy of nuclear generation – but its single largest impact was to destroy the basis of UK deep mining capacity and simultaneously, the coal field communities.

That this outcome was directly a consequence of a British government determined to destroy the National Union of Mineworkers is, perhaps, open to argument; that energy issues are essentially political issues is not debatable.

While small amounts of oil were produced on shore in the UK, from the late 1930s, it was not until the late 1960s that production of offshore oil was established. In 1989, the UK was eighth in world oil production with 91.1 million tonnes per annum. It is expected that production from the UK continental shelf in the North Sea will fall to between 40–70 million tonnes by 2000. It was estimated, in 1989, by the Department of Energy that 'proven reserves were 510 million tonnes' (Department of Energy, 1990). Natural gas was discovered in the southern sector of the North Sea in 1965, the West Sole field and began to come onshore in 1967. Annual UK consumption is around 50 x 10^9 m^3. Proven reserves are put at 560 x 10^9 m^3 (Department of Energy, 1990). Indeed, proven reserve estimates are not just physical estimates but also take into account the technology available for extraction. In turn, this implies some recognition of resource price, although proven reserve estimates pretend to be only physical estimates. Energy extraction, however, is always about price.

In the UK, electricity is generated mainly by conventional coal power stations, with small contributions from nuclear and hydro-electric generation. However, gas-turbine generation is also increasingly important in the post-privatized generation mix.

Table 1.3 provides a breakdown of (UK) final energy consumption. The annual percentage change, for 1991, shows that final energy consumption rose by 3.3 per cent as opposed to the 1986–91 average of 1.4 per cent. This 1991 increase in final energy consumption has to be seen against an average annual GDP increase of 2 per cent, as well as an energy intensity reduction of 1.1 per cent per year.

Industrial energy consumption remained static between 1986 and 1991 while the 1991/90 industrial average showed a decrease in energy consumption in all fuels with the exception of oil. An increase of 11.9 per cent in electricity used in the transport sector between 1986 and 1991 represented the largest percentage increase for electricity – a direct consequence of rail

Table 1.3 *UK final energy consumption (Mtoe)*

	1986	1987	1988	1989	1990	1991	91/86 Annual	91/90 % Change
Industry	32.57	33.79	35.14	34.85	34.00	33.56	0.6	(1.3)
Solids	7.17	7.06	7.61	6.74	6.86	6.47	(2.0)	(5.3)
Oil	7.45	6.61	7.44	7.62	6.89	7.50	0.1	8.9
Gas	10.32	12.11	11.29	11.50	11.15	10.60	0.5	(4.9)
Electricity	7.63	8.01	8.36	8.55	8.65	8.56	2.3	(1.1)
Heat	0.00	0.00	0.44	0.44	0.45	0.43	0.0	(2.7)
Transport	37.17	39.20	41.66	44.34	45.45	44.70	3.8	(1.7)
Solids	0.00	0.00	0.00	0.00	0.00	0.00		
Oil	36.91	36.93	41.38	44.06	45.00	44.24	3.7	(1.7)
Gas	0.00	0.00	0.00	0.00	0.00	0.00		
Electricity	0.26	0.25	0.28	0.27	0.45	0.45	11.9	(0.2)
Other	60.98	60.07	59.05	56.92	56.44	62.13	0.4	10.1
Solids	8.69	7.88	7.23	6.31	5.16	6.00	(7.1)	16.0
Oil	8.45	7.60	7.59	7.08	6.90	7.31	(2.8)	6.0
Gas	30.20	30.60	30.06	29.10	29.87	33.67	2.2	12.7
Electricity	13.63	13.99	14.18	14.43	14.49	15.15	2.1	4.6
Heat	0.01	0.00	0.00	0.00	0.00	0.00		
Total	130.71	133.06	135.84	136.10	135.88	140.39	1.4	3.3

Source: *Annual Energy Review*, DGXVII, 1993

electrification. Meanwhile, gas continued to penetrate the market in the domestic and tertiary sectors with an increase from 29.87 Mtoe in 1990 to 33.67 Mtoe in 1991.

In the UK primary energy production includes oil, coal and natural gas. Although a small increase in oil production occurred in 1991 (0.6 per cent) the production of UK oil has been decreasing since its peak of 129.9 Mtoe in 1985. In 1991 the UK was a net oil importer. While coal continued as the second largest primary energy source, an average drop since 1986 of 2.3 per cent in conjunction with the penetration of natural gas into domestic and tertiary markets signals the continued decline of UK coal production. The increasing importance of natural gas as an indigenous primary energy source is reflected in a decrease in gas imports from 11.39 Mtoe in 1985 to just 5.57 Mtoe in 1991.

Final electricity demand increased in 1991 by 2.4 per cent as opposed to an average increase of 2.3 per cent per year for the period 1986 to 1991. During 1991, nuclear output increased by 7.3 per cent as opposed to an annual average of 3.6 per cent from 1986 to 1991. Energy intensity increased by 4.7 per cent in 1991. This runs against the average annual decrease of 1.1 per cent since 1986. This is due in part to the loss in efficiency of 1.7 per cent in 1991 for the industrial sector.

In 1991 CO_2 emissions increased to 10.2 (t/capita) compared to 10.1 (t/capita) in 1990, an increase of 1.1 per cent. This small growth in emissions, compared to an increase in final electricity demand of 2.4 per cent for 1991, is due in part to an increase in nuclear generation. An increase in renewables was registered, for 1991, but no exact figures are available. However, in 1991 'seven new wind farms totalling 29 MW' had been completed and were feeding the national grid.

It is expected that natural gas and nuclear generation will increase their share in final energy consumption for the foreseeable short term future. Coal production in the UK will continue to decline as cheap imports enter the UK market. Renewables are likely to increase but their overall energy impact, in the short term, is low. Emissions of CO_2 are likely to increase, although at a lesser rate as nuclear and natural gas generation increase: the increase in CO_2 emissions will occur more because of the expanded utilization of private transport rather than because of expanding electricity production.

The European Community (EC)

Table 1.4 provides a breakdown of final EC energy consumption. In 1991, final energy consumption increased by 4.9 per cent as opposed to a 1.9 per cent per year average between 1986 and 1991. Of particular note is the increase of 11.5 per cent in domestic and tertiary sectors in 1991. However, a number of countries such as Italy and Portugal saw their final energy demand decrease compared to the previous five-year average. In 1991 the decreasing trend in industrial solids, down 5.4 per cent, appears to be compensated for by an increase in gas consumption, up 2.9 per cent. While industrial demand stagnated in much of Europe in Germany, Denmark and Spain it increased faster than the previous five-year average. This was, in

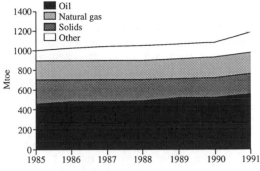

Source: *Annual Energy Review*, DGXVIII, 1993

Figure 1.13 *Gross inland consumption for Europe, 1985–91*

Denmark's case, a reflection of increased energy efficiency.

Figure 1.13 shows the gross inland consumption (GIC) by main fuel for the years 1985 to 1991. Current trends show a large percentage increase in natural gas consumption of 8.8 per cent, as opposed to 3.8 per cent average per year for 1985 to 1991, but a decrease in nuclear and renewable consumption down 1.1 per cent from the five-year average at 2.5 per cent. Net gross inland consumption increased by 3.4 per cent in 1991. Estimates for 1992 show that an increase

Table 1.4 *European final energy consumption (Mtoe)*

	1986	1987	1988	1989	1990	1991	91/86	91/90
Industry	209.66	216.50	219.05	222.31	220.24	230.00	1.0	0.00
Solids	42.90	42.49	42.82	43.05	42.71	43.58	(1.2)	(8.40)
Oil	52.08	50.63	40.73	46.92	44.37	45.46	(3.1)	0.03
Gas	61.20	67.69	66.31	72.39	72.54	77.36	4.1	2.90
Electricity	51.17	52.91	55.40	57.30	58.07	61.20	2.7	0.50
Heat	2.31	2.79	2.78	2.64	2.65	2.36	0.6	(10.00)
Transport	191.46	198.64	211.40	222.61	229.74	241.50	4.1	2.00
Solids	0.11	0.14	0.08	0.03	0.07	0.00		
Oil	188.26	195.38	206.16	219.37	226.15	237.56	4.1	2.00
Gas	0.24	0.24	0.22	0.21	0.21	0.21	(2.5)	2.40
Electricity	2.84	2.88	2.94	3.00	3.32	3.73	4.0	4.00
Other	287.94	288.81	276.78	266.96	271.01	319.51	1.0	11.50
Solids	19.02	17.00	15.08	12.62	11.27	21.60	(6.6)	20.30
Oil	110.23		99.89	89.11	89.17	98.87	(2.6)	8.50
Gas	94.79	99.10	94.10	95.26	98.68	116.61	3.9	16.30
Electricity	61.82	64.84	65.46	67.80	69.80	76.29	3.6	5.70
Heat	2.08	2.45	2.24	2.17	2.10	6.15	9.2	53.80
Total	689.06	703.95	707.23	711.68	721.10	791.01	1.9	4.90

Source: *Annual Energy Review*, DGXVII, 1993

of 0.5 per cent could largely be explained by warmer climatic conditions and the state of the European economy. Of all member states five showed a decrease in energy demand and Denmark (–16.0 per cent) and The Netherlands (–3.1 per cent) in particular showed the greatest. Nuclear production will increase slightly in Germany and the UK, however in most other countries output is stable. In general, final electricity consumption increased faster than GDP at about 3 per cent per year. During 1991 electricity intensity increased by 5.7 per cent in the domestic and tertiary sectors, whereas increased electricity demand in industry only increased by 0.5 per cent.

In 1991 total electricity generation increased by 4.1 per cent over 1990. The particular fuel mix shows that hydro-generation (without pumping) is up 10.5 per cent from 144.72 TWh in 1990 to 159.90 TWh in 1991 and that renewables are up 7.1 per cent in 1991 over 1990 levels. Although renewables are increasingly supplying electricity to the European grid, their overall contribution is still small. Overall European energy efficiency has decreased in 1991 as measured by increased energy intensity. However, this indicator relies on the ratio of GIC to GDP and as such is influenced by variations in mean temperature. Indeed, energy intensity can fluctuate rapidly from year to year purely as a result of annual temperature variation. Greater statistical accuracy can be gained by comparing years of like mean temperatures.

During the period 1985 to 1991, import dependency increased from 43.25 per cent in 1985 to 50.26 per cent in 1991, as has oil dependency from 31.60 per cent to 35.99 per cent respectively. During the same period CO_2 emissions increased from 2635.8 (Mt of CO_2) in 1985 to 2863 (Mt of CO_2) in 1991, an annual percentage change of 1.6 per cent.

Following the signing of the Framework Convention on Climate Change during the Earth Summit in June 1992 the EC will try to stabilize CO_2 emissions. This will partly become possible by changes to less polluting fuels as well as drives towards efficiency.

According to the *Annual Energy Review* of the Directorate General for Energy, energy consumption in Europe is strongly influenced by weather conditions and economic activity. Taking both the slow-down of economic growth

and assuming normal weather conditions it is anticipated that total energy demand will increase by 0.7 per cent in 1993 and 1.0 per cent in 1994. In addition, total deliveries of oil are expected to grow by 0.5 per cent in 1993 and 0.9 per cent in 1994. It is also anticipated that increases in the use of gas and renewables will continue into the twenty-first century. Although the changing fuel make-up is likely to reflect a move away from solid fuels towards renewables, gas and oil, this change is likely to be gradual.

Final electricity demand is likely to carry on increasing at least during the short term and increases of 2.0 per cent are being forecast. Total primary energy production fell by 2.8 per cent in 1992 and no further increase is expected. As a result net imports are likely to rise.

The world

The fuel mix associated with the developing world provides a view of the diverse nature of energy resources. In Africa, for example, annual biomass dependency is put at about 35 per cent of total energy needs. This, of course, hides figures like the 98 per cent dependence in Ethiopia. Although woodfuel and its charcoal derivative is the predominant energy source in many of the

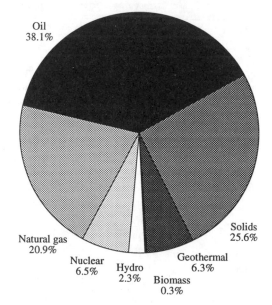

Source: *Annual Energy Review*, 1993

Figure 1.14 *World share of primary fuels, 1991*

18

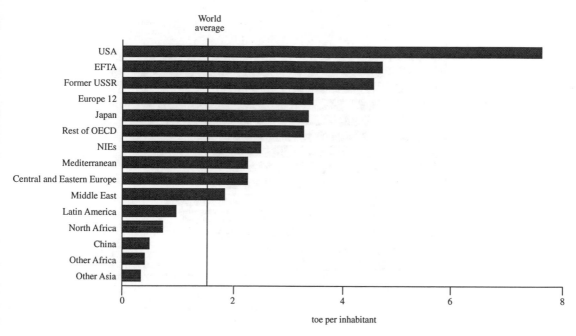

World
average

toe per inhabitant

Source: *Annual Energy Review*, DGXVIII, 1993

Figure 1.15 *Energy consumption per capita in 1991*

poorest nations, it is by no means always the case. In India, energy from burning dung and agricultural residues totalled over 110 million tonnes against '133 million tonnes of fuel wood' (K Smith, 1992). In Bangladesh, fuelwood is even less important, representing only 17 per cent of the total energy consumption against '66 per cent of crop residues' (FAO, 1986).

Between 1985 and 1990 total gross energy consumption increased annually by 2.2 per cent, however, in 1991, this was reduced to 0.9 per cent. These composite figures hide regional variations such as a fall of 9.5 per cent in 1991 for Central and Eastern Europe, as well as an increase of 10.2 per cent in the newly industrialized countries (NICs). This wide variation in energy consumption makes an analysis of global trends difficult. During the 1990s, oil demand showed little increase, dropping 0.2 per cent per annum, natural gas, on the other hand, continued to grow by 3.7 per cent. Figure 1.14 shows world shares of primary fuels in 1991. World energy consumption was dominated by oil with 38.1 per cent of the total. Solids make up 25.6 per cent and natural gas 20.9 per cent. The total renewable gross consumption makes up 8.9 per cent of the total. Once again these composite indicators hide wide variations in fuel mix. In

1991, the dominant primary fuel in China was solid fuel at 73.2 per cent. This dependence on solid fuel is reflected in CO_2 emissions where China is ranked as having the highest CO_2 to energy ratio. The primary fuel consumption in the Mediterranean reflects a 90.6 per cent oil dependence and 9.1 per cent solid consumption.

Figure 1.15 represents energy consumption per capita for 1991. According to these figures the average American used 7.5 toe/inhabitant compared to 3.3 toe/inhabitant in Europe and 0.5 toe/inhabitant in China. The average USA inhabitant consumes 14.5 times more energy in one year than a Chinese inhabitant. Figure 1.16 presents CO_2/energy ratio by region for 1991. While the highest CO_2 to energy ratio is exhibited in China, its share of total emissions is small because of a low per capita energy consumption. The CO_2 to energy ratio for USA equals the world average, but the USA was responsible for 20 per cent of annual CO_2 emissions.

Total final energy demand showed an increase from 4824.8 Mtoe in 1985 to 5326.8 Mtoe in 1990, an increase of some 2.0 per cent per annum over the period. Major fuel changes in this period include an increase in electricity demand by 3.6 per cent and a drop in biomass demand of 0.9 per cent. This is due in part to

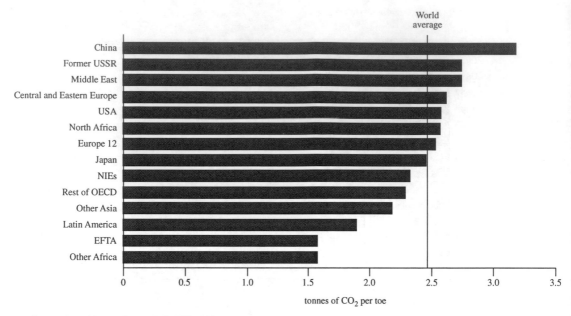

Source: *Annual Energy Review*, DGXVIII, 1993

Figure 1.16 *CO$_2$ to energy ratio by region in 1991*

rural electrification schemes, improved combustion efficiencies and decreased biomass availability.

It is anticipated that biomass and solid fuel energy will continue to decline as oil, gas, nuclear and renewable energy penetrate the economies of NICs and developing countries. World energy production will expand most rapidly in non Organization for Economic Co-operation and Development (OECD) areas, such as NICs, which provide new markets for oil and gas. The Middle East is expected to hold its share of exports at about 58 per cent of world export markets.

ENERGY AND ECONOMIC DEVELOPMENT

Increased energy consumption has often been used as an indicator for economic growth. However, a fundamental problem exists with this general correlation. Two different economies, one supplying large quantities of energy very inefficiently and the other supplying smaller quantities of energy with greater efficiency, may deliver the same volume of energy services but the amount of energy consumed varies enormously. The ideal society is one that achieves high efficiency, through renewable technology, and thus has a low relative energy demand.

Improving the quality of life, and enabling economic and industrial growth, calls for increased amounts of usable energy; but what is also required is an increase in end-use efficiency. An understanding of the difference is fundamental to understanding the relationship between energy and economic development.

Imagine two households, one using incandescent light bulbs drawing 100 watts of electricity, the other using a 20 watt compact fluorescent bulb. The incandescent bulb uses energy very inefficiently, while the compact fluorescent bulb requires a much smaller amount of energy. However, the energy services provided by both bulbs are identical. This is important because this investment in end-use efficiency, if taken up nationally, substantially reduces the requirement for energy provision. The economic benefit of investing in energy efficiency can outweigh the economic costs of building additional electricity generating stations. In turn, this means large savings to the utility, increased services to the customer and fewer emissions of greenhouse gases.

Energy opportunities and constraints

The steady take-up of renewable energy technologies provides perhaps the greatest opportunity for change in energy supply. The opportunity to supply present and future global energy requirements while conserving resources and promoting environmental sustainability is very great. Seizing the opportunity is particularly vital at a time when excessive CO_2 production, largely the result of fossil fuel use, threatens the stability of the global climatic system. Given the seriousness of the present energy/environment relationship, a number of opportunities can be highlighted as essential to long term sustainability. These are:

* an investment in renewable energy (wind, solar, biomass etc);
* nuclear generation (providing suitable disposal arrangements are delivered);
* savings on energy conversion (eg combined heat and power);
* savings on end use (eg building insulation);
* intra fossil switch (eg from coal to gas);
* recycling (eg waste plastics);
* CO_2 removal (eg at coal power stations).

(Okken et al, 1991)

Fifteen years ago, such an energy strategy would have seemed unsuitable for the provision of future energy requirements. However, changes in the efficiency and cost of renewable technologies, along with present environmental deterioration, mean that this strategy is quickly becoming the blueprint for a sustainable energy future. These changes will radically alter the conventional patterns of energy supply.

In the UK, the energy demand has largely stabilized, although slight increases in consumption will continue. During the 1970s, threats to the stability of the UK's energy supply came from the Middle East. However, the discovery of and investment in indigenous oil means that the UK has suitable oil reserves to fulfil the medium term UK requirement. One direct constraint, a product of the Earth Summit, on all fossil fuel generation will be the requirement to reduce CO_2 emissions to 1990 levels by the year 2000. This alone will provide an institutional incentive to change from conventional to non-conventional generation.

Constraints on nuclear energy supply will largely depend on the success of efforts to store low, medium and high level nuclear waste safely. This has always been a problem for the nuclear industry and seems likely to remain so largely because of public opposition to such measures.

There are a number of restraints on the development of renewables in the UK. Enormous sums were spent on the nuclear industry which was developed for military purposes before being transferred to the public sector. Renewables, on the other hand, enjoy only limited funds for research and development. But even if that funding were to improve, there are several additional constraints. The main one has to do with pricing policy. At present the cost of cleaning up the environmental damage caused by conventional electricity production is not included in the end price. If these costs, externalities, were included the price to the consumer would double. Such a move would tip the balance in favour of environmentally benign renewables and would actually help in the abatement of global warming. There are a number of other benefits to be derived from the use of renewable energy resources which are not at present included in standard economic accounts.

The development of renewables would provide new opportunities both for employment and for economic development. This would particularly be so in rural areas where their generation sites are likely to be built. Rural poverty and rates of urbanization would thus decline and, as one consequence of the use, for example, of methanol or hydrogen technologies, air pollution would be reduced. Biomass production would mean increased land restoration and so would also increase the productivity of denuded land. The creation of large areas of multi-purpose biofuels would also provide wildlife habitats.

END-USE ANALYSIS

Plans and analyses of the kind spelled out in this introduction, and discussed throughout this book, demand a shift from thinking only in terms of possible energy supplies to the demands made on those supplies. To make rational energy policies possible an account of end-use must come first.

Supplies of energy are needed for two kinds of end-use, the provision of goods and services, and the provision of fuel to run them. For example, energy is used in the manufacture of motor cars and of houses, and, subsequently, to make the one move and to heat the other.

It is possible to treat the 'energy system' as a distinct sub-system of a national economy. It can be distinguished from the other sub-systems of labour, land, capital and material resources; it is also possible to separate production and consumption within it. This means that, in principle, a path can be followed through the economic system from the desired goods and services to the amount of primary energy required to supply them.

In the introduction we have argued that energy supplies are essential to the maintenance of contemporary societies because they are, in effect, substituted for land, time, labour and capital. We have also remarked that the laws of thermodynamics decree that, once used, energy supplies cannot be replaced. This makes it vital that the raw materials of energy production are used carefully.

The hitherto common supply-side analysis of production processes first considered the supply of fuels, and then their translation into goods and services (this is illustrated by Figure 1.17). But this does not reflect the actual purposes of an economy, which are to produce those things needed to satisfy the desires of the consumers. If, instead, our analysis begins with the goods and services demanded by consumers, and then considers only what is absolutely needed for their production, then a strategy for the provision of the minimum energy and resources needed can be devised. This 'demand-side' approach, in looking at end-uses, leads to its own ways of building the infrastructure of the economy. We are concerned here only with energy needs, but these are closely linked with all other inputs.

To make use of this method it is necessary to know how much energy is needed to produce particular goods and services at the various stages of, for example, those given in Figure 1.18. Techniques for energy accounting or for energy analysis are available to help in this and the following sections will consider the relevant areas in more detail.

It is obvious that energy is needed for the reduction of raw materials to a usable condition, for example, the refining of ores into pure metals. But energy is also needed to produce the various usable fuels (petrol, diesel, coal, coke, uranium etc) from fossil deposits.

The production of each fuel has its own energy requirement (see Figure 1.19), which depends on its natural source and on the technology needed to bring it in a usable state to the market. Thus oil derived from oil shale or from

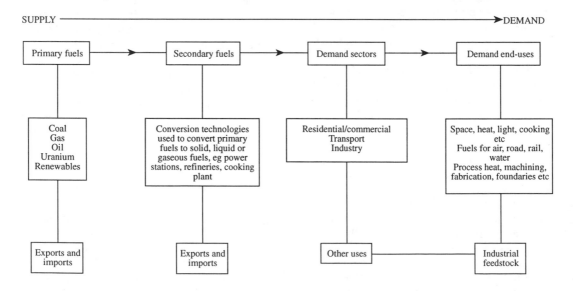

Figure 1.17 *Supply–demand energy flow*

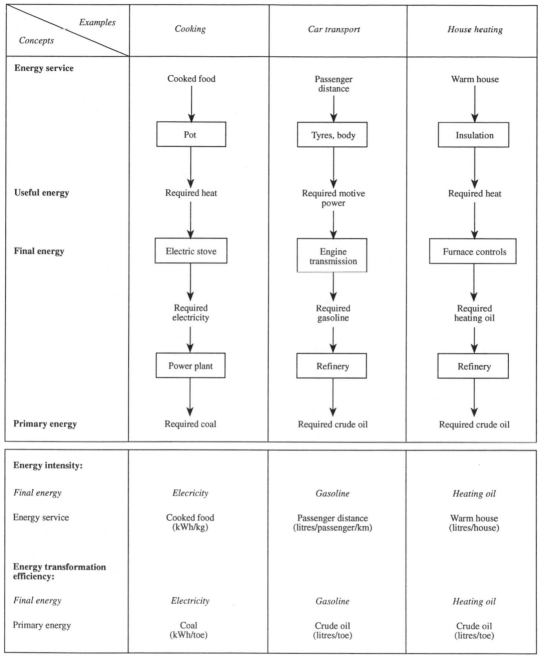

	Cooking	*Car transport*	*House heating*
Energy service	Cooked food	Passenger distance	Warm house
	Pot	Tyres, body	Insulation
Useful energy	Required heat	Required motive power	Required heat
	Electric stove	Engine transmission	Furnace controls
	Required electricity	Required gasoline	Required heating oil
	Power plant	Refinery	Refinery
Primary energy	Required coal	Required crude oil	Required crude oil

Energy intensity:			
Final energy	*Elecricity*	*Gasoline*	*Heating oil*
Energy service	Cooked food (kWh/kg)	Passenger distance (litres/passenger/km)	Warm house (litres/house)
Energy transformation efficiency:			
Final energy	*Electricity*	*Gasoline*	*Heating oil*
Primary energy	Coal (kWh/toe)	Crude oil (litres/toe)	Crude oil (litres/toe)

Source: Leach G et al, 1986

Figure 1.18 *Energy needed for energy services*

coal needs more energy for its processing than does oil extracted from crude oil. But energy used in transport has also to be taken into account. Thus oil arriving in the UK by pipeline from the North Sea uses less energy for its movement than oil shipped from the Gulf.

Energy savings in transport are enough, in this case, to balance the increased energy investment in offshore platforms against the cheaper land based production in the Gulf.

It follows from these interconnections between new facilities and present production

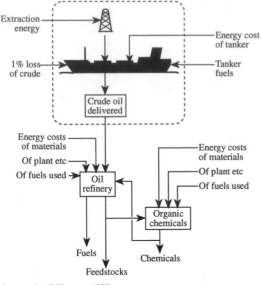

Source: J A G Thomas, 1977

Figure 1.19 *Energy inputs to provide fuels from crude oils*

that as fuel prices rise so it becomes progressively more expensive to build new facilities. This difficulty is compounded by a further problem. When estimates are made of the likely cost of producing a new fuel (liquid fuels from coal, for example), it is always priced in comparison with the cost of oil at the time of the estimate. This means that there can never be an oil

price against which the new fuel seems competitive. It also follows that new energy production facilities may only be built at a rate which does not compromise the ability of the rest of the economy to provide adequate levels of other goods and services. There is then a limit to the rate at which coal mines, power stations or oil fields may be developed if, in exceeding that rate, too large a proportion of materials and energy are diverted from the wider economy.

To make a true comparison between the levels of investment in energy required by the different means of energy supply it is necessary to take into account all, even the remotest, sources of each facility's needs. English nuclear power production, for example, depends not only on the construction of the power stations, but also on mines in the USA, South Africa and Australia. Then the production of enriched uranium fuel for nuclear reactors by the gaseous diffusion method is very energy intensive.

It is possible to calculate the efficiency of an energy industry by comparing its products with its primary energy intake (both its ongoing intake and the amortization of the energy sequestered in its construction and maintenance). The calculation is complicated by the fact that each energy industry makes either direct or indirect inputs to all the others. For example, they all use electricity, which is a

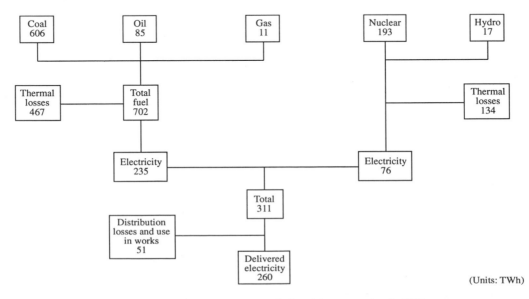

(Units: TWh)

Figure 1.20 *Energy inputs to UK electricity generation in 1989*

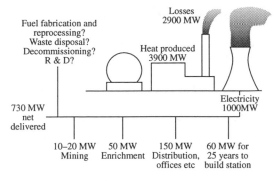

Fuel fabrication and
reprocessing?
Waste disposal?
Decommissioning?
R & D?

Losses
2900 MW

Heat produced
3900 MW

Electricity
1000MW

730 MW
net
delivered

| 10–20 MW Mining | 50 MW Enrichment | 150 MW Distribution, offices etc | 60 MW for 25 years to build station |

Source: J A G Thomas, 1977

Figure 1.21 *Energy flows in a 1000 MW station*

direct input, or they all use materials like steel, aluminium or concrete which, because they all use energy in their production, are indirect inputs. These inter-relationships can be quantified and the resulting equations solved to give the efficiencies required.

The efficiency of the energy industry is defined as:

$$\frac{\text{Calorific value of its outputs}}{\text{Fuel cost of its inputs}}$$

The fuel cost of one tonne of fuel = its calorific value + the energy expended in producing it.

(NB 'Calorific value' and 'energy content' are synonymous. In some texts the terms 'energy cost' or 'gross energy requirement (GER)' are used instead of 'fuel cost'.)

Table 1.5 *Efficiencies of the energy industries, 1972*

Coal	95.5%
Coke	88.0%
Gas (Gas manufactured from coal and oil)	81.1%
Oil	89.6%
Electricity	25.2%

Source: J A G Thomas, 1977

Figures 1.20 and 1.21 look in different ways at the electricity industry. In Figure 1.20 fuel inputs alone are considered for the whole network, and an efficiency based on this can be calculated, but this misses some of the energy costs involved. A more detailed look at a nuclear power station is shown in Figure 1.21 and includes some further energy costs. Inclusion of these causes the efficiency to fall from 1000/3900 = 25.6 per cent to 730/3900 = 18.7 per cent. Even then reprocessing, waste disposal, research and development, decommissioning and other peripheral energy costs are not included.

Although the electricity industry is the least efficient, all the energy industries deliver less to the consumer than their own intake and Table 1.5 gives some values calculated for their efficiencies in 1972.

Table 1.6 shows how the amounts of primary fuels used in the UK in 1987 differed from the corresponding amounts of fuels delivered to

Table 1.6 *Primary inputs compared with delivered fuels, 1987*

Fuel	Primary Inputs Quantity	kWht (x 10⁹)	%	Delivered Fuels Quantity	kWht(x 10⁹)	%
Coal	116.2 x 10⁶ tonnes	870	34.5	1.6 x 10⁶ tonnes	130.0	7.6
Coke	nil	nil	nil	9.8 x 10⁶ tonnes	74.9	4.4
Oil	64.3 x 10⁶ tonnes	804	31.9	nil	nil	nil
Oil products	nil	nil	nil	53.7 x 10⁶ tonnes	686.8	40.2
Gas	21473.0 x 10⁶ therms	640	25.4	19383.0 x 10⁶ therms	567.9	33.2
Hydro	nil	4	0.2	nil	nil	nil
Nuclear heat	nil	193*	7.6	nil	nil	nil
Electricity (Imported)	nil	11.6	0.5	249690 GWh	249.7	14.6
Total		2522.0	100.0		1709.0	100.0

*The amount of heat to generate 48205 GWh at 25% efficiency.
NB 1. Per cent mixes are NOT the same.
    2. Delivered energy is only 68 per cent of the primary input

consumers. Notice that primary fuels with a total calorific value of 2522 x 10^9 kWh have been used to supply consumers with fuels totalling 1709 x 10^9 kWh. The overall efficiency of the energy supply industries is therefore about 68 per cent. Notice also that the mix of fuels delivered is not the same as that entering the system, in particular, coal and oil are mostly processed to other more convenient fuels.

(NB the calorific value of nuclear power is the amount of heat necessary to produce the recorded amount of nuclear electricity at an efficiency of 25 per cent. This convention is adopted to treat nuclear power in a similar way to the other fossil fuels. A similar approach could have been taken for hydro and imported electricity but as they comprise in total less than 1 per cent of the primary input they are included as the actual amount of electricity to make explicit the amount they contribute to electricity supplies.)

To estimate the energy supplies needed for a given level of goods and services, a way of working at the energy required for any given item is needed. This must reveal the primary energy (fuel cost) involved by including the energy needs of the energy industries, as well as the energy content of the goods and services. Care must be taken not to count the same amount of energy twice.

A key table in the annual *Digest of UK Energy Statistics* (HMSO) lists energy consumption by final users. This gives a breakdown of the fuels supplied to various sectors of the economy which are subdivided into the broad categories of industry, transport, domestic, public administration, agriculture and miscellaneous. For many economic (that is, financial accounting) purposes this subdivision is conve-

nient. But for our present purpose the organization of the input data (illustrated in Figure 1.22) into the goods and services subsequently provided is more appropriate because it allows their fuel inputs to be estimated in a straightforward way. The distribution of energy between the various sectors is shown in Figure 1.22 and is based on the energy content of the fuels purchased by final users. The losses shown in Figure 1.22 represent the energy used by the fuel industries to process and deliver these fuels, and so the allocations will need to be revised to take account of this before the consumption of primary fuels of a range of goods and services can be found.

The effect of this procedure is to share out the losses shown in Figure 1.22 to incorporate the fuel they represent into appropriate sectors. Each of the sectors in Figure 1.22 will use a different mix of fuels and this mix must be known for the appropriate consumption of primary fuels (fuel cost) to be calculated. The calculation must also take into account the manufactured products used by the fuel industries. A convention is adopted that 100 units of primary fuel entering the economy should be seen to produce 100 net units of goods and services. The 4.2 units of fuel used by the fuel industries is diverted to the fuel industries before calculating the final output. This has the effect of making the input to the fuel industries 104.2 units. Figure 1.23 shows the division of fuel use according to fuel cost.

FUEL COST IN PRODUCTION OF GOODS AND SERVICES

In estimating the fuel costs of an item, fuel costs must be assigned to each element in its manufacture and these must be combined to give a total cost. The energy needed in the manufacture of many raw materials may be estimated and a fuel cost per kilogram can be assigned to them. These estimates are based on particular processes and different processes will give different fuel costs. It is possible, using thermodynamic arguments, to calculate the minimum energy required to produce a given raw material. However an absolute minimum could only be achieved through infinitely slow equilibrium processes. Real, commercial processes demand much more energy.

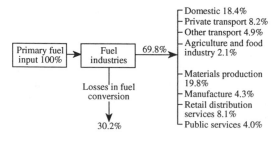

Source: P Chapman, 1975

Figure 1.22 *Energy content of fuel in different economic sectors*

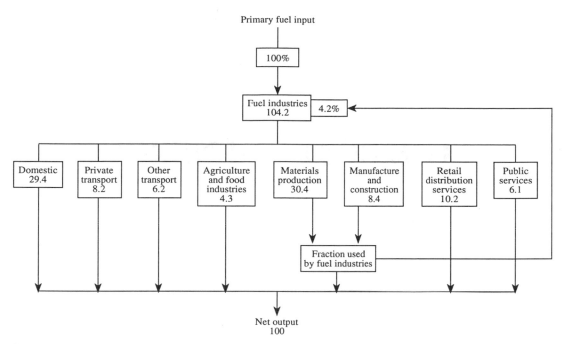

Source: P Chapman, 1975

Figure 1.23 *Fuel cost of fuels in different economic sectors*

The limits on the number of elements which must be included in a fuel cost estimate are not always self-evident. For example, Figure 1.24 shows the possible sub-systems associated with the manufacture of a loaf of bread. The fuel cost must include the fuel used in the bakery, but should it also include its share of the fuel costs of the shop, the mill and the factory which made the compressor used to pump up the tyres of the bakery van? Our pragmatic solution to this problem is to disregard contributory costs below a certain small percentage. These costs collectively usually come to about 10 per cent of the total, while the major costs make up at least 90 per cent of the final result. For our loaf of bread the major items are found to be fuel for transport, milling, baking, and heat and light which comprises 65.5 per cent of the total, packaging which is 10.5 per cent, and fertilizer which is 7.3 per cent. These items together make up over 80 per cent of the total energy input.

Such analysis can now be undertaken for proposed projects or energy policies and give an indication of the energy use implied by the proposal, an idea of the size of one of the financial costs and for an energy supply project an estimate of its useful net energy contribution to the economy.

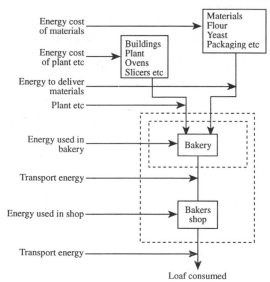

Source: J A G Thomas, 1977

Figure 1.24 *Possible sub-sectors associated with bread production*

2

THE COST OF ENERGY

In this chapter an overview of both world and country specific trends demonstrates the need for energy policy options to become firmly contextualized in regional end-use. Even so, it is clear that successful energy planning is fraught with complex management decisions that relate as much to national and international energy markets as to the complexities of global warming. It is this need for multi-perspective planning and control that is likely to provide the greatest challenge to the effective fulfilment of energy and environmental security.

'What is the cost of energy?' seems to be a reasonable and simple question. It is, indeed, simple, but the answer is complex. In this chapter we will examine these complexities and show why simple answers are misleading and unsatisfactory.

The cost of energy, for most of us, is represented in our electricity, gas or petrol bills. These, however, show only the prices charged by the companies to the consumer and usually have a fairly tenuous relationship to the costs of energy. Government tax policies, tax credits for investment or for research and development, and energy policies all have a great influence on prices, as do company policies on rates of return and on marketing.

However, estimating the real cost of energy from any given source is necessary if decisions on new investment are to be made. Investments may be in the supply of energy, its distribution or in the technologies for converting the distributed energy into the energy services demanded by the customer. Most public controversy surrounds the construction of new electricity generation plant and the electricity industry will be used as the main example in this chapter. It is chosen not only because of the controversy over nuclear, coal, gas or renewable sources of supply, but also because it is the most intensively analysed of the energy industries and the issues are more clearly understood. Other energy sectors, such as space heating, use a larger fraction of the nation's delivered energy and transport is becoming the largest polluter of the environment. But the multiplicity of buildings and of vehicles, each with their different characteristics, make them difficult examples to use.

THE COSTS OF ELECTRICITY GENERATION

There are many components in the cost of electricity generation. Costs borne by the generating company are called 'direct' or 'internal' costs and are paid by the utility concerned. When one technology is claimed to be cheaper than another, it is these costs which are usually quoted. However, there are many others not paid by the utility, or by its customers. These are the 'indirect' or 'external' costs and are paid by society, or by parts of it, either through direct taxation or by reduced well-being. External costs are much less familiar than direct costs, but they are not small and we do pay them – not as energy consumers, but as taxpayers or as members of society. In the past few years it has been calculated that the environmental costs of fossil fuels are at least equal to, and possibly much greater than, the direct costs. If we may, uncharitably, allocate the total cost of the various wars in the Persian Gulf to the defence of oil supplies rather than to some noble defence of freedom, then the indirect political cost of this oil exceeds $75 per barrel.

In most cases it is clearly very difficult to quantify the social and political costs of energy, none the less they do influence energy policy. The industrialized nations maintain large stocks of oil for purposes of national security and governments see the cost as an insurance against economic disruption. For similar reasons, governments prefer to rely on a diversity of sources of supply and usually favour indigenous rather than imported supplies. Such factors are included in national energy policy decisions as a consequence of political choice rather than of economic analysis, but they do incur costs which, although borne by the taxpayer, should ideally be charged to the users if the energy market is to work effectively.

Two classes of energy cost amenable to economic analysis are the direct and the environmental costs. The next two sections will outline the techniques which may be used to analyse them.

The direct cost of electricity generation

Direct costs can be divided into two kinds: capital and recurrent. Capital costs include those for all the land, structures, buildings and equipment needed to handle, use and dispose of the primary fuel, and to convert it into electrical energy. They may also include those costs incurred

because of legislation to protect the environment. For example, the installation of flue-gas desulphurization equipment adds to the capital cost of coal-fired stations but reduces the environmental costs of acid gas emissions. Similarly, health and safety legislation may increase capital costs to the industry and its suppliers, but will reduce the external costs of fatal and non-fatal injuries, and illnesses both to workers and to the general public. Finally, to make a fair comparison between differing energy technologies, capital costs should include the cost of restoring the site to its original state at the end of the plant's working life.

Recurrent costs include the labour and supplies needed for the operation and maintenance of plant during its lifetime, and, of course, the cost of fuel. For a fair comparison of differing energy technologies fuel costs should include the safe disposal of any waste products like ash from coal-fired stations or radioactive material from nuclear stations.

If a choice is to be made between two designs of a coal station with identical lifetimes, burning identical coal with identical efficiencies, then it may be made simply on the basis of comparative costs. However, if we are to compare differing energy technologies the choice is not so clear. Each technology has different capital and recurrent costs, different construction and lifetimes. We must find a way of comparing a fossil fuel plant with low capital but high recurrent costs and a lifetime of 30–40 years with, say, a tidal plant with high capital but low recurrent costs (zero fuel costs) and a lifetime of 100–150 years. This may be done by estimating the net present value (NPV) of income and expenditure over the lifetime of the plant.

The NPV of the expenditure in building and running a plant is the sum of money, at a given rate of interest, which must be deposited so that all bills may be paid throughout the lifetime of the plant. We shall give two examples in which figures are simplified for illustrative purposes (see Appendix II for the equations needed for working to more realistic figures).

Let us take as our first example a wind generator costing £1 million on commencement and £1 million on its delivery one year later. This would call immediately for the first £1 million. But the second could be paid by investing £0.9 million at 10 per cent per annum to yield the final sum. Thus the NPV of the capital cost would be £1.9 million. The second £1 million might also be raised by investing £0.8 million at 20 per cent per annum or £0.93 million at 5 per cent per annum. In this case the NPV would respectively be £1.8 million and £1.93 million. Calculating the NPV of any plant depends on the assumed discount rate, that is the notional interest at which the money could be invested.

The NPV of the income is the sum which, if invested now at a given rate of interest, would be equal to the total income generated over the lifetime of the plant. Imagine, for our second example, a thousand trees planted now to be harvested in five years' time when they will be sold at £10 each. The NPV of those trees is the sum which must be invested now and left for five years to earn interest equal to £10,000. If interest at 10 per cent per annum were available, then it would be necessary to invest only £6,000 now to reach £10,000 in five years' time. The NPV at a 10 per cent per annum discount rate is thus £6,000. If the discount rate were 20 per cent per annum, the NPV would be only £4,000. The higher the discount rate, the lower the NPV of future income.

Note also that income accruing in the distant future is very heavily discounted; it has a very low NPV. If £1 is left on deposit at 10 per cent per annum for 50 years, it will be worth £117, thus the NPV of £117 of income in 50 years' time is, at a discount rate of 10 per cent per annum, only £1. This has serious consequences for any generating plant with a long life because its income later in that life has a very small NPV and so counts for little in any cost/benefit analysis (the terms and equations needed for cost/benefit analysis are given in Appendix II).

Another factor which influences the future value of income and expenditure is inflation. If the price of goods and services increases each year, then money invested now will purchase less in the future. However, if rates of inflation and investment are equal, then £1 invested now will pay for future goods also costing £1, which means that the NPV of future expenditure on goods and services will equal the present costs. The effect of inflation is to reduce the effective discount rate applied to future income and expenditure. Since NPV is so dependent on rates of discount and inflation, the assumptions made

about them can alter totally any comparisons between differing energy technologies. The value selected for these rates is thus of crucial importance to any discussion of investment in energy technology.

Inflation and interest rates vary widely over time and between different countries. Inflation can vary from virtually 0.0 per cent per annum to, in collapsing economies, as much as 100 per cent per month. Even in stable economies, particularly in developing countries, it can reach 100 per cent per annum. Interest varies not just in time and geographically, but also between customers who have differing credit ratings. At the time of writing, UK interest rates on borrowings by banks or government was about 7 per cent, mortgages were about 9 per cent, a large company would borrow at about 12 per cent and a small one at 17 per cent, while personal overdrafts ran between 18 and 20 per cent.

To calculate NPVs, one value must be chosen from among these rates which will be representative for the lifetime of the plant.

Some comfort may be gained by noting that the difference between rates of inflation and interest varies much less than the rates themselves. The difference between rates of interest and inflation is called the 'real interest rate', since it represents the real growth of the value of investments. NPVs are usually calculated in 'real money', but even though this narrows the range of interest rates, the question of the precise value to be adopted remains.

Interest rates depend not only on the rate at which the investment can generate wealth but also, partly, on the degree of the risk of failure that the lender supposes the investment to entail. Government borrowing is usually thought to be risk-free and discount rates for public infrastructural development are usually set to equal the long-run rate of increase in national capital. In industrial countries, in real terms, this is about 5 per cent per annum and is the rate applied to those investments in energy which are part of the public infrastructure.

Now that the UK electricity industry has been privatized it can no longer be treated in that way and discount rates similar to the rest of private industry must now be applied. Electricity utilities are large companies with enormous capital stocks and high credit ratings, and so can borrow money at about 12 per cent per annum.

In this case, with an underlying inflation rate of about 4 per cent per annum, the real discount rate is about 8 per cent per annum.

Some investments in the generation of electricity are not, however, seen as entailing low risks. Increasing costs in operating coal or nuclear plant following new legislation, the uncertain costs of decommissioning nuclear plant and the uncertainty surrounding new renewable technologies are all seen as adding to the risks of investment. In consequence, rates of 15–19 per cent per annum are being charged which give real discount rates of 11–15 per cent per annum. Test discount rates for NPV calculations for generating equipment, now applied by the Energy Division of the Department of Trade and Industry, are 8 per cent and 13 per cent per annum. These rates reflect the real interest rates charged on investment in new electricity plant quite fairly and are appropriate to the current financial circumstances of the UK. But the extent to which, together with the public sector rate of 5 per cent, they will continue to be so 100 or even 20 years hence is neither known nor knowable. Our crystal ball is dim and uncertain.

There are good arguments for each of these three discount rates, but the effect of each is quite different and can have a dramatic effect on investment priorities. Consider the following cases.

1   A coal-fired station with an output of 1 GW, a construction cost of £1400/kW, a construction time of 4 years and a lifetime of 40 years and burning 2 million tonnes of coal per annum at £40 per tonne; other recurrent costs are estimated at £30/kW per annum and decommissioning, to take place 1 year after closure, at 10 per cent of the construction cost; the plant will be assumed to have 80 per cent availability, generating 7×10^9 kWh per annum.

2   A nuclear station with an output of 1 GW, a construction cost of £1500/kW, a construction time of 8 years and a lifetime of 30 years; recurrent costs, including fuel, are estimated at £40/kW per annum; decommissioning will take 10 years from closure and will come to 50 per cent of the construction cost; the plant will be assumed to have 74 per cent availability generating 6.6×10^9 kWh per annum.

3   A wind generator with an output of 300 kW, a construction cost of £900/kW (the capital costs to be treated as a one-off initial charge), a construction time of 3 months and a lifetime of 25 years; recurrent costs are estimated at £18/kW per annum; the machine can be moved within 1 week of its life's end at a cost of about £40/kW; the wind site is good with a load factor of about 46 per cent, the machine availability is 95 per cent generating 1.2 million kWh per annum.

4   A tidal barrage with an output of 7 GW, a construction cost of £800/kW, a construction time of 15 years and a lifetime of 100 years; recurrent costs (operation and maintenance) are estimated at £20/kW; at the end of its lifetime the plant is removed or refurbished at a cost of £500/kW over 10 years; the annual output is 17×10^9 kWh.

In each of these cases both construction and decommissioning costs are assumed to be spread equally over each of the years taken.

Table 2.1 shows the NPVs for all four technologies, at all three discount rates and the consequent costs of electricity.

In the case of the coal-fired plant costs, at the 5 per cent discount rate, are dominated by the recurrent costs; but both recurrent costs and output are so heavily discounted at the 13 per cent rate that the capital costs dominate. Because the current commercial discount rate is 13 per cent gas-fired plants, which cost about £500/kW, are, at present, usually chosen.

The large decommissioning costs for a nuclear plant become negligible when discounted at the 13 per cent rate. Even if those costs were greater than the cost of construction they would still, even at a 5 per cent rate, have a small NPV compared to other factors. Note that, using the assumptions made in these examples, nuclear-generated power is cheaper than that from coal except for 13 per cent discount rate.

If discounted over its full 25-year span, the costs for the wind generator, so long as the wind regime is as good as that assumed here, are the lowest of all. But the development of wind power in the UK is inhibited at present because the non-fossil fuel obligation (NFFO) is of limited duration and wind machines must pay their costs in only five to ten years (the NFFO is a

Net present values	Discount rates p.a		
	5%	8%	13%
Coal			
Construction (£M)	1225.0	1155.0	1040.0
Decomissioning (£M)	10.5	3.05	0.4
Recurrent (£M)	1727.0	957.0	511.5
Output (kWh x 10^9)	109.9	60.9	32.6
Cost (p/kWh)	2.7	3.5	4.76
Nuclear			
Construction (£M)	1211.0	1078.0	900.0
Decomissioning (£M)	120.0	34.0	5.0
Recurrent (£M)	419.0	244.0	114.0
Output (Kwh x 10^9)	69.3	40.0	18.8
Cost (p/Kwh)	2.5	3.4	5.4
WEG			
Construction (£M)	270.0	270.0	270.0
Decomissioning (£M)	3.5	1.8	0.6
Recurrent (£M)	76.1	57.6	39.6
	(23.4)	(21.5)	(19.0)
Output (kWh x 10^9)	16.9	12.8	8.8
	(5.2)	(4.8)	(4.2)
Cost (p/kWh)	2.1	2.6	3.5
	(5.7)	(6.1)	(6.9)
Tidal			
Construction (£M)	3879.0	3204.0	2410.0
Decomissioning (£M)	9.8	0.3	0.0015
Recurrent (£M)	1334.0	552.0	172.0
Output (kWh x 10^9)	162.0	67.0	21.0
Cost (p/kWh)	3.2	5.6	12.3

Table 2.1 *Net present values of expenditure and output, and electricity costs for the power plants*

levy imposed, following their privatization, on conventional facilities and which is used to support renewable technologies). The figures in brackets are those for a five-year payback which instantly moves wind energy from the cheapest option to the most expensive. A political decision to extend the NFFO to the full lifetime of the machines would redress the situation and save considerable sums of money.

At a 5 per cent discount rate, the tidal plant looks quite attractive, but it becomes quite uneconomic at 13 per cent. Construction costs dominate at all discount rates, so the heavy discounting of future output leads to high costs per kWh. It is interesting to see that, at 13 per cent, the NPV of the £3500 million refurbishment or decommissioning costs are only £1500

If investment in electricity generation is seen as being similar in kind to any other commercial investment, then the arguments in favour of using the private sector discount rates of either 8 per cent or 13 per cent per annum are strong. In that case, investments which maximize the return on capital as quickly as possible must always be chosen, because the swift increase in the net wealth of society makes more funds for future investment available sooner. That high discount rates work against long term projects is not taken seriously (the view seems to be 'what has the future ever done for me?').

But there are equally strong arguments in favour of the public sector discount rate or, in some cases, an even lower rate. If we see ourselves as trustees of our planet and not its owners, then the future may not be so heavily discounted. At a rate of 13 per cent per annum, the interests of our children count for little and those of our grandchildren are worthless. The issue of inter-generational equity becomes more acute when calculating environmental costs. In this context we have only to remember that we benefit from the long term investments made by our forebears. For example, the capital costs of the Scottish hydro-electrical plants were paid long ago and the cheapest electricity in the UK is now generated in Scotland at marginal cost.

Which of these two views is to be adopted is a political, not a technical, decision. But it is important, if that decision is to be well informed, to recognize the impact that it will have on investment priorities. At present, in public enquiries and debate, no one questions the discount rate, it is simply a background assumption. The result is that the cost of electricity generated by differing technologies is always presented to at least two decimal places as if they represented some 'true' and unalterable situation. Debate on energy technologies will be much more fruitful once it is recognized that the projections depend as much on politically determined discount rates as they do on the technologies themselves.

External costs

It has long been recognized that energy sources are significant contributors to environmental damage, and that the extent and the type of that damage depends on the magnitude of the power source and the type of technology it uses. Costs associated with this damage are treated as external to the energy economy and are known to economists as 'externalities' or 'external costs'. Because the environment and its resources are thought to be free for everyone, power utilities do not take the costs of pollution into account either in their internal costing or in their charges to their customers, but, in effect, pass them on to society. In most cases, neither the utilities nor their customers take any economic responsibility for the non-marketed resources that make up environmental quality.

In recent years a number of studies have been undertaken to estimate the indirect costs of energy technology. The Centre for Renewable Resources in the USA discovered that subsidies from general taxation to energy industries, a political external cost, amounted to $44 billion, roughly equivalent to the total energy bills for all US families in 1984.

Another study, undertaken by O Hohmeyer in Germany, concluded that costs not included in the market price of electricity were of the same order of magnitude as the internal costs of generation. At present, further studies in, among other countries, the USA, the UK, Germany and The Netherlands are being undertaken to reach a consensus on the value of the external costs of conventional as well as of renewable energy technologies.

NON-ENVIRONMENTAL EXTERNALITIES

Some hidden costs arise from government intervention in the economy. These include taxation policy, subsidies for research and development, limits to liability (see below), administrative costs, lost employment and costs arising from energy security. These costs are thought to be controversial, and there is a continuing debate about their importance, their magnitude and the extent to which they should be included in cost calculations. Recent studies in the USA have shown that some of these non-environmental costs can take on quite significant proportions. For example, in 1989 the US Department of Defence spent $15 billion on safeguarding oil supplies and more than $30 billion on the war in the Gulf. Hohmeyer's study, published in 1988, estimated that Germany spent, at 1982 prices, DM3210 million on subsidies, and research and development grants for the conventional energy sector. As his study does not cover all non-environmental externalities, he regards this sum as a gross underestimate.

Some of these externalities can result in considerable costs to society, so that their inclusion in or exclusion from the calculations of external costs should be considered very carefully. Government activities and market conditions must be examined thoroughly to make sure that all possible externalities have been identified.

There are some non-environmental externalities, like administrative costs or regulatory inefficiencies, which may be ignored. But others, like energy security, natural resource management, limits to liability, employment and politico-economic instruments, must be included because the amounts of money involved will be substantial.

Energy security

Energy security is a major externality and aspects of it are part of all energy policy considerations. To demonstrate the relationship between energy policy and the costs of energy security, we have divided it into three sub-sections.

Security of energy supply

This usually involves high military spending both to secure access to resources and to ensure their uninterrupted supply. The Gulf oil crisis is a good example. Countries which rely largely on one energy resource, particularly if it is near depletion, will spend heavily and take high risks to secure access to a constant supply.

Vulnerability of energy systems

Any highly centralized energy system, or one which depends on very few energy resources, is vulnerable both to routine breakdown or to sabotage. Funds must therefore be found both for the storage of resources against emergency and to provide extra capacity to cope with short-falls in supply or with extra demand. By spending on decentralization and diversification much of this vulnerability may be reduced.

Nuclear security

Nuclear security involves both civil installations and military uses. Substantial external costs are involved in securing civil reactors, in developing their fuel cycle technology, in maintaining security in high level waste disposal and in any major nuclear accident. But nuclear technology is developed not only to produce energy, but also to make weapons and to build reactors which may be sold on an international market. It is this last which conceals a further major 'cost'. Nuclear power stations sold for the production of energy may, as Iraq demonstrated, be refitted as reactors capable of producing materials for nuclear weapons.

Natural resource management

The non-renewable character of fossil fuels gives rise to three types of external cost. The first has to do with the allocation of non-renewable resources: are we simply to satisfy ourselves or are we to accept the cost of taking into account the needs of future generations? The second is a matter of management: do we accept the cost of using resources in the most economically and socially efficient and acceptable way, and is resource scarcity reflected in the price that we pay for energy? The third deals with the depletion of non-renewable resources: do we take depletion into account when national and international prices are fixed? Depletion, of course, may lead to international conflicts over access to scarce resources, but this is related to the issue of energy security.

Limits to liability

Energy production, particularly in the nuclear industry, has high levels of occupational health risk and of accident or disaster. These impose heavy insurance costs on the industry. Governments sometimes intervene either by taking over part of the insurance costs or simply by accepting liability for those accidents for which the producer has no, or inadequate, insurance. The effect of thus limiting the producer's liability is to transfer these costs from producers and consumers to society.

Quite apart from accident or catastrophe, energy production can, of its nature, create messes which need expensive cleaning up. These, too, are sometimes underwritten by the state. One example may be seen in the cost of disposing of nuclear waste generated in only one of two reprocessing plants in the former German Democratic Republic. German taxpayers will now have to find DM15 to DM20 billion to clean it up.

Employment

Changes in energy technology can have major implications for employment. They can influence both the total of the employed and the kinds of skill the industry requires. Indeed, unemployment may be caused as much by changes in the industry's demands for skills as by any other structural change. In places where an energy industry is a major employer, such changes can have both local and regional effects. Unemployment has a psychological impact on its victims, but it can also produce changes in the quality of life and in patterns of education for an entire region. Any area dominated by just one energy sector, coal for example, can be drastically affected by a shift in energy policy or technology. Because the effects of such changes are specific both to sites and to regions the links may be seen, and we may talk of them as non-environmental externalities.

Politico-economic instruments

In the energy sector subsidies and tax incentives are the most important macro-economic tools, and make up much of the non-environmental external expenditure. Subsidies have financed research and development which, in turn, has ensured continuity and competitiveness in technology, and has helped to maintain dominance in national and international markets. They have also, usually as a result of intense lobbying, been used to keep fuel prices down.

Where non-environmental externalities can be identified, they should be valued and included in the calculations of external costs. It is important to make sure that they have not already been included elsewhere in the utilities' private internal costs or in market prices. It is also necessary that these externalities should be site-specific and that links between expenditure and a particular region can be established.

ENVIRONMENTAL EXTERNALITIES

Environmental externalities remain, however, the most prominent external costs in energy generation. How to internalize them is a matter of growing urgency, not least because of the ever increasing rate of environmental damage. Environmental concern has also been enlarged to include not just local and regional damage, but also the alarming levels of global damage. That 'global warming' is caused by an enhanced greenhouse effect is a theory now widely accepted by both scientists and decision makers. This has focused attention on the energy industry and its emission of gases such as carbon dioxide (CO_2), sulphur dioxide (SO_2) and nitrous oxide (N_2O) as sources of environmental damage. The industry is confronted by demands that it should minimize its emissions from fossil fuel fired power stations, and consider a shift to less environmentally damaging and more sustainable energy technologies.

The drastic reduction of polluting emissions becomes an even more urgent demand when we consider that, by the year 2010, the world's population will have risen from its present 5.5 billion to more than 7 billion and most of this increase will be in the developing world. The demand for energy outside the industrial countries will rise considerably.

Since the need for changes in energy policies was acknowledged some time ago there have been several different politically and economically justified attempts at achieving change. Various options have been tried, mostly in Western industrialized countries, with differing degrees of success.

Environmental regulations were among the first administrative measures introduced to control pollution from energy sources. Emission targets were at first set locally and regionally. They compelled the introduction of abatement technologies on power plants using conventional fuels and, hence, the inclusion of some environmental costs in their internal calculations. However, following the increasing recognition of the global scale of environmental damage, international regulations setting emission targets for the most hazardous and damaging of air pollutants are being drawn up. The rate of national compliance with these international regulations is patchy and is probably less than compliance with local or regional targets. Despite this, international environmental regulation will have to be one way of altering energy generation policies.

Another approach would be to compel utilities to monetize both environmental and non-environmental externalities and to include them in their internal accounts; this would give the real costs of both producing and consuming energy. Utilities, decision-makers and consumers alike would then, for the first time, be able to compare the real costs of competing energy technologies. This would allow informed choices, and would encourage investment in more energy efficient and environmentally benign technologies, not the least because it would remove the existing unreasonable bias in favour of fossil fuels. A positive effect on energy conservation and on renewable technologies would also follow from the inevitable increase in prices caused by identifying the real costs.

Fuel cycles

Environmental costs are incurred not only during the operation of power plant, energy transmission and use, but also during the various stages of the fuel cycle. Any detailed analysis of external costs must account for the environmental damage created by activities throughout the fuel cycle, from extraction, processing and transport, to plant construction and energy conversion, to distribution and waste disposal. It is important to identify environmental impacts in both 'upstream' and 'downstream' activities from all energy technologies. Furthermore, some technologies adversely affect the environment mainly at the front end or, alternatively, at the plant disposal stage, of their activities and not, as with some fossil fuels, during the actual production of energy.

This applies in particular to renewable resources such as photovoltaics. While they seem not to have any particular impact during their operation, the manufacture of their cells – an upstream activity – calls for the use of hazardous materials and their disposal – a downstream activity – may involve the release of heavy metals such as cadmium. But it also applies to conventional technologies. Nuclear power, for example, has major effects on the environment quite outside the stage at which it generates energy. The most significant environmental costs are those attached to decommissioning, and to the disposal of both high and low level radioactive waste. These downstream activities are of particular concern because of the substantial uncertainties surrounding their long term environmental cost to society which will affect not only present, but also future generations. The problem of evaluating these costs has only just begun to be

addressed, and the debate about the future of nuclear power as an 'environmentally friendly' technology and, thus, as a viable source of energy, will not easily be resolved.

To ignore the costs of environmental externalities will impede calculations and render impossible a fair comparison of differing technologies. Computer models exist that compile data on the different steps of fuel cycles and that may be used to facilitate calculations of environmental and non-environmental externalities. Examples are the TEMIS system developed by the German Öko-Institute and LEAP developed by the Tellus Institute in the USA.

Quantification

A first and decisive step in attributing costs to environmental externalities is to quantify the environmental impacts. This means estimating their physical magnitude and relating each effect to its originating pollutant. Pollutants must be traced from their source to their receptors and to the damage caused and the procedure may be described thus:

pollution–emission–burden–impact–valuation
  source   level   level   level   costs

Emissions are counted in tonnes of pollution per MWh, for example tonnes of CO_2, or CO_2 equivalent, per MWh. Burdens are the intermediate effects of those emissions such as concentrations of ambient SO_2. Impacts are physical changes to the environment, including effects on human health, which follow from the emissions and the burdens. Examples are increased human mortality, losses in crop yields or fish deaths.

Any analyst of environmental impacts must realize that the relationships between emission and burden, and burden and impact are not always easily determined. Although some are well documented, can easily be identified and measured, and even show a simple linear relationship between cause and effect, this is not universally so. In cases like global warming, acid deposition or loss of species the relationships are fraught with uncertainties. Some are due to the limits of scientific understanding or to the lack of accurate data. Other uncertainties arise because environmental damage may be a response to a multiplicity of causes or because of the unpredictability of ecological response to disturbance.

Difficulties may emerge for yet other reasons. For example, emissions may, as a consequence of meteorological factors, be chemically transformed in ways which produce further primary or secondary pollutants. The former are those which are generated with little change to their structure (particulate matter or lead) or which result from relatively simple interactions (SO_2, NO_x and CO_2). The latter are those produced by complex interactions between their inputs. For example, ozone (O_3) is produced by synergistic reaction between NO and hydrocarbons, or volatile organic compounds, in the presence of sunlight or ultraviolet radiation. Aerosols and acid deposition are the best-known examples of these secondary pollutants. Other difficulties may arise from the impact of topographical conditions on pollutants and their settling.

All the consequences of emissions are subject to substantial uncertainties. Both acid deposition and global warming demonstrate this, for both offer examples of local emissions leading to burdens and impacts which may be felt anywhere. Besides, ecosystems are very complex and when change occurs in one part it can result in changes in other parts. They are also very stable which allows them to cope with much ecological disturbance, for example, fluctuations in climate. This stability is threatened when different parts of the system are put simultaneously under stress by differing pollutants or by natural disturbance. Trees, for example, already under stress from drought are more likely to succumb to acid deposition than those which are not.

Another point to remember is that some environmental impacts may not be felt for a long time because the pollutants may have to accumulate before the ecosystem shows any response. Complex and highly interactive sub-systems often manage to minimize the overall effects of pollution loads until some threshold is reached where a vital link in the interactive chain is broken and the ecosystem rapidly deteriorates.

All these considerations must be kept in mind when quantifying environmental impacts. But, as many of the effects of environmental pollution cannot yet be determined unambiguously, further work will be needed to find appropriate methods of defining and measuring the relationships between emissions and burdens and burdens and impacts.

Valuation

Although various economic methods are available for costing environmental impacts, it still proves to be the most difficult and controversial step. Difficulties arise because environmental goods are not bought and sold, and so most environmental impacts are not directly reflected in markets, so it is difficult to work out their economic values.

Environmental value relationships

None the less it is possible to work out the costs of some environmental impacts as, for example, in the case of lost output or in the case of the repair of buildings damaged by acid deposition. However, conventional economic methods which would work in these cases fail when it comes to costing a beautiful view or a historic building.

Again some environmental impacts are quantifiable but not, or not yet, priceable; greenhouse gases, in particular CO_2 emissions, are good examples. While the amount of CO_2 emitted by power stations is easily determined, the economic damage associated with it has not yet unambiguously been derived. Monetizing these emissions is still controversial because there are so many unknown variables in the risks of global warming. For these reasons the costs of reducing emissions, calculated so far, also vary considerably.

Where the loss of biodiversity or of species is at issue, or the uniqueness of natural sites or biotopes, it may be impossible, in general, to work out direct monetary costs. We do not know what potential costs might be involved if these assets are eliminated and future choice forgone. Besides, these assets are non-marketable commodities and their values may only be expressed in qualitative terms. The most likely way of getting round this is by a system of contingent valuation (for example, hedonic pricing and 'willingness to pay', see below), in which the societal valuation is derived from the expressed preferences of individuals.

Another problem arises in forecasting environmental impacts. This is not only complicated but also subject to much uncertainty. Our knowledge of the future is limited, as is our scientific understanding of the extensive bio-chemical and bio-physical feedback mechanisms which determine environmental impacts and the working of ecosystems.

Irreversibility and uniqueness

Many decisions about energy sources have irreversible effects. If an environmental asset is not preserved, it is likely to be eliminated with little or no chance of ever being restored. Radioactive waste, once produced, cannot be destroyed, it must be stored, perhaps for centuries, with all its attendant risks. If an ancient monument is pulled down to make way for inner city development it will be lost for ever unless it is dismantled and reassembled elsewhere. Obviously not to build nuclear power stations or not to develop inner cities will mean forgoing benefits. Any damage avoided by not taking a development decision must be weighed carefully against the consequent loss of benefits had it been taken. The same considerations hold for natural species which, once destroyed, can never be regenerated. But not only is extinction irreversible, also our knowledge of what such losses will mean to ecosystems is very vague.

Discounting

As the effects of pollution are often slow to work, time is of the first importance in estimating environmental damage, not the least because existing damage may not be an adequate guide to future effects. As we have seen the choice of discount rate can change the relative costs of different technologies, particularly those with long working lives. Equally, the choice of discount rates radically alters the estimates of the external costs of long term effects and so reflects our concern for the well-being of future generations. Assuming that society is wise enough to avoid human-made catastrophes and lucky enough not to suffer natural ones, future generations will be more wealthy than our own. Future wealth will come from constant investment in wealth generating activities. If we defer an important investment now, because we feel that the rate of return is inadequate, then we reduce the wealth of future generations and their ability to meet the cost of that investment when it can no longer be put off. We need some principle from which to derive a balance between legitimate concern for ourselves and our concern for the future. One might be to consider what we would wish our ancestors to have done to maximize the well-being of all generations up to and including our own. Similarly, we might guess at what some future generation might wish that we had done for all generations up to and including theirs. Intergenerational equity demands that we maximize the benefits of investment while counting the costs in such a way that they do not impinge more, or less, heavily than if they were incurred today. This suggests that long-term costs should be discounted at the same rate as the growth in wealth. We remarked before that investments in social infrastructure are discounted at a rate equal to the rate of growth of capital which is about 5 per cent. However, this is not an appropriate measure for discounting external costs, many of which relate to the health and well-being of individuals, and so increase with increasing populations. In this case the discount rate should be equal to the rate of growth in wealth per capita. For the past 100 years or so, in Europe and the USA, this has averaged about 1–2 per cent. It is higher in newly industrializing countries, but mature economies all seem to have similar rates of growth. It seems equitable to use a discount rate of 1 per cent, either for benefits or for costs which extend over many generations.

For short term effects where the costs are borne by the generation which enjoys the benefits, a discount rate which reflects the opportunity cost of the resources should be used. There is still room for argument whether this should be the social discount rate or the private market rate of 8–13 per cent. It would seem that since, by definition, external costs are borne by society as a whole, the social discount rate is the most appropriate. However, any calculation of external costs must use the entire range of discount rates in order to determine their sensitivity to them. The value for external cost eventually agreed by the general public, the energy utilities, politicians and so on, can then be the subject of informed debate.

Monetization

Costing environmental goods and the damage from pollution remains controversial because pricing externalities which involve non-marketable goods is fraught with uncertainty and difficulty. None the less there are several reasons why they should be monetized, and why the method should always be used in making decisions and in planning utility systems. If environmental externalities are not monetized, they may well be ignored or, at best, given insufficient weight. Mere difficulty of achievement should not stand in the way, but should act as a spur to the development of new valuation techniques.

Money may be regarded as a measuring rod for both gains and losses. Its use, in the form of common units, allows precise comparisons to be made between direct, environmental and external costs of each energy technology. Monetization makes consistency in the evaluation and treatment of environmental issues possible.

Economic value

The period in which environmental resources may be valued can extend over many generations. But the effects of distributing these resources both intra-generationally (in the present) and inter-generationally (across time) pose important ethical and conceptual questions. 'Environmental value' is one term to be considered because it is interpreted in various ways. Environmental economists have tried to develop some kind of taxonomy of economic values as they relate to natural environments. In order to derive an economic value its components have to be identified. They consist of user, option and existence values, and the sum of all three is defined as the total economic value of an environmental resource. For individuals the environment has mainly a user value, ie a benefit derived from the use of the resource. The option value is worked out by discovering the extent of an individual's willingness to pay for the preservation of the resource so that they might make use of it if they so wished. Existence values try to identify the willingness to pay for the preservation of environmental goods (forests, species, the Antarctic wilderness) just so that they continue to exist even though the individual may make no use of them.

The two basic tools of environmental valuation are the estimates of 'willingness to pay' (WTP) and 'willingness to accept' (WTA – the amount an individual will accept in compensation for a reduction in environmental quality), and they are commonly used together. Common sense might suggest that there should be little difference between the two measures, but this may not always be the case. In valuation the two measures must be reconciled and there is much debate about how this might best be done.

VALUATION METHODS

Because so many valuation methods are now available, placing an economic cost on environmental impacts which affect people both directly and indirectly seems to be achievable. Neither of the two most commonly used approaches, 'control costs' and 'damage costs', is universally accepted, and much debate rages around whether environmental externalities should be valued on the basis of either controlling or preventing pollution, or on the basis of the costs which are passed onto society.

Control costs

Because it is difficult to value externalities directly, utilities tend to use the costs of control or prevention as surrogates for the costs of damage. Control costs are the average costs of using emission reduction technologies to reach standards set by government regulation. These technologies include gas desulphurization devices, switching to other fuels, reducing loads by conserving energy or a combination of several methods. The advantages of using control costs are that data are readily available and the costs are easier to determine.

The disadvantage of control costs is that the cost of complying with existing regulations usually bears little or no relation to the actual costs of pollution damage to society. Another problem is that as the cost calculations are specific to particular pollutants and their abatement technologies they may not be worked out on a least-cost basis and they seldom address the environmental risks involved.

A more nuanced technique has, however, been developed, and this is the so-called 'implied valuation' or the 'revealed preference' approach. The difference from conventional control costs lies in its use of costing control measures as an estimate of the price which society is willing to pay to reduce pollution. However, it only considers the marginal costs of abatement, which means that it accounts only for the cost of reducing those final units of emission which breach the target level.

One difficulty arises in both forms of control costing. It is that for many pollutants emitted by power plants there are no environmental control standards. Thus, if control costs designed to protect the public are adopted with 'an adequate margin of safety', they are often set without reference to the real damage to health and environment.

Damage costs

Damage costs may be derived from measuring actual damage and will reflect more accurately the real costs to society. Monetizing damage to non-marketable environmental goods calls for sophisticated techniques, some of which have been developed in the last two decades. There are four criteria for selecting valuation techniques.

1   The methods must be technically accept able. Any technique must be reliable (in design and in susceptibility to biases); it must be valid (in methodology, and in the extent and accuracy of the predictions it allows about the real world); it must measure what it is required to measure and it must be consistent with the perspective of the study.
2   Techniques must be institutionally acceptable. Although those involved in the valuation process agree that environmental damage and benefits should be assessed and evaluated, they still disagree about the acceptability of quantifying and monetizing environmental assets, particularly 'soft' ones. They also disagree about the ethical issues of environmental degradation so that while decision-makers are mainly interested in environmental and economic trade-offs, environmentalists tend to be deeply troubled by the 'trade-off mentality' which they see as a war of attrition on environmental assets.

3   Techniques must be easily understood. Not only must the technique be understood by specialized researchers, but also by decision-makers and by those most affected by it. If the technique is easily understood then it will be possible to see that it is properly applied and that the results are credible.
4   Techniques must be cost-effective. As all techniques will provide some information, it is important to ensure that only the most cost-effective are used. Should a given study need additional information, then a decision about the value of getting it must be made, if necessary by the application of yet another valuation technique. Decisions must also be made about the use of cheaper techniques which may provide only approximate values or if the subsequent cost of refining them might not prove to be too high.

Valuation techniques are usually divided into 'direct' and 'indirect' methods. Four direct methods need further description: hedonic pricing, travel cost, contingent valuation and wage-risk. We shall then describe 'dose response relationships' which are the root of indirect methods.

Hedonic pricing

This method is commonly used to determine the effects of pollution of all kinds on property prices. A decrease in house or land values is one reasonable way of assessing the costs. In hedonic pricing it is important to get at how much of any difference in value is a consequence of environmental differences between properties and how much is due to pollution. It is also necessary to discover how much people are willing to pay for improvements in environmental quality and, also, what the societal value of such improvement would be.

To get at the effect of pollution on property prices data may be collected about a small number of properties over several years or about a large number of differing properties at a particular time. Sometimes both methods may be used and the results collated, but usually, because it is simpler and quicker, the general survey is employed.

Many things can affect property prices, so it is necessary to include factors like accessibility, local transport, the quality and size of accommodation, facilities, costs and so on. Obviously, air pollution, traffic or aircraft noise, water quality, access to recreational open spaces etc have also to be included in such a survey. Care must be taken because the exclusion of any significant factor will simply bias the study.

David Pearce and Anil Markandya (1989) assembled data from a widespread study of the effects on property prices in North America of, among other forms of pollution, traffic and aircraft noise. Assuming that economic and housing conditions are still much the same as they were at the time of the study, then the data suggest that every one decibel rise in traffic noise would lead to a £250 decrease on a £50,000 house. In the case of aircraft the units of measurement are different and are known as the 'noise and number index' (NNI). The authors calculate that for every single unit of increase in the NNI £3750 would be lopped off the value of the house. These price changes may be used as a measure of what people are prepared to pay to avoid pollution or, conversely, what they are willing to accept in compensation.

Hedonic pricing is a crude measure and its accuracy has to be tested against surveys in other, but similar, contexts, by comparing its results with those obtained by other methods and, where possible, by looking at what is actually happening in the market. This is not least the case because, on occasions, its estimates of the costs of pollution have been shown to be mistaken by an order of magnitude.

Travel cost

This technique may be used to value recreational facilities like parks, lakes and forests. A number of elements go into the process: the time taken by visitors to travel to the facility (on the assumption that time may be priced by treating the hours spent at leisure as equivalent to the cost of giving up work at an hourly rate); the cost of travel; and, where applicable, the cost of entry and the frequency with which particular individuals or groups visit the facility. As in the case of hedonic pricing, there is a large number of variables that must be taken into account in order to avoid bias. Extended surveys of the sort described for hedonic pricing will be conducted over a large range of households and individuals. Some people may want to visit the facility at issue, but be too poor to do so very often. Others

may have access to some other recreational area. Yet more may simply not enjoy that kind of recreation. Distance and transport must also be factors, and so on. The object of these complex enquiries is to establish a number of 'demand curves' for the facility at issue among households with similar incomes and responses. By combining the differing levels of expenditure the value of the facility may be determined. Much more work would be needed to discover how much these people would be willing to pay for an environmental improvement to the facility, but the principles would be much the same. This approach is largely only applicable to recreational facilities. The accuracy of its results falls within a range of ±60 per cent. The method also provides only the 'user value' component of the full economic value of the resource.

Contingent valuation (CV)

Elements of this method are to be found in most of the others. It relies on surveys which determine people's expressed preferences. Individuals are asked what they would be willing to pay to avoid hypothetical reductions in health, and increases in environmental risks or impacts and, conversely, what they would accept by way of compensation for putting up with them.

However, CV is difficult to control because respondents may answer strategically, hoping for increased influence on the outcome of the decision. This problem can be overcome by taking care in the design of the questions. But it is also important to ensure that respondents taking part in CV are familiar with the goods at issue, familiar, too, with the hypothetical means of payment and, above all, they must be given enough information from which to form an opinion.

CV is the only system really able to make use of WTP and WTA estimates, and thus of putting prices on future risks like global warming or nuclear accidents. It is technically applicable to all circumstances and is the only consistent approach to valuing environmental impacts. It has been widely used in the USA to value environmental goods. Like the travel cost method the range of accuracy is ±60 per cent.

Wage/risk

These studies are based on the assumption that money may be substituted for reducing health and safety risks at work, and a look at the wage markets will, in theory, show whether workers in riskier jobs are paid premiums. It should then be possible to asses the value of risk by means of the WTP and WTA techniques. Data are generally easier to get than in other studies, but the difficulties presented by independent variables remain. The biggest single problem in using this approach is that it assumes that labour markets are free and ignores the ways in which government activity and trade union achievements affect wage differentials. It is also unable to cope with individual reactions to risk and the differing values put on life. Hence its levels of accuracy are too low for most purposes.

Dose response relationships

Indirect methods set out to calculate the value of the relationship between pollution and its effects, and their use is appropriate when people are unaware of what they are. This dose response analysis includes, for example, the effects of pollution on health, on material assets, on aquatic ecosystems and on vegetation. However, it should be noted that some of these can be valued directly by applying the contingent valuation method as in the case, for example, of the impact of acid deposition on the rivers and lakes of Norway.

The dose response technique is applicable to those environmental problems where links between damage and cause may be established. Use of the technique need not imply that the extent or the limits of such links are precisely known, merely that there is a physical relationship. The damage is divided into units, each of which is given a 'price' (value) and the cost is estimated by multiplying the units by their prices. The cost of the damage is thus related to the actual level of pollution (damage function).

There are several problems in this approach. It can be difficult to identify, with any accuracy, the precise links between pollutants, or combinations of pollutants, and particular damage. The approach calls for large amounts of data, especially for those studies which have to do with the effects of pollution on health. It may be difficult to correlate things like the relationships between pollutants and the levels that they must reach before having discernible effects. Different people and different ecosystems react differently to pollutants. Accuracy depends on the state of knowledge about the ecological inter-relationships, the degree of understanding of localized elements and the probability distribution of random variables. Despite these problems, the dose response methodology has been successfully applied to the valuation of many environmental costs, particularly of gaseous emissions.

The evaluation of health and safety

The first concern of most studies of health and safety is, unsurprisingly, with risks to life. Chronic sickness and injury attract marginally less attention.

There are a number of ways of costing a reduction in risks to life and the two most commonly used are, in the case of occupational risks, wage/risk studies and, for general environmental risk, contingent valuation. In 1989 a study of the relationship between wages and risks suggested that a life lost at work should be valued in a range from £1 million to £10 million, with a mean around £3 million. The upper percentiles ranged from £9.1 million to £20 million respectively.

Few CV studies have been produced which try to estimate the WTP for reducing the risk of death from pollution. One such, in the USA, considered the WTP for reductions in the risk of cancer caused by trihalomethanes in drinking water. It was discovered that in the event of a change in risk of four in one million, the value of a statistical life (VSL) could be set at about £1.6 million.

Research into the means of costing chronic illness has been very limited, probably because what is to be valued is so complex that any realistic outcome is uncertain. On the other hand, acute illness is easily valued, not the least because it is so common. People are familiar with the good to be valued and, in consequence, it is straightforward to work out the WTP for specified reductions in the duration of the symptoms. Three CV studies of days in which respiratory symptoms were suffered, valued them in a range from £1 to £16 or more.

CV surveys show that occupational morbidity is commonly costed in a range from £5000 to

£500,000, while morbidity occasioned among the general public is costed in a range from £10,000 to £1 million. These ranges are below those for mortality by about one order of magnitude. Minor injury tends to be costed by two orders of magnitude less than major injury.

Costing operational health and safety

Only some of the impacts of energy production and consumption on occupational health and safety need concern us here. These are accidents occurring during the extraction of coal, gas and oil, and the effects of radiation from accidents in nuclear plant.

Accidents during the extraction of fossil fuels are best costed on the basis of rates of morbidity and mortality, and on the values proposed for health and safety. A review of wage/risk studies concluded that the cost of preventing non-fatal injury lies in a range from £10,000 to £20,000 in each case.

To assess the costs of the impact of radiation on health and safety, it is necessary to know exactly how much radiation is being emitted by each particular site at issue. This is because radiation from the nuclear fuel cycle may be significant. It follows that the radiation emitted by each fuel cycle must also be known.

A study designed to estimate the effects of a possible major accident in a UK pressurized water reactor concluded that costs could be as high as 0.5–5 pence per kWh. The US PACE University study, based on figures from Chernobyl, put the costs of nuclear accidents at 2.3 cents per kWh (1.5 p per kWh). In a recent revision of his 1988 study of 'social cost', Hohmeyer noted that taking into account the latest German reactor safety study (1989), Germany's population density (ten times that of the USA) and the latest estimates of mortality costs, nuclear accidents would add from 1–7 pence per kWh.

Global warming

Predictions about the effects of global warming, as working groups two and three of the International Panel on Climate Change (IPCC) pointed out, are unreliable. Much depends on the levels of future greenhouse gas emissions and on the international response to the dangers, but even so, in the nature of the case, accurate predictions cannot be achieved.

It is equally impossible to be certain about the risk of global warming to human life, however it seems probable that over the next hundred years it will cause the deaths of at least one million people each year. The upper limit is usually taken to be ten million deaths a year or one billion over the next century. Fatality estimates thus range from 10^7 to 10^8 and, if we take the costings of public mortality given above then the total costs will lie in a range of £10^{14} to £10^{16}.

As significant rises in greenhouse gas emissions are expected, particularly as developing countries industrialize, the IPCC (1990) considers that world emissions of CO_2 must be reduced by 60 to 80 per cent for atmospheric concentrations to stabilize at their present levels. The current rate of emission is said by the IPCC to be 26 giga-tonnes which, accumulating over 100 years, will amount to 61 per cent of all greenhouse gas emissions. Taking the mortality costs of global warming, an environmental cost of £10^2 to £10^4 per tonne of CO_2 results. Since coal-fired electricity generation produces about 1 kg per kWh, this would result in environmental costs of about 10 pence to £10 per kWh.

The PACE University study estimates that the average value of reducing emissions is 1.4 cents per kWh for coal, 1.2 cents per kWh for oil and 0.7 cents per kWh for gas.

Acid deposition

Estimates of the costs of acid deposition show that there are no major health costs associated with sulphur emissions in Europe. The levels neither exceed the World Health Organization (WHO) guidelines (50 g/m^3), nor the lowest levels at which effects from long-term exposure to CO_2 and to particulate matter (100 g/m^3) may be observed. The health costs of sulphur emissions are not, therefore, at issue.

However, present levels do cause environmental damage. Expert opinion holds that deposits of 100 g/m^3 will damage all soils, even those least sensitive to acidification, irreparably. This means that all European soils are in danger.

The UK produces about one-tenth of Europe's sulphur emissions and contributes, proportionately, one-tenth of the deposition rates. Cleaning this up would add costs in a range from £0.12 to £2 per kWh. These costs assume that a coal-fired power station (using coal with a 1 per cent sulphur content) emits about 40×10^3 tonnes of sulphur per GWy.

One study of the effects of emissions on forestry suggests that ten years of emissions are needed to make a significant impact on forests for the next century. If the figure really is ten rather than one before effects are observable, then costs would be reduced to a range from 2 to 20 pence per kWh.

Results of recent US studies of acidification indicate costs in the range of 0.83 cents to 1.53 cents per kWh. EPRI puts these costs much lower in a range of 0.14 cents to 0.67 cents per kWh, but the Californian Energy Commission suggests the far higher figure of 7.09 cents per kWh.

A contingent valuation study in Norway of the benefits of a 30–70 per cent reduction in sulphur emissions, with a consequent fall in acid deposition, would be approximately £48 million at 1986 prices. This is 0.009 per cent of Norway's 1986 gross domestic product (GDP). This study, like others, indicates that the economic value of environmental improvements can be large.

Ozone effects
Ultraviolet radiation causes about 10^4 cancer deaths per year. If there is further damage to the ozone layer, then that figure could rise by an additional 10^3–10^4. Against these costs there are some curious benefits for atmospheric ozone: studies undertaken in the USA indicate that a reduction in atmospheric ozone can significantly reduce the damage to a variety of fruit and vegetable crops. Reductions of between 10 and 20 per cent in seasonal average ozone levels have increased agricultural productivity and, for the major field crops the benefits have exceeded £1 billion.

Areas of differing environmental value
The amenity value of land is very variable and the value of recreational areas is quite site-specific, and can only be determined for each site. Parts of the natural environment are valued for their outstanding beauty, as wilderness areas or as sites of scientific interest. In contrast, others have little to commend them except as workplaces for their inhabitants. While clearly it would offend people if their area were to be despoiled, changes to the landscape which enhance employment in such country are more likely to be welcomed than opposed.

Although the visual element of a given development has no effect on living species, considerable costs can follow from the visual degradation of the environment. These costs particularly need to be determined if large technologies like power stations or wind turbines are to be installed. The cost of visual impacts cannot be expressed by some simple equation because they depend on individual aesthetic values which, in turn, depend on the value systems of both individuals and of society.

The installation of wind turbines is a case in point. Assuming that the visual impact of each would destroy 0.2 km^2 of beautiful landscape, then the cost of installing the 330 kw machines in an area of outstanding beauty or in a national park would reach between £4 million and £40 million each. If this cost is paid off over the 20-year lifetime of the machine at a discount rate of 8 per cent, then the annual cost would be from £40–£400. As the wind energy converter (WEC) would generate around 10^6 kWh per year in good conditions, the external cost would amount to 4–40 pence per kWh.

These figures are based on the assumption that the wind farm would totally degrade the beauty of the area. If it was supposed that the effect was less than total, or if the area were of less outstanding beauty, then the costs could be very much lower, becoming close to zero for landscape of little amenity value.

Noise pollution is also site specific, and the calculation of its impact is complicated by levels of intensity and distance from the source. In general the costs of noise pollution from turbines or other technologies need to be studied in detail for every site.

INTERNALIZING EXTERNAL COSTS

To determine the real costs of energy, and to allow for a comparison of conventional and renewable energy sources, we must be able to calculate external costs. But simply knowing these costs is not enough to overcome market distortions and to guarantee any change in present energy policies. External costs must be internalized to affect future resource planning, acquisition and operational decisions.

Future decision-makers will have to consider two strategies when internalizing externalities. One, the use of subsidies and taxation, will bring about change in the short term. The other must include long term policy measures such as the use of alternative resources and changes in operational practice. This is particularly important as the choice of resources entails long term commitments, so that making the wrong choice could have disastrous consequences for health and the environment, not just in our lifetime, but also for the next generation. Both utilities and society in general must be pushed, by regulation and legislation, into environmentally benign and sustainable energy policies.

In this section four ways of internalizing external costs are addressed: fiscal policy; environmental regulation; resource options; operational practice.

Fiscal policy

Fiscal policies include subsidies and taxes. Subsidies for the development of conventional energy technologies have been in existence for a long time. They could be cut altogether or diverted to investment in both alternative and renewable resources, and in the development of energy efficiency which would help to stimulate their introduction to the market. Several European countries and some states in the US have already started to do this. For example, both Denmark and The Netherlands subsidize investment in wind turbines. So, too, does Germany which subsidizes small, locally sponsored turbines for the kWh that they generate and, also, in proportion to their effect in cutting environmental and social costs. The UK uses the NFFO to encourage the installation of renewable energy. In the US the Californian Energy Commission is considering a fund for energy research and development which is directly tied to environmental costs.

The most general way to internalize external costs is to introduce fuel and emission taxes, and fees for the disposal of nuclear waste. In the US 19 states have adopted coal severance taxes based on the value of production or on the volume of mined coal. These revenues are used to offset the environmental and social costs of burning coal. In some states, all or part of the revenues are deposited in restricted accounts to ensure that they are used for these purposes. Taxes on emissions are another means of internalizing the costs of pollution. Sweden introduced carbon and sulphur emission taxes on fossil fuels on 1 January 1991. The EU is also considering the introduction of carbon taxes.

The main advantage of introducing fuel or emission taxes is that they can be adjusted to reach certain targets for abatement. They also provide a mechanism for raising revenue for pollution control equipment, for scientific research, for inequity reduction, and for investment in technologies for renewable resources and energy efficiency.

Taxes generate large amounts of revenue, for example, a carbon tax of $15 per tonne, if applied throughout the world today, would generate $84 billion annually. Would it be used for mitigating pollution or for remedial action, or would it become part of general tax revenue? Another problem is that if high taxes are put on to fuels and energy consumption, other taxes would have to be reduced to compensate, otherwise the overall effect would be further to disadvantage the poor.

Environmental regulation

Direct environmental regulations for emission reductions, for the control of air and water pollution, and for dealing with hazardous waste are widely applied in many countries. However, as emission reduction targets are, in most cases, insufficiently stringent, the regulations will only lead to the introduction of alternative energy technologies in the long term. It is possible to introduce a system in which permissions to pollute up to a certain level are sold at auction. Although, in this system, market forces would determine the cost of such permits, the administrative problems would be horrendous.

Resource options

Integrated resource planning and least-cost planning are directed to meeting energy demand at the least possible overall cost. There are always several options for energy acquisition and they are examined before any planning decision is taken. Should a utility consider changing

Author	Average coal power station		Nuclear power	Wind power
	Global warming	*Acid deposition*	*Catastrophe*	*Visual intrusion*
Ferguson[1]	1–100	0.3–3	0.15–5	8–30 (AONB) Negligible for most sites
Hohmeyer	40–100	1–3	1–7	
Pearce	~0.5	~5	0.5	
Ottinger[2]		3–7		
California Energy Commission[2]		7–20 (for plant in California)		

1 Ferguson emphasizes the uncertainty in costs due to the uncertainty in understanding of the effects of global warming, acid deposits and the public perception of catastrophes, His costs for wind turbines in national parks and areas of outstanding natural beauty are reflected in the fierce opposition to siting in these areas. Turbines in undistinguished landscapes have negligible costs for visual intrusion.

2 The studies by Ottinger (PACE University) and the California Energy Commission do not separate costs into the two categories.

This is not a complete survey of all the published data but it is representative of the work throughout the world.

Table 2.2 *Environmental costs of energy technologies (p/kWh)*

its resources and introducing demand-side management to its long term planning, then regulation can determine that only those options which have included environmental costs and which conform to environmental 'standards' should be considered. In the US 26 states have begun to introduce this kind of planning by requiring public utilities to account for external costs in their integrated resource plans.

Operational practice

Environmental costs should be included not only in utility planning, but also in operational decisions. This would allow the calculation of the economic costs of the environmental impact of both existing and planned capacity, which is summed up as 'the dispatch of energy generating facilities'. Known as 'the least full cost dispatch', the advantage of this approach is that it includes existing plant which is, invariably, the most polluting.

Other approaches

Several other approaches to internalizing externalities have been developed. Some states in the US add a certain amount per kWh to the expected price of electricity from each source, based on the cost of air and water pollution. Yet other states have adopted a method developed by Buchanan and his colleagues from the Bonneville Power Administration (BPA). In this the costs per kWh of both power generation and power conservation are compared, but conservation is given a bonus of 10 per cent because of its obvious environmental benefits. According to BPA, energy efficiency and conservation are the most cost-effective resources, while new nuclear power plant, coal-fired plant and co-generation are the most expensive.

All these approaches can be used in one way or another for resource planning and acquisition. However, as none of them by themselves provides a completely adequate way of internalizing external costs, it might be advisable to use several of them simultaneously to arrive at a combination of options.

CONCLUSION

Over the last few years the calculation of the external costs of energy has become widely accepted by decision-makers and utilities alike. Even if some externalities cannot be estimated without diffi-

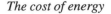

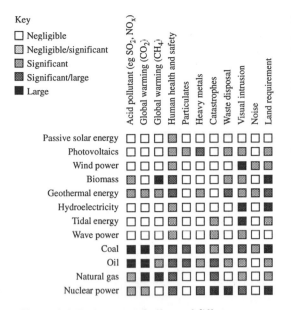

Figure 2.1 *Environmental effects of different energy technologies*

culty, neglecting them results in a bias against technologies in which they are small or negligible.

Internalizing environmental externalities allows for a comparison of the costs of competing technologies, and thus enables both decision-makers and utilities to base their resource planning and acquisition on comparable and less biased data.

It also means that more appropriate price signals could be sent to planners and consumers, and this, in turn, should lead to a change in the magnitude and mix of resources needed to satisfy energy demand. A change in the sources of energy would be beneficial as the costs associated with replacing such sources would not be additional but would reflect investments that have in any case to be made because investment turnover in the energy sector takes place every 25–30 years.

Estimating the external costs, as in Table 2.1, reveals that those accruing from generation from fossil fuels and nuclear power are quite significant compared to the costs of renewable technologies. Although further studies estimating the complete range of environmental costs are called for, it is already evident from those in Table 2.2 that, if further damage to environment and to health is to be avoided, then the course for restructuring the current energy policy has to be set now. As energy policies include long term commitments, decision-makers and utilities should put into effect energy policies based on least cost planning and the use of several analytical approaches. Policies that should distinguish themselves by imposing the lowest overall cost to society and which should be economically and environmentally sustainable.

We have made clear that the discussion of the environmental costs of energy provision and use is complicated. Figure 2.1 provides a crude overview of environmental damage caused by supply technologies. It lacks numbers and this is in order to emphasize the need for detailed, site-specific investigations in every case at issue.

3

ENERGY PLANNING

This chapter is about the development of the principles that underlie energy policy. They are commitments to a sustainable energy economy and to energy security, and are not only important for long term co-operation with development partners but also an opportunity to minimize ecological risk. This is particularly important at a time when global warming and acid deposition threaten to undermine the very basis of a sustainable environment.

Given these concerns a commitment to a model of 'best practice' must be constructed and implemented in both developed and developing countries. This inevitably demands a reflexive policy that takes into direct consideration the heterogenous nature of energy supply technologies, and local, regional and national cultural traditions. The following discussion suggests socio-economic, technical and environmental considerations for designing a sustainable energy economy. Their implementation is illustrated by a case study of agroforestry in Africa.

ENERGY IN THE GLOBAL VILLAGE

The world is rapidly becoming a single global village. In it, developed families cannot deny the existence of the poor. The major initiative for changing matters must, however, lie with the poor themselves. Development aid is no more than a small contribution to the alleviation of poverty.

Developing countries face three serious problems. These are:

1 increasing ecological destruction;
2 low levels of economic development;
3 problems with maintaining political pluralism.

Problems, addressed correctly, can produce solutions that generate new opportunities and these must be opportunities for sustainability.

In the past decade, as aid has increasingly been focused on poverty alleviation, discussion on designing sustainable responses to development challenges has emerged. But there is little point in addressing vital issues if they simply re-emerge, in a more acute manner, in another generation. The basic policy aim of development can be summarized by the wish: 'May today's children die of old age, having confidence in the future.'

Several development problems, particularly those concerned with the environment, such as population growth, the greenhouse effect, ecological degradation and natural resource exhaustion, only appear as problems after a long delay. If such problems are not addressed immediately they accumulate, creating conditions in the system that cannot be repaired. Prevention is usually cheaper than cure and, even if a firm diagnosis is not yet available, paying now for prevention is a wise precaution. It is precisely because these time-delayed problems are difficult to handle in the future that they need to be addressed as policy issues now. A starting point is the definition of a clear energy policy with a long term perspective.

We have in mind a perspective which runs to the mid twenty-first century when, although many readers of this chapter will be dead, power plant built now will still be operating. Medium term policies, up to 2010, will have to make significant progress towards long term objectives. This means the full implementation of energy efficiency measures and the use of renewable energy sources. Short term action, which includes formulating an energy policy, must be focused on institutional developments that can secure a sustainable energy future and on the immediate introduction of efficiency measures. Efficiency is the key which, among other things, makes energy resources available for alternative purposes. Short term initiatives must not undermine the longer term.

It is not immediately evident that an energy policy for development is needed. For most economic activity, energy is just an input and it is neither difficult nor expensive to obtain. However, precisely because of this, energy markets are a poor guide to developing a sustainable energy future. Energy is never an item of final consumption, but only a means of providing services and satisfying basic needs. Energy however, differs from other economic inputs in that it is associated with a number of macro-economic problems with a wide spatial and a long temporal impact.

Energy is used in all sectors of society. In energy policy, however, it is important to distinguish different levels of energy issues. The first and most important is energy as an environmental issue where it codetermines the level of sustainable development. Crudely, this is a situation where energy issues put the existence of a nation state at risk. At a global level, climate change resulting from enhanced global warming is another such issue.

Energy is also a strategic issue influencing national development and energy scarcity. Policies here address issues of natural resource exploitation, fuel switching, energy for industrialization, transport and rural electrification. Separate from these two levels are matters relating to secondary energy, including discussion of energy forms, pricing, availability and quality as well as of management techniques, institutions and technologies for the delivery of energy. These secondary questions must be dealt within a broader policy framework which demonstrates a commitment to long term institutional development.

The parameters for the global village energy future

Present energy consumption in developed countries is 7 kW per capita, but only 1.1 kW per capita in the developing countries. Technology already exists for a reduction from 7 to 3 kW per capita in the developed world and it is theoretically possible to achieve a 3 kW per capita world by 2060, but only if, both for economic and environmental reasons, energy efficiency and the use of renewables are adopted more or less everywhere.

Fossil fuel prices, when left to the market, have not provided an incentive for improving energy efficiency or for employing renewable energy on a large scale. The prices of hydrocarbons must be monitored because, although these resources are underpriced, neither the costs for resource depletion nor for the externalities associated with production and use are included, they are the benchmark for costing any intervention in the energy sector. Governments also need to monitor energy markets proactively so as to determine how they should intervene to create a sustainable energy future. This problem is particularly acute when addressing policy issues to minimize environmental damage.

Current world energy use is 10 TW (10^{12} watts) and rising rapidly, and most of it is obtained from non-renewable resources. Gross world annual photosynthesis, the essential but only conditionally renewable resource, is some 100 TW. In the longer term, photosynthetic production will neither be a major energy source nor a carbon sink. This points up the need to address long term problems of sustainability by concentrating on efficiency and on the use of renewables that directly convert incoming solar radiation to productive energy.

Global warming is the problem that most clearly establishes the direction of a long term sustainable energy future. To avoid the enhanced greenhouse effect and, by implication, climatic disaster, the human population must emit no more carbon dioxide than it does today. In crude terms, this probably means an upper limit of carbon emissions of 5 billion tonnes per year. Assuming that demographic change produces a steady state population of 15 billion, per capita consumption would have to be reduced to 0.5 kW per year. This is roughly 10–20 times less than developed countries use now.

The trend towards greater urbanization in developing countries is unlikely to change, so an accelerating transition to hydrocarbon fuels is inevitable. However, experience has shown that the potential for change is much greater in urban than in rural environments. The urban opportunity is the 'Coca-Cola' opportunity because energy, like soft drinks, is a universal service already commoditized and advertised. Assistance for urban development should be designed to ensure that best practice prevails. Energy efficiency programmes, coupled with health, sanitation and waste programmes, can be integrated into urban development as a priority. There should also be a renewed emphasis on efficient public transport.

The section below highlights two possible and contrasting trends in development which will produce different commercial energy futures. They suggest that, for some countries, there will be an increase in energy use at a rate above the growth of gross national product.

ENERGY POLICY AND MARKETS

It is necessary to recognize that to design a sustainable energy policy for the future, it is not enough to rely on market signals which are derived from the appraisal of volume and price for energy commodities. Market information does not include the costs of resource depletion and of pollution. It also excludes those substantial energy resources collected as 'free goods' for use in households in developing countries. At best, the market indicates what energy future is profitable, not what is sustainable. By focusing on profitability, the market emphasizes short term solutions: by focusing on least cost investment, the market reinforces the short term outlook.

The limitations of the market cannot be addressed by a simple technology push involving the rapid transfer of existing technology from developed to developing countries. Such a transfer is focused on energy supply, not on energy consumption. In most cases, developed countries themselves do not supply technologies designed for a sustainable energy future and the beneficiaries of investment in developing countries tend to be the rich, not the poor.

The design of energy policy calls for a focus on energy consumers by sector of economic activity. This will require the strengthening of institutional arrangements so that consumer need can be secured. An emphasis on security, on economic maximization, successfully pervades the energy policy of developed countries – the best demonstration of this was the minimal impact of the Gulf War on energy supplies. Security for energy consumers must be matched by an emphasis on energy efficiency. Again, reliance on market signals gives the wrong message – while it is cheaper to save a unit of energy than to produce a new one, it is more profitable, for any individual electricity company, to produce a new unit of energy than to save one.

Beyond the market, in the household energy sector dominated by woody biomass fuels, it is difficult to price energy goods. A tree, for example, is usually a free good available to an entire community or, often, to all. Even a nominal price for the tree as wood energy is difficult to calculate because it is simultaneously a resource for fodder, fencing and fruit. Designing woody biomass projects, if a nominal price for woodfuel can be accepted, is hazardous at best. Signals from the energy market are important but they cannot drive an energy policy committed to a long term sustainable energy future focused on securing stable supplies for consumers. Such security is provided by emphasizing efficiency and by supporting the local management of renewable energy resources.

Towards a sustainable energy future

The present concept of 'development' is based on the Western model of society. Europe uses about 5 kW and the US 10 kW per person, and are dominated by production from fossil fuels. But these levels are only possible so long as they are limited to no more than a small fraction of the global population.

If non-carbon energy sources are to become dominant, then the world energy price must be significantly higher than it is today. The present Northern societal structure (large turnover of goods, high mobility etc) is poorly adapted for the sorts of price level needed and its technologies are far from optimal. The Western model is therefore not one for best future practice in developing countries. Developing countries must aim to achieve well-being at historically high international energy prices and the developed world will have to transform itself within the same framework.

Figure 3.1 demonstrates the route that developing countries must take to achieve the goal of sustainable energy and they should be helped to find the shortest route to it. This will need both societal and technological change, the beginnings of which exist neither in the developed nor in the developing world. Introducing them is the challenge to societal and technological research and innovation, and a task to be shared by all countries.

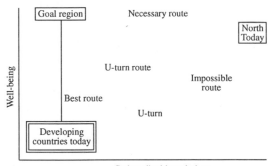

Source: after Ferguson

Figure 3.1 *Future environmental paths*

National energy and environment policy

In The Netherlands, the national energy policy, focused on conservation, got enormous encouragement in the wake of the oil crisis. Overall, energy consumption was reduced by almost 2 per cent per year, while the economy continued to grow. At the beginning of the 1980s, however, the economic growth rate was not high. This, combined with a small shift towards less energy intensive sectors of industry, made total energy consumption in 1985 just about the same as it had been in 1973. The annual energy efficiency improvement rate has, at the present time, fallen to less than half of what it was in the period 1973–85.

The CO_2 and climate issue is taking a prominent position in the concerns of the industrialized nations, particularly through the International Energy Agency, the IPCC and the EU. It is becoming so serious that it has prompted international action. However, developing countries with large fossil fuel reserves (China, with its coal, and the Organization of Petroleum Exporting Countries (OPEC) countries) might have less interest in participating in CO_2 reductions, as international sales and inland use of these fuels are a major source of income and a motor for development: in the short term, economic constraint can override environmental concerns.

Designing sustainable energy policy

Developing countries have been excluded from much of the discussion on global environmental change. Furthermore, their short term economic and energy security problems imply that, if a new mode of energy and development is not found, they will increasingly contribute a substantial proportion of carbon emissions.

Sustainable energy policies start from the point of consumption, not of supply. This is an emphasis on end-use which, in turn, allows for a focus on energy efficiency. Looking at end-use also allows certain sectors of the energy economies of developing countries to be highlighted, particularly those of household energy and of energy transition in urban areas, notably in transport. In fact the main objective of an end-use orientation is to enable a sustainable energy economy, which gives particular emphasis to household energy needs, to be built in developing countries.

End-use

End-use is a worm's eye view of the energy problem. It starts with the people or organizations using energy rather than with supply.

End-use and supply are the opposite ends of a chain which runs from the energy source, through transformation and distribution to the services the end-user wants. End-use analysis begins by defining major energy consumption sectors. In general, these are households, industry, transport, agriculture and commerce. Major sub-sectors within the household sector are used to differentiate between driving power and heating requirements; within transport, the major sub-sectors are passenger and freight requirements.

In rural households, the dominant end-use is cooking, although there are numerous others such as space and water heating, ironing, and light. These end-uses vary from region to region depending on socio-economic, cultural and ecological considerations. A disaggregated end-use approach can capture the complexity of this situation, allowing a range of solutions to be offered.

For each end-use, such as cooking, there is a further level of disaggregation associated with:

- fuel type;
- technology;
- energy intensity;
- social class of users.

Examining each end-use from this level of disaggregation allows for a clear analysis of policy options. These run from fuel switching, through technology transfer and energy intensity, to government intervention on behalf of certain end-users.

Global warming

The major environmental challenge facing humanity over the next 100 years is climate change. Scientific advisers and policy-makers now accept that the rate of climatic change might be more substantial than at any point in the last 10,000 years. This is because the greenhouse effect, which produces temperatures that allow people to live on earth, is being enhanced.

The earth's climate is driven by many factors. The primary force is radiant energy from the sun, and the reflection or absorption and reradiation of this energy by atmospheric gas molecules, clouds, and the surface of the earth itself. A portion of this reradiated energy leaves the atmosphere, and over the long term, a balance is maintained between the solar energy entering the atmosphere and the

energy leaving it. The net result of these natural processes is the 'greenhouse effect' – a warming of the earth's atmosphere and surface. Water vapour (in the form of clouds) and carbon dioxide (CO_2) are major contributors to this effect, with smaller but still significant contributions coming from methane (CH_4), nitrous oxide (N_2O) and ozone (O_3).

Human activities during the last century have resulted in significant increases in concentrations of CO_2, CH_4 and N_2O, as well as the introduction of chlorofluorocarbons (CFCs). As concentrations increase more radiation should be trapped to further warm the earth's surface and atmosphere. This should lead to an 'enhanced' greenhouse effect and a warmer climate which, in turn, will probably produce a parallel rise in sea level of between 0.4–0.6 m (OTA, 1990). The consequent threat of flooding is not limited only to The Netherlands. Some ten million of the world's population live less than 3m above sea level. Substantial areas, from inhabited Pacific atolls to the coastal areas of Egypt and Bangladesh, will become increasingly prone to flooding. If flooding is accompanied by major shifts in global atmospheric pressure, substantial alterations in global food production systems could occur. The impact of such change is difficult to predict but has to be considered as potentially enormous.

The cause of this enhancement of the greenhouse gases is readily identifiable. Over half comes from burning fossil fuel which releases carbon dioxide. A second substantial contribution comes from change in land use, particularly deforestation which accompanies the clearance of land for agriculture. A third is of chlorofluorocarbons (CFCs) used for coolants, propellants and solvents (CFCs also damage the ozone layer). In addition to these three dominant gases, there are others such as methane and nitrous oxide which are related to agriculture but which also contribute to the enhanced greenhouse effect. Natural gas is predominantly methane and so, when it is released, it, too, adds to greenhouse enhancement. The problem, however, is that the developed and the developing world produce these gases in different quantities.

The developing world is largely responsible for changes in land use as it seeks to bring more land into productive agricultural activity: the developed world is, however, responsible for most of the production of carbon dioxide and

CFCs. In the not too distant future, the newly emerging industrial countries (NEICs) including India and China, are likely to develop energy intensive industries which will substantially increase their releases of both carbon dioxides and CFCs. Their demand for access to functions of the ecoscope is likely to increase the problems of the enhanced greenhouse effect.

Urban air pollution

Developing countries are urbanizing rapidly and, by 2050, half the world's population will live in cities. This change of habitat is itself producing environmental problems. The combustion of hydrocarbons has led to levels of air pollution in the cities of developing countries which rank among the highest in the world. Transport is the largest contributor but the combustion of hydrocarbons, in electricity generating units and households, also add to them. Emissions of nitrogen oxides, particulates, sulphur dioxide, carbon dioxide and carbon monoxide are high. Coal is the most polluting of all of the fossil fuels in terms of emissions per unit of energy consumed, particularly when fired in inefficient plants, as in many developing countries.

These urban environmental problems are paralleled by more regional problems, of which the greatest is acid rain. Sulphur oxides and nitrogen oxides, emitted by the combustion of carbon fuels, have increased acid precipitation. On a global scale, over 60 per cent of this problem is currently due to the emission of sulphur oxides, largely from coal fired power stations. Smoke stacks work against the local dry deposition of sulphur oxides which, because of the altitude of emission, tend to be transported from the site of pollution. Prevailing meteorological conditions, notably wind direction and rainfall, tend to deposit sulphur and nitrogen oxides in mountainous areas from which they flow into fresh water systems, including reservoirs and lakes. The acidification of lakes and rivers is linked to acid precipitation and has impacts on a variety of aquatic organisms in the food chain. The growing use of coal in the Third World, particularly of high sulphur coal, will increase acid deposition unless suitable scrubbing technology is attached to coal fired power plants. Urbanization can consequently produce not just urban but also rural pollution. More emphasis

will be placed in our policy on reducing the effects of air pollution by supporting energy efficiency in the transport sector, by energy and environmental audits in industry, and by increasing accessibility to environmentally benign technology in the power production sector.

Deforestation

It is a mistake to attribute large scale deforestation to wood cutting for energy; more important processes are land clearance, grazing and bushfires. However, in local instances, fuelwood consumption can be a major contributing process, particularly near settlements and in sensitive eco-systems. For example, in the arid zones of developing countries, like the Sahel in Africa, stands of trees are being destroyed or threatened by fuelwood cutting. Either there is no replanting or it is insufficient to maintain existing stocks and yields: natural recovery is also hampered by livestock grazing. The most serious problems arise not from the rural population, but from the urban population which demands a steady supply of fuelwood and charcoal. Loggers have a wide variety of resources from which to cut and will simply look elsewhere if any village or rural region tries to collect a selling price (in stumpage fees). In short, local people have no bargaining power with which to enhance their management of local resources.

Experience shows, however, that the only people who can protect and replant trees are local villagers. Planting by authorities is difficult to manage on the required scale and it is expensive. But as long as prices to producers remain low and levels of responsibility remain unclear, local people often have little interest in planting or protecting trees and, consequently, sustainable wood production is virtually impossible.

Charcoal

In rural areas cutting fuelwood for conversion to charcoal (essentially an urban fuel) is a major source of income and non-agricultural employment. End-users prefer charcoal to woodfuels for a number of reasons. It is cleaner, produces less smoke, is easier to handle, easier to light, involves shorter cooking times, and is free from insect attack and wetting. It is usually made by stacking wood, covering it with a layer of earth and letting it burn with a limited supply of air. The efficiency of these simple earthen kilns is low, typically ranging from 40 to 60 per cent (Nkonoki and Sorensen, 1984). One bag of charcoal is equivalent in volume to ten bags of wood.

Charcoal is a 'priced' fuel and because it is popular, and its method of production is poor, a number of ways to promote efficiency in both production and use now exist. The introduction of more efficient kilns is one obvious move. If capital investment is made, ranging from a few hundred dollars for simple modifications to traditional kilns (Christopherson et al, 1988) to $100,000 or more for a modern continuous retort, higher energy efficiencies can be achieved (OTA, 1990).

The source of wood is also a matter for concern. Indiscriminate felling for charcoal has had detrimental effects, especially when it happens close to urban areas, where, among other things, woodland as an amenity is destroyed. One option is to identify charcoal production areas which can then be institutionalized and improved. It is a mistake to ban charcoal production altogether, as in the Gambia, because, where there is sufficient demand, banning simply leads to cross-frontier transfers. This, in turn, can impoverish other areas (in the case of the Gambia it is the Cassamance region of Senegal) which have no forms of redress.

As even the best traditional rural technologies lose 60 per cent of the energy content of wood in converting it into charcoal, and as the more customary loss is around 75 per cent, urban household demand exacerbates deforestation. Even though charcoal stoves use slightly less energy than the corresponding wood stoves, in the end changing over from wood to charcoal doubles, if not triples, wood consumption.

A global problem that parallels both energy use and changes in land use is the conservation of tropical rainforests and their biological diversity. They account, very roughly, for 50 per cent of all species of flora and fauna. Since 1950, over ten thousand species have been lost, largely through the destruction of tropical rain forests. However, although it does not have such an immediate impact on biodiversity, deforestation is larger in scale in semi arid and arid regions than in tropical rain forests, where logging and land clearance are for agriculture, not for fuelwood.

More emphasis has to be given, in energy policies, to the sustainable management of local land-use systems in which woody biomass for energy is just one component. Energy efficiency technologies that reduce the cost and secure the supplies of energy for rural and low income urban households must also be emphasized.

ENERGY AND EQUITY

Meeting the challenge of maintaining and enhancing the ecoscope is not simply a matter of polluting less and moving from non-renewable to renewable resources, but also of equity. Solving one environmental problem can frequently lead to others and, in the end, no solution will work without greater equity in access to the ecoscope.

The operation of an expanding, open economic system in a finite closed ecoscope poses several policy issues. It is important to screen technologies to minimize ecoscope disruption, to use environmental impact (EIA) and cost-benefit (CBA) analyses, and environmental profiles to outline the impact of investment on the ecoscope. But the major problem remains. It is that current energy production technologies are largely hydrocarbon based and cause significant environmental damage. Yet it is precisely these technologies that developing countries need most for their national economic development.

We have already remarked that there is a significant difference in the consumption of primary energy between developed and developing countries. The latter consume less than 28 per cent of world energy – taken together, all developing countries consume only the equivalent of 25 per cent of US fossil energy consumption. In developing countries, changes in energy prices do not have an immediate impact on fuel consumption, because household use is fixed at a virtually irreducible level by the need to cook food.

Rural women and children pay an increasing price in time in gathering biomass fuels to secure their energy subsistence. It is commonly two to three hours per day and in some cases can be up to five hours. Poorer urban households pay an increasing cash price because, for most of them, collecting fuel is not possible as supplies around towns become more and more depleted.

A proportion of income in urban areas is spent on switching to more advanced fuels. In Addis Ababa, Ethiopia, for example, by 1986, 70 per cent of households had switched to kerosene because wood and charcoal prices had risen. Paradoxically, as the price of energy rises, the demand does not fall. Therefore in developing countries, over the last 20 years, oil consumption continued to grow steadily, reflecting the original low consumption base, while in developed countries it varied, following the movement in oil prices. This indicated both a higher volume of consumption and an ability to lower consumption through investment in energy efficiency.

Developing countries must have a right to the economic opportunities enjoyed by developed countries. For that purpose, more investment in state-of-the-art technologies that maximize efficiency, minimize environmental damage and are budget neutral, especially for poor people, is needed. Furthermore, the concentration of energy investment in urban economic centres does not encourage significant rural development without which rural resource depletion and migration to urban centres will grow.

Economics and politics of energy resource depletion

The very size of energy production and consumption technologies, and the environmental problems associated with them, have made their impact global rather than local. The scale of this impact poses special problems for the costing of global environmental damage. Conventional economic analysis cannot handle the costs of pollution and of the depletion of common property resources because common property, like climate or air quality, cannot be privatized and thus is outside the market place. Different mechanisms have to be found to ensure equity in access to ecoscope both within and between nations, and, in the developing world, equity is closely tied to the alleviation of poverty, which will lead to an increase in energy consumption.

Several factors, in developing countries, will cause the use of commercial energy to rise more rapidly than gross national product. First, the growth of urban households will result in an increase in the commercial provision of goods and services, and thus in energy demand. Second, there will be a move from traditional biomass fuels to modern fuels and technologies at the very moment when they are available and affordable, especially in urban areas. Third, the building of commercial industrial and transport infrastructures will require the use of large quantities of energy intensive material. Fourth, modern manufacturing technologies have increased the access of the poor to a range of consumer goods which demand energy (radios, torches etc).

These factors are counter-balanced by others which will moderate a rapid increase in energy demand. First, the high cost of developing national energy infrastructure will limit its rapid expansion except in developing countries, notably China and India, which have sufficient hydrocarbon resources to pursue such investment. Second, energy efficiency improvements world-wide will become accessible to developing countries. Third, when poverty is alleviated by economic development, structural changes will shift investment from energy intensive infrastructure to higher value added goods.

Energy use in developing countries will depend on how these opposing economic factors operate. At low levels of development, the first set of factors predominate while, at higher levels of development, the converse is true. For rapidly industrializing countries, growth rates in energy use will be substantially slower than those in gross national product. The challenge for energy policy-makers is to establish strategies now without being able to predict the future for which they are designed.

Increased energy efficiency will enable developing countries to destroy the direct links between increases in standards of living and increases in energy use. To date, however, the energy transition model for developing countries that seems most probable is that followed by the former Soviet Union and Eastern Europe where a level of industrial development, and thus a level of improved income, was built on a high per capita consumption of primary energy. This is the route which will result in environmental problems. Within developing countries, economic development is an important determinant of energy consumption, and thus of equity, but it is not the only one. Energy intensity varies enormously between and within countries. In the years immediately before 1973, global energy intensity rose, but after 1973 there was a sharp drop in developed countries which reflected the growing importance of energy efficiency and conservation not matched in developing countries. Differences in energy intensity reflect differences in urbanization, the quality of industrial structure and levels of technology.

Some projections suggest that, by 2010, commercial energy consumption for developing countries could be 2.5 times higher than in 1985, suggesting a growth rate of 3.8 per cent (OTA, 1991). More conservative figures suggest that with an annual increase of 3.3 per cent, commercial consumption in developing countries will be 3 times higher than in 1985 while consumption of traditional fuels will grow by 25 per cent over the same period. Policies addressing the probable environmental impact of such a growth of commercial energy, which will largely be a growth in hydrocarbon consumption, will require an emphasis on models of best practice for urban energy consumption. This emphasis must include energy intensity in industry by concentrating on value adding processes and by improving accessibility to best practice technology from developed to developing countries. Most importantly, it requires an end-use analysis of energy, where energy consumption requirements are accurately matched to energy supplies. Such an approach will limit reliance on over-engineered single supply solutions, and will create space for energy efficiency improvements, and an expanded use of new and renewable sources of energy. The Dutch government's policy emphasizes an end-use approach because it maximizes equity in, and access to, energy services, while simultaneously minimizing environmental damage.

There is little doubt that a key issue in equity is the access of poorer households to fuel supplies. Their need for energy is irreducible but the cost in collection time or in cash has been rising over the last 20 years. Institutional support for poorer households must concentrate on minimizing the risk of fuel shortage. In rural areas, especially in the case of refugees (the most vulnerable of the vulnerable), where fuel scarcity is compounded by large local increases in population, policy must provide greater access to and control of productive resources by local people. In the case of refugee settlements in Sudan, gov-ernment policy puts a ceiling on their access to resources by insisting that it should be no better than that of other local people. At the same time, the activities of commercial farmers and commercial charcoal producers have led to a great reduction in the amount of fuelwood available. Initiatives aimed at improving local fuel supplies through farm woodlands, social forestry and community forestry have, however, in some cases, been successful.

Another way of supporting the more disadvantaged in both rural and urban areas is through income support schemes that allow for the purchase of energy. In rural areas such income may be achieved by smallholder cash cropping, service industry and domestic based manufacturing industries. Experience of Dutch supported refugee schemes in Tanzania and Sudan shows that, even in the case of refugees, it is possible to achieve sustainable development within a project.

Energy and national development

The use of different fuels in developing countries varies enormously – they use 80 per cent of biomass fuel but only 23 per cent of commercial energy. Several developing countries – China, India, Mexico, Brazil and South Africa – are among the largest energy consumers. Just three – China, India and Brazil – account for 45 per cent while, at the other end of the scale, the 50 countries of Africa use less than 3 per cent of total energy consumption in the developing world. The developing countries are expected to increase their share of global energy consumption to 40 per cent by 2020, which will account for almost 60 per cent of the global increase.

Most public investment is in electricity production and transmission, a commitment to capital expenditure that seems increasingly unsustainable. Africa alone requires $110 billion of capital investment in energy technology by 2010, largely in the electricity sector. Such investment is unlikely to occur without substantial private capital resources.

It is not just capital investment, but also recurrent expenditure which dominates discussion of the impact of energy costs on the national economy. Energy imports are, for the non-oil producing countries, a significant factor of recurrent expenditure.

In the energy sector, the level and stability of prices are of great influence on national economies. Stable prices encourage short term financial stability and make possible opportunities for long term sustainable development. Commercial energy markets are dominated by oil so that, quintessentially, sustainable energy development needs a stable oil market. In the medium to long term, the long run marginal supply price of oil is expected to be relatively constant. National, European and global policy aimed at limiting price instability in the oil market caused by political upheaval must be accompanied by questions about the real cost of energy, including the externalities of pollution, so that the global issue of carbon taxes can be addressed. The best investment in the energy sector for minimizing the impact of political and price disruption is efficiency rather than an expansion in supply lines.

The scale of future investment in the energy sector is projected as being very large. The World Bank estimates that $125 billion (which is double current investment) is needed to supply developing countries with electricity. It also estimates that electricity currently accounts for 50 per cent of all investment; oil, including refineries, 40 per cent; and natural gas and coal 5 per cent each. Over half the cost of energy investment is in foreign exchange and only coal has low foreign exchange costs. Financing this level of foreign capital resources will prove increasingly difficult for national economies over the next investment cycle, leading them, where resources are nationally available, to coal fired commercial energy futures. Developing countries need support to build a policy framework that enables them to seek less energy intensive development paths.

Energy as a productive factor

The productive sector of developing countries consumes between 40 and 60 per cent of commercial energy. The primary energy services are process heat and, to a lesser degree, mechanical drive. The form of energy provision is basically determined by whether industries are cottage, small factories or large scale processing units. In developing countries, although the modern sector is the largest energy consumer, as much as 70 per cent of industrial production can be in cottage industries which causes severe problems for energy delivery.

Process heat, ranging from low temperature heat for food processing through to high temperature processing of steel and cement, are energy demands with lower efficiencies than those obtainable in the developed world. Modern large scale industries operate at significantly lower efficiencies in developing countries and a few energy intensive materials – steel, cement, fertilizer and paper – account for most of industrial energy use. Mechanical drive is largely met by electric motors. Again, efficiencies are low because of poor maintenance, repair and rewind, as well as power variation. Energy use is dominated by the provision of basic metals and this could be the emerging energy pattern for all developing countries if a positive emphasis on energy efficiency is not pursued.

Other major sectors of energy demand are transport, residential and services. They consume slightly less energy but are none the less extremely important in consumption patterns. In many developing countries transport consumes more than a quarter of total commercial energy and most of it is oil derived. Although developing countries have only a small fraction of automobiles per person compared with developed countries, that fraction is growing. These automobiles are, in many cases, very inefficient and are a major cause of pollution. This is partly due to the 'transfer of relics' from the North to the South (vehicles that could not get a sale in the North are sold or donated to developing countries) and partly due to low scrappage rates.

The increase in the private ownership of cars and the rapid rates of urbanization combine to create urban congestion, which lowers vehicle efficiency and, in turn, adds to urban air pollution. Improvements both in engine efficiency and to infrastructure could lead to greater energy efficiency. The major challenge, however, is mass public transport.

Public services include health, education, utilities and government institutions. These tend to be arranged so that the highest level and most energy consuming activities are concentrated in large urban and élite areas, particularly in capital cities, which often have public service facilities comparable to those of developed countries. These include high energy consumption for lighting, office facilities and other equipment. Electrification has been extended to the level of small towns in many places, but intensity of use in secondary institutions (for example, small hospitals and clinics) is much less than in large administrative centres.

Most opportunities for efficient energy use in developed countries are relevant to developing countries. In particular, where energy efficiency investment reduces overall capital requirements, such investments should be made, since capital is scarce. It is difficult to achieve this because many policy instruments available to developed countries, such as rebate programmes, cannot work in developing countries where there are few fiscal mechanisms for delivering rebates to the poor. What is needed is a review of the product cycle of the entire energy system, from end-use to supply, which examines the effect of improved efficiency on saving foreign exchange and in minimizing environmental damage.

It should be noted that energy efficiency, and the use of a localized resource base, together with an emphasis on the production and use of renewable resources, can lead to the development of less energy intensive industries which will maintain prosperity while minimizing damage to the ecoscope.

Energy and basic needs

Enhancing economic development and improving opportunities has not lead to the eradication of poverty. Consequently, more tailor-made programmes have been developed that concentrate on basic human needs. This, it is hoped, will reduce the rate of migration from country to towns and, therefore, the cost of rapid uncontrolled urbanization.

Basic needs programmes aim to provide minimum standards of nutrition, shelter, clothing, sanitation, health, education and employment in rural areas. Energy is not specifically part of these programmes, but is indirectly required for the satisfaction of these needs and it usually comes from biomass fuels. Two-thirds of the world's developing population, some 2.6 billion people, live in rural areas with little access to commercial energy supplies and technologies. Biomass fuels provide the heating and cooking needs of these populations, and we

have already commented on some of the problems associated with them.

Traditional energy products are part of a complex, interdependent biological system, not of a simple, geological resource like fossil fuels. Despite frequently being outside the commercial energy market, there are benefits and costs associated with traditional energy use. The benefits associated with the integration of biomass fuel production integrated into local land-use management systems include the maintenance of ecological stability, and the provision of a range of products for food, fodder and shelter. The costs associated with deforestation are related to the environment (soil erosion, land degradation and loss of carbon sink), as well as the time women and children spend travelling to seek energy supplies. Cooking is the single largest end-use of biomass in rural areas, and responsibility for producing, collecting and purchasing fuel falls largely to women. Biomass fuels are frequently sold in urban markets and are thus sources of family income.

Investing in fuel switching in urban areas is a positive way of reducing demand for biomass fuels, particularly when the urban energy economy relies on charcoal which is more demanding on biomass resources than burning wood. The introduction of improved cooking stoves which conserve energy is helpful, particularly when such programmes are focused on urban areas where both the fuel and the technologies are already commercialized. An emphasis on enhancing biomass fuel supplies is useful but only when such programmes have an integrated approach to total land-use and to household production. It is also crucial to strengthen local organization in sharing energy conservation practices, like fire and food management techniques.

Access to biomass fuels is restricted by rules and regulations that govern the local management of common property resources. This remains a relatively unexplored area since, while customary controls have been eroded by the imposition of statutory government, government has not been able to replicate traditional resource management. Building local environmental management capacity is a central challenge if basic needs, and the parallel provision of biomass energy resources, are to be met. More attention should be given to the structure of management of natural resources at local levels, of which sustainable land-use management should form an integral part.

Women and energy

Women not only provide the backbone of rural Third World agriculture, undertaking some 70 per cent of all farming activities, but they also dominate household energy collection and utilization. Added to the time spent collecting wood (bundles may weigh up to 50 kilos) is an hour and a half pounding or grinding foods, and anything from one to six hours fetching water.

As land degradation spreads, especially in sensitive environments, women have to spend more hours walking greater distances to collect fuelwood. In this situation there may also be a corresponding shortage of water. This dual increase in the burden on women creates serious problems for other tasks such as planting, weeding and harvesting, and this accelerates the impoverishment of women. So far, it has proved difficult to design specific energy projects for women which can successfully break this vicious circle. Attaching an energy component to an ongoing women's project offers better development opportunities.

The burden on women is caused by the gender division of labour; men are largely the income generators and women largely do the unpaid, unrecognized work. Women frequently do not have access to opportunities which generate income and, as a consequence, have few opportunities for purchasing energy or labour saving devices. They are not only constrained by societal traps but also by finance. In a systematic end-use approach, the views of women will be central to the design of programmes and projects, in which energy is included.

Training and extension programmes in agroforestry specifically designed for women must be strengthened to include income generation and security of energy supply. To this end, more support should be given to 'training of trainers' programmes in local biomass production, linked to the continuing training programmes for low investment agriculture.

Energy efficiency

A central feature of an end-use energy strategy is the pursuit of cost-effective opportunities for more efficient energy use in the modern sector. Just as many of the energy efficient technologies used in industrialized countries are relevant to the modern sectors of developing countries, so also are many measures being considered for promoting the adoption of energy efficient technologies.

Improving energy efficiency is influenced by market forces and they are clearly important. A properly functioning market has a more important role in implementing end-use energy strategies than in implementing those for conventional energy. The complexities of energy end-use decision-making can generally be dealt with more effectively by buyers and sellers; they know what is needed, what is affordable and what energy using devices cost to produce. The public sector is relatively bad at monitoring users' needs and preferences, besides, replacing the myriad interactions of buyers and sellers with procedures and rules invariably produces black markets. There is a clear advocative and stimulating role for non-governmental organizations (NGOs) here.

Nevertheless, public sector interactions in the market are needed because of market biases, market frictions and inherent market failings. Existing 'market biases' in the form of price controls, and various energy producer and consumer subsidies, promote economic inefficiency and are slowing adjustments to a new sustainable energy economy based on real prices. Market interventions are needed to remove such biases, to create a more evenhanded treatment of investments in energy supply and energy efficiency improvements.

Compared to developed countries energy efficiency investment in developing countries is low, but there are several possible interventionary policy instruments for promoting it:

*   eliminating energy supply subsidies;
*   rationalizing energy prices;
*   improving the flow of information;
*   targeting energy performance;
*   promoting comprehensive energy service delivery;
*   making finance available for energy efficiency investments.

Power output and costs of generation technology

Generation technologies, of which there is a large range, must be judged by their power output and cost, and both must match end-use.

Fossil fuel and hydro-generation dominate all power requirements. By 1995 they will account for some 55 and 37 per cent, respectively, of all electricity supply in developing countries and both can be scaled down to power demands of less than 1 kW. Renewables other than hydro-generation can deal with low power demands; solar and wind power are particularly suited to the purpose. Table 3.1 outlines the minimum and maximum figures for each fuel source. Actual economic performance depends on the type of technology and, especially with renewables, on local conditions. Economic capacity must also be considered against the nature of demand for base and peak electricity. Given the low demand for electricity in rural areas, generation flexibility is important, which suggests a system based on peak power, not on base-load requirements.

Table 3.1 gives a range of costs associated with different combinations of fuel technology for electricity generation. Comparative capital costs favour fossil generation rather than renewables, but fuel, operation and maintenance costs, which together are recurrent, are higher for conventional fuels than for renewables. Of particular note is the recurrent cost of small scale diesel generation. The comparative delivered cost per unit of electricity indicates the relative cheapness of conventional generation, with the exception of small scale diesel generation, and the high maximum costs of all renewables except hydro-generation. Comparative costs do not totally explain the dominance of grid extension and stand alone diesel generation for rural electrification programmes. To understand the complexity of this issue, analysis of end-use demand is necessary.

Fuel switch and renewable energies

Fuel substitution and renewables (including biomass) are the joint priorities in any consideration of energy supply. Fuel substitution must be determined by end-use demands. Households, particularly those in urban areas of developing

	Comparative capital costs[1] (000's)	Comparative fuel and O & M costs[2]	Comparative costs of delivered power[2]
	Externalities not included		
Coal	1–2	2–4	5–10
Fuel oil	0.5–1	3–6	9–14
Natural gas	0.4–0.9	2.5–5.5	6–12
Nuclear	1–1.5	1.5–3	6–15
Small diesel	0.4–1	8–30	10–80
Solar	4–10	0–1	9–90

Note: [1] $/kW; [2] cents/kW
Source: World Bank, adapted from FINESSE

Table 3.1 *Costs associated with different fuel-technologies combinations for electricity generation*

countries, must be persuaded to a switch from biomass to kerosene. In the world at large, a move from non-renewable to renewable resources and, within the hydrocarbon sub-sector, from coal to natural gas should be encouraged. Rural households will continue to depend heavily on woody biomass for their sources of energy, but our policy will promote the establishment of local small scale generation plant for development opportunities.

The quality, reliability and durability of small scale electricity generation plant has often been assessed in the field, and what is apparent is that performance is largely determined by the characteristics of the site. Thus biomass fired plant depends on the availability of biomass feedstock, micro-hydro plant needs a river, even wind generation depends on a suitable site, though to a lesser extent than the other two. Because the technologies are place dependent, they tend to rely on local construction. Biomass generation in particular and, to a lesser extent, wind generation have encouraged local manufacturing with the consequence that quality, reliability and durability have been questionable. Even with photovoltaic generation, where the modules are internationally manufactured to a high standard, but parts of the system are locally made, there has been difficulty in maintaining electricity supply.

For a variety of reasons all renewable technologies are unable, from time to time, to provide continuous supply. Biomass and hydro resources are seasonal, although biomass generation can meet peak load more successfully. Wind generation is variable and is best paired with diesel generation back-up, although the size and costs of the back-up equipment have to be carefully considered. Solar generation varies by day, by season and with weather conditions. The product of all these technologies requires storage, essentially batteries, which increases both cost and maintenance problems.

Because renewable generation technologies are site specific, comparison between them is difficult, but photovoltaic generation is the simplest answer to the problem of rural electrification. Because the system will have been well manufactured and because it requires the least skilled servicing, it is the most reliable and durable technology. Furthermore, as its use becomes more widespread module costs are declining. However, all renewable technologies must be compared to stand-alone diesel generation, and any comparison between renewable energy technologies must recognize that they are site specific. Thus photovoltaic generation might not be the only answer for particular communities in particular places.

Policy support

It is only during the last 20 years that most government and donor agencies have paid any attention to energy as a policy issue, and the main approach during this time been to see the energy 'crisis' as a problem of supply. Diagnoses of problems and designs for their solution have both been premised on simple models of supply 'gaps'. Solutions have been sought by applying single technologies (whether forestry, stove technologies, individual renewables or large scale hydrocarbons) and, with a few notable exceptions, they have failed to have a lasting impact on the problems.

Some policies (for example, kerosene subsidies) can distort the operation of energy markets and prevent the setting of real energy prices. Strategies for each energy sub-sector should be developed and, at the same time, energy planning institutions should be strengthened and reformed, so creating a capacity for effective strategic implementation. There are four inter-related levels of policy support:

1. the improvement of the information base on which policies are developed;
2. the correction of market failures and the improved functioning of markets;
3. the development of energy sector strategies;
4. the strengthening of energy planning institutions.

Providing better information and removing policy distortions will create the preconditions for effective energy policies which need co-ordinating through strategies for energy sub-sectors which, in turn, are able to capture the local specificity of energy problems and opportunities. This will determine the mixes of technical packages appropriate to the enhancement of supply, of conservation and of fuel switching. It will also provide a structure for forming priorities and for institutional relationships between planning agencies and local communities.

ENVIRONMENTAL IMPACT ASSESSMENT

One of the most intractable, and at the same time long term, policy issues in environmental maintenance and sustainability, is the effect, direct and indirect, of energy use and resource development on the environment. Although lip service has in the past been paid to this issue, there are few examples of energy policies which have adequately fully accounted for environmental impacts and environmental opportunities. This neglect must be addressed.

The current practice in environmental impact assessment (EIA) restricts analysis to bio-physical factors, yet any accurate assessment of the effects of both energy production and energy consumption must include all the real costs, which means not only bio-physical externalities but also the socio-economic environments. Market prices also fail to recognize many of these costs, in fact they scarcely take any of the environmental and social costs of, for example, biomass fuels and hydrocarbons, into account at all.

Conventional EIA practice is to limit any given assessment to the spatial and temporal boundaries of the project concerned yet, if EIA is to be instrumental in policy decision-making, it is critically important that this should not be so. It is also essential that a full range of technical alternatives should be explicitly considered.

The contribution of rural fuelwood use to environmental degradation, and in particular to deforestation, has been debated for some time. The use of fuelwood makes little impact on the resource base when it is gathered for local use and the contention that a growing population will lead directly to resource depletion is questionable. Declining biomass resources are a product of changes in land-use, and in particular of agricultural colonization, but even this kind of structural change results in a new, relatively stable, level of biomass availability. The notion that, until the last tree is felled there is an inexorable depletion of wood resources, fails to comprehend the nature of rural land-use systems. What is true, however, is that the depletion of 'free' goods, common property resources, like natural woodland, is not adequately costed.

Coal mining destroys vegetation, interrupts natural drainage and pollutes water courses. It also widely affects land-use and causes serious erosion in cleared areas. Dust created by surface mining causes the loss of adjacent agricultural production. Deep mining creates surface spoil heaps which can add to erosion, sedimentation and the acidification of watercourses. Coal preparation releases carbon dioxide and methane gas. Its combustion significantly enhances global warming and also leads to the emission of gases such as sulphur dioxide that are associated with acid rain. These are all of minor importance in most developing countries, but are of some significance for China and India, which are both major and growing users of coal.

The exploitation of oil and natural gas also directly affects the environment. Large volumes of water are introduced into oil-bearing strata and some of this is brought to the surface with the crude oil as an emulsion. Unless this is carefully separated oil-bearing discharges can pollute watercourses and damage aquatic life. Oil spillages from offshore exploration can damage marine life, such as fish and birds. Explosions and fires caused in the cooling process or simply by unsafe equipment can occur in oil refineries. They can also be vulnerable to sabotage and present obvious targets in time of war. Refineries emit both airborne effluents (like sulphur oxides, nitrogen oxides and particulates) and liquid effluents (like oil, phenols and

ammonia). The combustion of oil and gas gives off gaseous effluents, the most important of which are carbon dioxide, sulphur oxides and carbon monoxide.

Hydro-electric power developments also have substantial environmental impacts. Storage dams can be immense. They can displace settlements and disrupt social relations, they modify agricultural and transport patterns, they can affect local health. The reduction in the transport of sediment below the dams alters the morphology of downstream rivers, and can also lead to the decay of deltas and to coastal erosion. The possibilities for downstream flood plain development are reduced because the fine sediments on which the natural fertility of their soils depend are trapped in reservoirs.

Central to any assessment of energy development is deciding how to provide for the expanding energy needs of developing countries with the minimum of negative environmental impacts. The form which development takes is of key importance here. The goal must be to provide for needs in the most efficient, environmentally sensible way possible. This raises a number of specific issues.

- Continuing research into the environmental implications of the enhanced greenhouse effect is needed. Forms of environmental change and possible vulnerable areas need to be identified. Policies to combat the dangers and to minimize the emission of greenhouse gases without jeopardizing energy supplies need to be developed.
- Energy efficiency in all sectors should be encouraged by active policies of promotion, technological development and, where appropriate, pricing mechanisms, like the 'carbon tax' to introduce prices which reflect the real costs of fuel use. In general, it is cheaper to save a unit of energy than to generate a new one.
- A fuel switch in power generation and in industrial use from coal to oil, and in particular to natural gas, would produce a reduction in the rate of carbon dioxide and other greenhouse gas emissions.
- Provided that wood used as fuel is replaced by the same amount of new planting, the carbon balance is maintained. However, a switch to kerosene in urban households

would reduce carbon emissions. Wood and charcoal combustion gives off up to five times more carbon dioxide per unit of energy than kerosene. A fuel switch, from wood and charcoal to liquid fuels or electricity, in urban informal manufacturing and service activities would similarly reduce the rate of emission of greenhouse gases. These changes would also improve urban environments while minimizing damage to wood resources.

- Making charcoal in primitive earth kilns destroys roots and seedlings, emits liquids and gases which, combined with the associated deforestation, can lead to soil deterioration and reduced agricultural yields. More experimentation with local, low cost design is clearly required.
- In rural areas action to protect the biomass resource base by the development of sustainable, multi-purpose land-use needs to be promoted through national and regional programmes.
- The long term demand for electricity in developing countries is likely to mean the use of large dams for the expansion of hydro-electric power generation. But a cost-benefit analysis of these schemes needs to incorporate the costs of mitigating environmental impacts, of compensation for social disruption and, if possible, it must take into account the biological diversity of the corresponding wetlands.

Table 3.2 summarizes the environmental issues associated with each energy source.

The process of the environmental impact assessment of energy related activities, in both large and small projects, must be strengthened. Furthermore, mass awareness campaigns that demonstrate the links between energy, environment and development should be promoted to ensure public support for environmentally benign energy consumption.

Applied research

Applied research is an essential step in developing more effective energy policies, not the least because energy systems in developing countries are complex and varied. The 'toolkit' of conventional energy planning is not well suited to policy

Resource/technology	Impact issue
Coal fired power plant	Carbon emission
	Air and water pollution
	Acid precipitation
	Waste disposal
	Safety and health impacts of mining
Large scale hydropower	Land requirements – especially associated resettlement requirements
	Dam safety
Oil and gas fired power plants	Carbon emissions, from oil fired plants
	Oil spills
Biomass energy systems	Land requirements
	Carbon emissions
	Ecological impacts of harvesting and transportation
	Loss of species diversity
Solar energy option	Land requirements for larger implementation

Source: T J Wilbanks, 1990

Table 3.2 *Typical environmental impact issues associated with energy*

and planning in the face of such complexity.

Past policies have been based on highly aggregated and ill-informed assumptions about the forces driving energy production and use. Effective monitoring is even rarer and, in most cases, the available information does not allow for an accurate (or even a crude) assessment of likely future fuel mixes, nor for the economic benefits and costs associated with different forms of provision, of investment in efficiency and of consumption. Better information is urgently needed in a number of areas. Among them are household energy use, fuel markets, opportunities for energy efficiency, the fuelwood resource base, and tree and woodland management systems, the speed, direction and causes of fuel transitions, the real costs of different fuels in different localities and, finally, the potential role of renewable sources of energy for different forms of energy demand.

Much has been written about the way that households respond to energy scarcity and which factors are important in influencing their fuel choices, but there is little empirical information. A number of household surveys have been undertaken, but most are census type 'snapshots' taken at one time, and which are notoriously poor at providing insights into the processes of change or the specific character of localized fuel production and use. Nor can they show the subtle, non-quantitative interactions between people and their resource base. Longitudinal data on patterns of fuel use and rigorous estimates of demand and supply elasticities are almost non-existent.

Carbon taxes

When the degradation of an environmental resource is not costed, there is no economic incentive for users to ensure its proper management. This is particularly true if the resource is, like air quality, a common property or open to everyone. It can be argued that a tax on the amount of carbon dioxide emitted by the burning of particular fuels would be effective in slowing the increase in the amount of carbon dioxide in the atmosphere. Such a tax may be fine-tuned to ensure its effectiveness, in the same way that leaded petrol suffers a calculated market disadvantage. Unfortunately, a carbon tax is regressive and poor people would be particularly hit by it because their demand for fuel cannot respond to price: they must have fuel with which to cook. In theory, a user has the choice of switching fuel to avoid the tax, but, in practice, many are locked into existing technologies; they may choose to economize on fuel but be unable to switch to one attracting a lower tax. Collecting the tax from numerous small users would be expensive and there is no reason to expect government to use the revenue other than as general income. On the principle of the 'tragedy of the commons' there is no incentive for a single country to impose such taxes on its citizens.

Fuel markets must be surveyed in depth to find out how fuels are produced, distributed, marketed and priced, how the economic cost of different fuels is built up and which stages in the marketing process are most susceptible to policy interventions. This is critical for urban areas and for those rural areas where fuels have become commoditized; policy-makers interfere in markets they do not understand at their peril.

There is very little reliable information on the resource base for fuelwood and, in particular,

little on the level of sustainable off-take from different ecozones. One particularly important gap is in information on trees and shrubs in the agricultural landscape, outside the forest, which are often the main source of rural fuel.

Data on the resource base for fossil fuels are better where substantial exploration has taken place, but there are still large, relatively unexplored regions, particularly offshore deposits and deposits in remote areas. There is also a need to improve the understanding of the potential of small scale deposits of fossil fuels, many of which are not considered viable by international companies concerned with supplying a world market, but which could make a major contribution to national energy needs in developing countries. Finally, there is often a paucity of reliable data on the potential of renewable sources of energy and again considerable work is needed to improve the information base for planning in this area.

In general, in applied research more emphasis should be given to socio-economic and environmental factors that support the formulation and implementation of an energy policy. More technically orientated research, particularly in energy efficiency, should support the broad goals of this policy or respond to a specific end-use need.

AGROFORESTRY AND THE FUELWOOD PROBLEM IN AFRICA

Fuelwood is the issue at the centre of energy planning. That wood energy cannot be provided by planting fuelwood trees is, at last, being recognized. Agroforestry, in which trees are a multi-purpose resource in a land-use system, seems to provide an opportunity for addressing the problem. However, women, who are usually the wood gatherers and farmers of Africa, need to be key participants in any solution. More importantly, energy systems in urban areas need to be addressed. Many of them still rely heavily on charcoal. By encouraging a change from charcoal to fuels which are both preferable and more easily obtained, the pressure on rural wood resources could be reduced. As we have already remarked, this transition will ease the problem of wood depletion and rural environmental degradation.

Given Africa's heavy dependence on wood for energy, the call is now for a form of forestry which will contribute to the process of sustainable development (sustainable development was characterized by the Brundtland Commission as that which is equitable and which meets the needs of the present without compromising the ability of future generations to meet their own needs). Implicit in this is a need for new forestry initiatives which contribute to a participatory, equitable, decentralized and self-sustaining process of rural development throughout Africa.

Fuelwood stress is also conditioned by social and demographic trends within African countries; both overall population growth and rates of urbanization are exacerbating the problems. In particular, fuelwood policies do not fully consider the significance of urbanization processes. Urban growth rates of 10 per cent are the norm in Africa and what were rural societies are becoming increasingly urban. Population growth in rural areas affects fuelwood use in much the same way as it does other forms of resource exploitation.

However, the varying circumstances of different people and places make generalization about fuelwood stress problematic and the problems can rarely be summarized. Fuelwood use and scarcity reflect complex and variable interactions between local production systems and the environmental resource on which they are based. The significance and origins of fuelwood problems vary as much as do local environments and societies.

Given this, a number of criteria must be satisfied before a sustainable energy policy can reflect the heterogenous nature of fuelwood supply and end-use.

* Biomass resources in different areas must be measured and this will give an indication of the maximum available as potential fuel. The areas taken will equate to agroclimatic zones, which are a broad indication of land productivity.
* The characteristic rural economy, including population densities, forms of settlement and dominant types of agriculture must be identified. This will indicate the level of demand for energy and the characteristic patterns of land management.
* The socio-economic condition of the area must be described because it determines access to the resource base for fuel by different sections of the local community.
* Factors which produce significant exports of woodfuel resources, such as commercial logging, and the influence of urban woodfuel and charcoal markets, must be incorporated.
* Major forms of structural change which seriously affect the fuelwood situation in a locality must be analysed. They will include land colonization, demographic change and urbanization, major developments such as roads and hydro-electric power schemes and catastrophic drought or conflict.

This is a complex list of criteria, but their consideration is essential if fuelwood problems and solutions are to relate to the condition of the people experiencing fuelwood stress.

The African fuelwood experience

Most forestry plans in the past 15 to 20 years have treated the biomass problem simply as one of supply and demand. It was argued that people were extracting more biomass than the environment could sustainably produce and the solution was self-evident – if projected demand exceeded supply, either plant more trees or devise policies to reduce demand. As a result, foresters tried to increase tree supplies by various large scale means like monocultural plantations, peri-urban woodlots, community woodlots, and increased policing of forests and woodlands. Their object was to plant as many trees as quickly as possible. Unfortunately, and all too often, decisions to spend large sums of money planting trees have been taken without considering other options or the consequences of existing market and policy failures. Foresters have only themselves to blame for excluding options and courting failure (Van Gelder and O'Keefe, 1992).

The Kenyan experience

From 1980, there was an attempt, in Kenya, to address the broad energy and development problem, particularly that of fuelwood, in a systematic manner. Fuel switching was considered but, because of the comparative expense of oil, it seemed insufficiently attractive. Energy conservation was mooted but, especially for fuelwood, there were substantial limits to investment in it. Finally, the analysts looked at the possibility of expanding wood energy supplies and this led to the formulation of the Kenyan Woodfuel Development Programme (KWDP). This programme was run from the Ministry of Energy but had a level of contact with the District Forestry administration.

The KWDP was focused on the Kakemega and Kisii districts of western Kenya. They are densely populated and undergoing rapid land consolidation, and were thought to be the best areas in which to explore potential models of agroforestry. Early surveys came to the striking conclusion that deforestation does not necessarily occur in densely populated areas. Quite the reverse – there is a great deal of evidence to suggest that farmers, given the necessary inputs, will increase the amount of woody biomass on their farms.

TOWARDS SOLUTIONS

Although there has been much work in recent years on local demand for trees and tree products, it has largely been led from social science and has not addressed the issues of local production. What is urgently needed is a new form of social forestry which provides wood near where people live. This requires integrating wood into existing land-use patterns in the farming system; it requires production design for a new agroforestry.

It is important, even at the risk of repetition, to correct the three most popular misconceptions about the problem of declining wood resources. First, it is frequently assumed that deforestation is caused by commercial logging and cutting for fuelwood; this is simply not true – agricultural colonization is the major cause. Second, it is frequently assumed that forests are a primary source of woodfuel for rural people; this is wrong – in Africa over 90 per cent of biomass fuel comes from agroforestry. Third, it is assumed that rural people fell trees for domestic energy use – this happens very infrequently because woodfuel is a residue from other uses of wood in the rural economy. Quite simply, woodfuel is what is left over.

Any new agroforestry project must recognize that:

- trees can be combined with crops and/or animals in many different systems of land use;
- a range of goods would be produced, not one single product;
- indigenous, multipurpose trees and shrubs are the core of intervention;
- such complex production systems are probably better suited to fertile environments rather than to fragile conditions;
- land-use systems will actively reflect socio-cultural values.

The integration of a project which takes these things into account is a step-by-step process which allows the people themselves to control it, to follow its progress and to adapt the programme in a gradual way without deviating from its objectives.

Five phases are distinguished in the process of integration. These are, of course, only indicative; in reality there may be more or fewer. They are largely based on the Kenyan experience where tree planting was integrated into programmes of rural development, especially in the National Dairy Development Programme.

Phase 1: Analysing the situation

Any attempt at developing something new must be based on local and existing agroforestry. Its restraints must be recognized and learning how to reduce or to remove them is the first important step.

To analyse a situation, project staff must consider the following issues:

- the present function of woody vegetation for rural people in relation to their priorities and to the objectives of the project;
- the present role of rural people and the relevant institutions in the management of woody biomass;
- the present problems or shortcomings in the woody biomass system;
- the present efforts being made by rural development institutions in the field of woody biomass development.

No detailed surveys are needed at this stage, but discussions with the main actors in woody biomass management are a must – farmers, foresters, agriculturalists, rural sociologists and policy-makers will all have something to add. As it is important to understand the technical, socio-economic and cultural factors influencing woody biomass management, it is advisable to use an analytical team with a wide range of expertise.

Phase 2: Identifying and formulating the agroforestry options

During this phase a number of promising agro-forestry options have to be identified and formulated so that the programme can start testing them, and for this, both the knowledge of farmers and information from outside has to be used. During each of the subsequent phases, agroforestry methods are reformulated and refined in response to the results of monitoring and evaluation.

Since testing the options for tree planting starts on a limited scale, it is unwise to address all the problems and priorities identified in Phase 1 at once. It is better to identify those specific focal points which are relevant to the goals of the project and to the target groups identified by the programme, and which are important enough to the people concerned. As forestry programmes commonly have a wide scope, a number of different focal points can be chosen. Examples are fodder production, the supply of tree seeds, the production of building materials, the production of firewood and the demand for specific species of tree.

The choice of options will have implications for the organization. It may mean changes in the tasks of the staff, in the supervision of nurseries and in collaboration with other organizations. It may also involve changes in the extent of the programme by refocusing target groups or changes in communication with the farmers, in publicity, in technical messages, and in seedling and seed distribution. But options, once formulated, must be concrete, clear, cheap, and easy to adopt and implement. Everyone involved should, as far as possible, agree with whatever decisions are taken – then the project must start with a bang!

In this phase the involvement and the training of project staff is important, because it will lay the foundation for their involvement and motivation. Besides, information and training sessions are

also the fora for the exchange of ideas. At this stage emphasis must be given to the following subjects: recognizing farmers' knowledge; understanding the process of formulating options for agroforestry; establishing and maintaining trials; monitoring and evaluating procedures.

Phase 3: Testing

The methods of agroforestry chosen for the programme must be tested to see if they qualify for inclusion. This first round of tests need not produce clear cut results and 'polished' systems ready for wide application, but it should produce a rough set of ideas which may be developed further.

How the trials are to be established must be determined during this phase. Are seedlings or seeds to be used? If seedlings, who is to raise them? If seedling distribution is chosen, what type of nursery is needed?

Training activities during this phase focus on the results of the trials, the reactions of farmers and the consequences for the next phase. Monitoring and evaluation procedures are also discussed.

Phase 4: Partial integration

In this phase agroforestry systems are reformulated on the basis of results from Phase 3 and are further developed within the programme; the result must be a set of systems which can be fully integrated into the programme.

Methods are tested on a larger scale, involving more farmers, while additional research is carried out in the project centre. Both the species and the management systems, which are gradually incorporated into the programme, become more varied, and research on both is based on information gathered in the process of monitoring and evaluating them.

Phase 5: Complete integration

By this phase agroforestry should have become fully integrated into the programme. The results of the work should be available to a wider audience for application elsewhere. This means that information about ways of extending agroforestry should be packaged in a form suitable for widespread dissemination; that these packages should be incorporated into extension programmes; that a broad range of species and of management systems are either offered or are being studied; that monitoring and evaluation are continuous; that the training of project staff is also continuous; that the results of the programme are handed over to local organizations by means of training and the use of demonstration plots. If frameworks of this kind are incorporated into national energy plans, then the likelihood of achieving sustainable energy economies will be greatly increased.

4

EFFICIENCY OF END-USE

Earlier chapters have covered patterns of energy use, end-use analysis, sustainability and the costs of energy. Later chapters will concentrate on supply, but of equal importance is the conservation of energy and it is relevant to all the other considerations.

There are at least five major reasons for encouraging it:

1   if less fuel is used in the provision of a given service, then money is saved;
2   the use of fossil fuels will be slowed down and so they will last longer;
3   greenhouse gas emissions would be reduced so that adverse climatic change would become less likely;
4   with smaller power requirements the prospect of using renewable sources of energy is enhanced, which will make the development of sustainable economies more possible;
5   less pressure on resources from developed nations will allow them to be shared more fairly with developing countries, and will also ensure that stocks are available for future generations.

Any one of these would be sufficient cause to take energy conservation seriously, but as all of them apply, conserving energy by using it efficiently must be central to any energy policy.

How energy is used, and the attitudes and aspirations of its consumers, must be known if significant reductions in use are to be achieved. An appropriate framework of institutions, standards and legislation favourable to improvements in energy efficiency is also required. In this chapter we present studies of the use of energy in transport and in buildings, the two sectors with the largest consumption in the UK. These will show how the same levels of service can be sustained with less fuel; they also reveal some of the obstacles to these reductions which we will consider further at the end of the chapter.

ENERGY IN TRANSPORT

One of the most striking changes in the use of energy over the past few decades has been the increase, absolutely and proportionately, of end-use energy for transport. Reducing this use would prolong the lifetime of oil reserves.

Among the strategies for such a reduction in both surface and freight transport are the introduction of legislation to limit the number of vehicles, fuel rationing and the improvement of fuel efficiency. Informed comment depends on a knowledge of the numbers of vehicles in use, the ways in which they are used and their fuel efficiency. The following sections present some of the available information.

Energy use in transport, past and present

Between 1965 and 1986, the proportion of fuel used by transport of various sorts increased from 17.6 to 28.1 per cent. In the same period the amount consumed by road transport doubled and in air transport the increase was by a factor of 2.25. However, aviation uses less than 20 per cent of the amount used by road transport. In 1986, between them, they accounted for 90 per cent of the fuel used in transport, all of it supplied as petroleum ('petroleum' is the term used by geologists and the energy industry for a range of hydrocarbon raw materials which include crude oil, natural gas and asphalt). The two industries used 65 per cent of all petroleum, 55 per cent for road and 10 per cent for air transport.

Passengers and freight within the UK mainly travel by surface transport, and over 90 per cent of the energy used at sea or by air (see Figure 4.1) is for travel to and from other countries. For this reason most of the ways of reducing the use of fuel will arise in domestic transport.

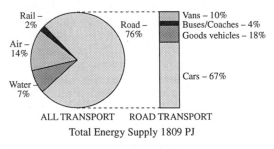

ALL TRANSPORT   ROAD TRANSPORT

Total Energy Supply 1809 PJ

Sources: R D Evans and H P J Herring, 1989

Figure 4.1 *Energy content of fuels for transport in the UK, 1986*

The number and uses of vehicles

Figure 4.2 shows the increasing number of road vehicles registered between 1950 and 1989, and the corresponding increase in the use of fuel. In

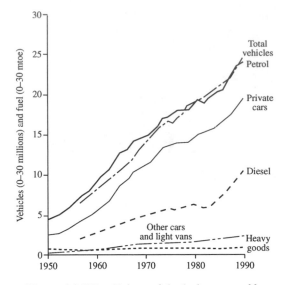

Figure 4.2 *UK vehicles and the fuel consumed by them, 1950–89*

the same period the passenger kilometres per annum for both road and rail increased from 170 to over 500 billion, and the tonne kilometres increased from 70 to 120 billion.

Rail accounts for about 7 per cent of passenger kilometres and about 16 per cent of tonne kilometres (9 per cent of total tonnage), which means that improvements in fuel use should first be sought in road transport.

One way of reducing fuel consumption might lie in substituting one form of transport for another, but for this to be possible we must first know what journeys are taken by which kinds of transport. For example, although journeys of all kinds are longer in rural than in urban areas, only 11 per cent of the population is involved and they often have little in the way of transport to choose from. Extending mass transport to rural areas would be both expensive and uneconomic (see Appendix III).

Energy use by road and rail transport

From 1950 to 1986 energy use rose from 400 PJ to 989 PJ in road and rail passenger transport, and from 340 PJ to 387 PJ (a more marginal increase) in freight transport.

One way to compare the relative efficiency in energy use in differing modes of transport is to calculate the 'specific energy consumption'

(SEC) of each of them. To do this it is, once again, necessary to know what kinds of journey by what means of transport are being undertaken and how many passengers or how much freight is carried on each one. The SEC, expressed either as MJ/passenger kilometre or as MJ/tonne kilometre, tells us which means of transport is the most energy efficient and, when it is calculated over a period, which is improving (see Appendix III for a detailed definition of SEC).

When steam locomotives were replaced by diesel traction the SEC for rail improved from 6.6 to 2 MJ/passenger kilometre, a figure around which all passenger transport hovered throughout the period 1950–86. Between 1950 and 1967 the SEC for rail freight fell, for the same reason, from 5 to 3 MJ/tonne kilometre, but in recent years there has been a slight rise.

Passenger transport

In 1987 the Department of Transport published estimates for surface passenger activity in Great Britain (see Table 4.1). We shall look in turn at each of the three categories in the table, but, obviously, private and business motoring consume the most fuel.

Private and business motoring

Private and business motoring absorbs almost 90 per cent of the energy devoted to moving passengers by road and rail, which reflects the value

Sub-sector	Passenger kilometres (10^9)	Vehicle kilometres (10^9)	Energy use (PJ)
Private and business motoring[1]	430	247.8	884
Road passenger transport	41	3.1	54
Rail passenger transport	37	0.37[2]	51
TOTALS	508	251.1	989

Notes:
1 Including motorcycles
2 Travelled by loaded trains
Source: Department of Transport

Table 4.1 *Surface passenger transport activity*

	Average $(KWh \times 10^4)$	toe.	%
Materials Production	0.85	0.68	4.7
Spares	0.82	0.68	4.5
Other	0.1	0.08	0.5
Total	1.77	1.42	9.7
Operation Fuels and lubricants	16.50	13.20	90.3
Total	18.27	14.62	100.0

Source:Energy and the Motor Industry.SMMT 1979

Table 4.2 *Lifetime energy use of a motor vehicle*

placed on personal, individual transport. Personal transport is used for travel to work and to school or college, for commercial and for personal business, for leisure, for shopping and for many other purposes (see Appendix III). For some people either their own or a hired car is the only means of transport available, but for many it is simply the way that they prefer to travel. Cars take the traveller from door to door, they are comfortable and have luggage space, they provide privacy and entertainment on the journey. Their drawbacks, principally expense and danger, are either not appreciated or are considered acceptable. In the UK, where there are now more than 19 million registered vehicles, more than 43 per cent of households have access to one car and another 17 per cent have access to two or more. Of these 232,500 ($\approx$1.25 per cent) are diesel engines.

It is impossible, accurately and in detail, to define the way in which fuel is used by such a large number of vehicles and for such a multitude of purposes. It is particularly hard to separate business from private use since many vehicles are used, at different times, for both purposes. The details which follow are, therefore, either averages or, sometimes, estimates.

We also deal only with the fuel and lubricants used in running the vehicles. In view of the arguments in Chapter 1, it might well be asked how the energy used in manufacturing and supporting them compares with their lifetime use, and whether or not it should be included. Table 4.2 gives an approximate breakdown of all the energy used in the lifetime of a car. Fuel and lubricants make up 90 per cent, and may reasonably be taken as the major element in the consumption of energy by motor vehicles.

Motor car fuel consumption

The amount of fuel used by cars, light vans and motorcycles is known from a combination of petrol sales, and an estimate of the amount of diesel fuel used by these vehicles (see Figure 4.2 for the history of its increase). Reliable data for individual models are harder to come by, partly because they depend on how the vehicles are driven. For example, when fuel consumption based on standardized government tests is compared with that based on ordinary road testing, the former is always greater. SEC figures (listed in Table 4.3), estimated for different kinds of journey by the Department of Transport, were based on the assumption that all kinds of vehicle were driven in the same way. But they do give some idea of the likely values when the kind of journey, road conditions, speed and passenger load are taken into account.

Public service vehicles

Public service vehicles (PSVs) are the various kinds of bus used on inner city, suburban or long distance routes, and hire cars and taxis used mainly for local journeys. Their SECs are typically in the range from 0.4 to 1.2 MJ/passenger kilometre (see Appendix III for details of the vehicle stock and the SECs).

Examples of types of journey	Number of occupants	Average SEC (MJ/passenger km)
Urban commuting in built-up areas	1.3	2.8
Other urban journeys, eg shopping	2.0	1.8
Non-urban journeys, eg leisure	2.3	1.3
Non-urban journeys eg personal business	1.7	1.8
Motorway journeys eg in course of work	1.1	2.6

Source: Department of Transport, 1988

Table 4.3 *SEC in 1986 for private and business*

Passenger transport by rail

Passenger transport by rail uses much the same amount of energy as PSVs. Again many types of journey, on trains varying from those drawn by the latest 225 electric main line locomotives to those on the London underground system, are involved. Their SECs range from 1.2 to 1.4 MJ/passenger kilometre (see Appendix III for details).

Freight transport

In 1986, energy amounting to 387 PJ was used in transporting freight; 240 PJ was used by heavy goods vehicles, 135 PJ by light vans and 12 PJ by rail. These figures may be compared to the total of 989 PJ used by surface passenger transport.

Since 1950 both the number and the average length of freight journeys on the roads has steadily increased, but the total tonnage has fallen slightly from a peak in 1968. This fall presumably reflects falls in the manufacture of heavy goods and in the movement of heavy loads of raw materials. Longer journeys have led to a small rise from about 3.5 to nearly 4 MJ/tonne kilometre in the SEC for road transport (see Appendix III for details).

Twenty per cent of the energy used on railways is accounted for by freight and in 1986 total movement amounted to 15.7×10^9 tonne kilometres. Of this coal and coke made up 31 per cent, metals 14 per cent, freightliners (containers) 13 per cent, construction materials 17 per cent, oil and petroleum 13 per cent and other cargoes 12 per cent (see Appendix III for details).

POTENTIAL FUEL SAVINGS

Fuel usually accounts for between 10 and 30 per cent of all operating costs, and it will only be at the higher end of this range that reducing consumption may become a priority. This is because saving fuel is only one factor influencing purchasers and users of transport; others include design, speed, comfort, convenience and control of emissions. But economies, as a consequence of technical developments in vehicles and changes in the ways that they are used, can be made in all forms of surface transport and we shall consider some of them. To bring out the general principles we shall consider cars in detail and give brief attention to other road and rail transport.

Private and business motoring

Among the ways of reducing the amount of petroleum by road transport are limiting the number of cars, reducing the number of miles each vehicle travels, heavily increasing the price of petrol, road pricing, improving public transport, rationing fuel, campaigning to change the attitudes of motorists and producing cars which use fuel more efficiently. This list is not exhaustive, nor are its elements mutually exclusive. Several are being considered at present, but motorists would probably find the last of them the most acceptable. It leaves the freedom that a car brings intact, it reduces costs, it can be done, it does not exclude any of the other options and it helps to use less fuel.

Energy use by cars

Technical advances which improve fuel efficiency will not only be a matter of engine design, but also of better design for the rest of the car. Thus, in order to pinpoint the most effective improvements it is necessary to understand what it is that the fuel does, which aspects of the car make the biggest demands and what factors influence them.

The forces opposing the movement of a car travelling along a flat road on a windless day are air resistance and the frictional drag of the road on the tyres – they are known as the drag and rolling resistance. When power from the engine is equal to the rate at which work is being done to overcome these forces, the car's speed is steady. Depressing the accelerator to give more power will, once the new level of power is just sufficient to balance the losses caused by the two resistive forces, give a new steady speed. The maximum speed of which a car is capable is that achieved when the greatest power that the engine can exert equals the new level of losses.

The maximum speeds of different makes of car with the same engine power are indicators of the size of their resistance to motion. The higher their maximum speed, the lower their resistance and the more fuel efficient they are at speeds

below their maximum. Head winds increase the relative speed between the car and the air, and air drag is increased. The maximum attainable speed is then lower and more power will be needed to maintain any speed.

More fuel is also used for acceleration and for climbing hills. If cars can be modified to reduce the fuel demanded for these two jobs, as well as for overcoming drag and rolling resistance, then less fuel will be used. Identifying the ways in which all these factors are modified by the car's shape and structure will make appropriate design changes possible. Lower fuel consumption may also be achieved by increasing the efficiency of the engine, the design of which determines how much power is provided for a particular amount of fuel. For maximum effect, shape, construction and engine all need to be analysed for possible improvements.

Looking in more detail at the forces involved allows them to be related to the relevant properties of the vehicle. Some of the forces opposing motion are dependent on the mass of the car, some on its size, some on its velocity and some on a combination of all three.

To stop, or to slow down, a controlled retarding force must be available and this is supplied by the brakes which dissipate the car's kinetic energy by using frictional forces to convert it to heat.

Overcoming the resistances to a moving vehicle
The forces needed to propel the vehicle may be expressed as:

F_r = the force needed to overcome rolling resistance

F_{ad} = the force needed to overcome air resistance

F_a = the additional force needed for acceleration

F_h = the additional force needed for hill climbing

And so at any particular time the engine may be required to overcome a total force of:

$$F = F_r + F_{ad} + F_a + F_h$$

The extra margin that an engine must have for

acceleration and hill climbing can be large, even for very small cars. F_r is proportional to the mass of the vehicle and its velocity. The constant of proportionality is C_r and so,

$$F_r = C_r mv$$

where m is the mass of the vehicle and v its velocity. C_r depends on bumps and holes in the road surface (1–5 per cent of the losses), air friction on the rotating tyre (1–3 per cent), flexing of the tyres (92–98 per cent) and frictional losses in moving parts of the vehicle (negligible).

F_{ad} is proportional to the frontal cross-sectional area of the car A_f, and its velocity squared. The constant of proportionality is $P/_2 C_d$, C_d is known as the drag coefficient and ρ is the density of air, and so

$$F_{ad} = P/_2 C_d A_f v^2$$

C_d has values ranging from 1.17 for a flat square plate held perpendicular to the direction of travel to 0.03 for the best theoretical teardrop

shape. Current production cars have values between 0.3 and 0.5 (see Table 4.4), vans between 0.4 and 0.6, and lorries between 0.6 and 1.0. Research vehicles have attained 0.15.

F_a depends on the mass of the vehicle and its acceleration, a, and so,

$$F_a = ma$$

F_h depends on the mass of the vehicle, the acceleration due to gravity, g, and the slope, s, of the road expressed as a fraction, ie 1/10 for 1 in 10, and so

$$F_h = mgs$$

Taking these together, the expression for the total of the forces becomes:

$$F = C_r m v + P/_2 C_d A_f v^2 + ma + mgs,$$

and the power needed is:

$$Fv = C_r mv^2 + P/_2 C_d A_f v^3 + mav + mvgs$$

Make and model	Drag factor	Make and model	Drag factor
Audi		Mercedes	
80	0.40	190	0.33
100	0.30	200	0.43
Quattro	0.43	250	0.29
Austin		Nissan	
Mini	0.48	Micra	0.39
Metro	0.38	Sunny	0.40
Maestro	0.38	Porsche	
Montego	0.37	944	0.33
Citroen		911	0.39
2CV	0.51	928	0.38
Visa	0.38	Renault	
BX	0.34	4	0.42
CX	0.35	5	0.35
Fiat		11	0.35
Panda	0.41	25	0.28
Uno	0.34	Rover	
Strada	0.37	213	0.43
Ford		2600	0.40
Fiesta	0.40	Vauxhall	
Escort	0.36	Nova	0.38
Sierra	0.34	Astra	0.32
Granada	0.33	Cavalier	0.38
Jaguar XJS	0.40	Volkswagen	
Lada Riva	0.48	Polo	0.39
		Golf	0.34

Table 4.4 *Drag factors of various car models*

Reducing C_r, m, C_d and A_f will reduce fuel consumption and some of the possibilities are looked at below.

Engine losses
As far as the engine is concerned, we must remember that its primary function is to convert heat, derived from the fuel, into work. This is a second law process and, as such, there being little flexibility available with the temperatures involved, is very inefficient. Typically, the power available 'at the wheels', ie that available to overcome the resistances discussed above, is about 18 per cent of that provided by the fuel.

In 1982 the OECD estimated that for a car travelling over a representative mixed route with urban roads, motorways, hills and starting, that the energy from the fuel was dissipated in the following proportions:

Transmission	2 per cent	⎫ Thermodynamic
Auxiliaries	8 per cent	⎪ and mechanical
Radiation	12 per cent	⎬ losses, mostly
Exhaust	20 per cent	⎪ associated with the
Coolant	40 per cent	⎭ operation of the engine
Air drag	4 per cent	⎫ Overcoming
Rolling resistance	6 per cent	⎪ resistances to
		⎬ motion. Braking
Braking	8 per cent	⎭ dissipates energy acquired in acceleration and going downhill

Improvements in engines
A recent report from the Energy Technology Support Unit (ETSU) for the Department of Energy has considered the outlook for technologies for improved fuel efficiency in engines and has estimated that an improvement of 6 per cent over 1986 figures could be achieved in conventional engine design. The main areas would be in precision cooling, reduced friction and reduced pumping losses. If lean burn, four stroke petrol engines with four valves per cylinder are used, then an improvement of 5 to 15 per cent might be realized. Two stroke, direct injection petrol engines could yield savings of up to 10 per cent, while replacing petrol with diesel engines offers reductions of up to 20 per cent. The widespread adoption of electronic engine management systems to optimize fuel consumption in prevailing conditions and engine load could bring savings of between 5 and 20 per cent.

Petrol engines are very inefficient at low loads because of the amount of power that it takes to drive the auxiliary equipment, to overcome mechanical and fluid friction, and to pump mixture into the engine against a partially open throttle. When a car is idling, over-running or braking, fuel is being consumed to no good purpose. Engine management systems can improve this and novel types of transmission may enable the engine to be run continuously at its most efficient power output and speed.

Improvements in transmission etc
Fuel consumption can be improved slightly by optimizing gearing and by using five speed gearboxes of conventional design, which are now common, or by using overdrives, both of which give more efficient high speed cruising. But constantly variable transmission makes possible the use of a constant optimum engine speed with continuously varying gearing matching engine to road speed. A reliable development in this area would offer savings in fuel of about 15 per cent against conventional transmission. Ford recently introduced it as an option on their smaller cars, calling it the CTX system, but, like Volvo before them, withdrew it because it was mechanically unreliable.

Improvements in body, tyres etc
Acceleration, retardation, hill climbing and rolling resistance all vary with the weight of the car. Reductions in weight will reduce the amount of fuel used and, over the last few years, some advances have been made. It is thought that between 3 and 9 per cent more fuel might be saved by a further reduction in weight of 10 per cent. The body represents 28 per cent of the weight of a typical car, the engine and transmission 21 per cent, and the trim (including glass) 16 per cent. The remainder is made up of the assumed combined weights of the passengers and the fuel.

A reduction in drag (achieved by a smaller C_d and a smaller cross-sectional area) might bring about a 7 per cent improvement in consumption. The average C_d for new cars, now around 0.40, could be reduced to 0.30 with little compromise in function and, in the long term, there is no reason why 0.20 should not be achievable.

Radial rather than cross-ply tyres reduce rolling resistance by about 25 per cent and maintaining correct pressures gives a 3 per cent increase in efficiency. The ETSU estimates that further savings of between 5 and 10 per cent are possible following improvements to tyres, lubricants and accessories.

Emissions control

Controlling exhaust emissions which damage health and pollute the air can increase fuel consumption, as in the cases of unleaded petrol and catalytic converters. The incorporation of stringent emission controls will tend to counteract the measures taken to improve fuel consumption, but it is unlikely that they will wipe fuel savings out completely.

Passenger transport

Public service vehicles

Urban buses stop frequently and average 18 to 22 km/h. At these speeds aerodynamic drag is minimal and the estimated breakdown of fuel use is thus:

Thermodynamic and mechanical losses	80%
Acceleration and gradients	10%
Rolling resistance	6%
Aerodynamic drag	2%
Idling	2%

In contrast the consumption of fuel by long distance buses is dependent on their speed and the type of route. At 100 km/h fuel use is estimated as:

Thermodynamic and mechanical losses	80%
Aerodynamic drag	12%
Rolling resistance	8%

ETSU's study, looking at the effect of rapid technical change on fuel consumption in this sector, concluded that improvements from 4 to 7 per cent were possible, depending on the type of vehicle and its route. When the effects of strict emission controls were investigated it was discovered that the 4 per cent savings achieved by improvements to minibuses and taxis were reduced to about 2 per cent. But in the case of both double and single decker buses, based on 1986 figures, strict emission controls converted savings of up to 7 per cent to increases in consumption of between 1 and 3 per cent (see Appendix III for details).

Rail

The change from coal to diesel in rail transport brought major reductions in fuel consumption. An 8 to 10 per cent efficiency was standard for steam, whereas the figure for diesel is about 25 per cent. Electrification will bring a small increase in efficiency, but its main saving will be in the lower operating and maintenance costs, and extended the lifetime of the power units.

Freight transport: road and rail

An analysis of fuel consumed by road transport shows:

Thermodynamic and mechanical losses	62%
Idling and accessories	3%
Rolling resistance	15%
Aerodynamic drag	12%
Transmission losses	4%
Braking	4%

Fuel distribution between the last four is dependent on route, speed and load.

Techniques for improving fuel consumption are similar to those for passenger transport. While current emission controls remain in force, improvements in engines, transmission, weight and the aerodynamic drag for light and heavy goods vehicles could yield reductions from 8 to 14 per cent. If strict emission controls are introduced then any savings will, at best, be marginal and may be converted into as much as an 8 per cent increase in fuel consumption.

In rail transport, technical improvements, which could be introduced quite rapidly, could yield a reduction in consumption of 8 per cent in both diesel and electric trains.

ENERGY IN BUILDINGS

Buildings which concern us here are those used for domestic, public administration (for example, national and local government, defence, health and education) and miscellaneous purposes (for example, offices, shops, warehouses and hotels).

Private housing absorbs about 28 per cent (1639 PJ) of the energy delivered to UK consumers and about 13 per cent (760 PJ) is used in commercial and public premises. Substantial reductions in this use of energy are possible.

Table 4.5 gives the percentages of the fuels used in these sectors in 1977 and 1987, and compares them with the total for all final users in the UK.

The aggregation of these three sectors shows that the following percentages of a particular fuel were used in buildings in the UK.

In 1977
57.7 per cent of the total use of natural gas
59.4 per cent of the total use of electricity
60.3 per cent of the total use of coal, burnt as coal
28.1 per cent of the total use of coke and manufactured solid fuels
16.4 per cent of the total use of oil

In 1987
69.5 per cent of the total use of natural gas
63.5 per cent of the total use of electricity
54.5 per cent of the total use of coal, burnt as coal
26.8 per cent of the total use of coke and manufactured solid fuels
11.1 per cent of the total use of oil

The domestic sector uses more natural gas, electricity and coal than any other individual sector.

End-uses

The fuels referred to in the previous section have a number of uses which are estimated by ETSU as shown in Table 4.6. These estimates show that 66 per cent of the energy used in buildings is for space heating and 16 per cent for water heating, both low temperature applications; 6 per cent for cooking, a medium temperature application; 9 per cent for lighting; and 3 per cent for other applications in the service sector. The last two categories both use electricity, for lighting and applications dependent on electric motors and electronics, and so are end-uses which cannot use other fuels.

Fuel	% of total fuel used in sector		% of all of that fuel used in the UK	
1 Domestic sector				
	1977	1987	1977	1987
Natural gas	44	60.9	46.8	54.2
Electricity	19.3	18.4	38.87	37.3
Coal (as coal)	21.3	11.9	51.6	46.3
Coke/manufactured fuels	6.0	3.1	22.5	20.7
Oil	9.3	5.7	5.2	4.2
2 Public administration and miscellaneous sectors				
	1977	1987	1977	1987
Natural gas	23	40.4	10.9	15.3
Electricity	22.6	30.4	20.7	26.2
Coal (as coal)	7.8	5.0	8.7	8.2
Coke/manufactured fuels	2.3	2.1	5.6	6.1
Oil	44.3	22.0	11.4	6.9

Source: HMSO, annually

Table 4.5 *Fuel used in buildings*

	Domestic		Commercial and public	
	PJ	%	PJ	%
Space heating	1102	67	484	64
Water heating	305	19	78	10
Lighting	136*	8	76	10
Cooking	97	6	4	6
Other	–		73	1
Total	1639	100	7	100

Note: * Includes other electrical appliances

Table 4.6 *End-use of fuels in domestic, commercial and public buildings*

Improving fuel efficiency

Space heating

Clearly, any scheme for improving fuel efficiency in buildings must begin with space heating. The means will vary from building to building depending on their size, age, state of repair and the uses to which they are put. Whether or not any action is taken at all will depend on cost and the extent to which modifications will interfere with the use of the building.

Both the heat put into and the heat lost from any given building must be considered. In the first of these, possible steps are boiler replacement, servicing existing controls or installing new ones, introducing computerized energy management systems and optimizing 'free' heat gains. The steps for reducing heat losses include insulation (both roof and walls, together with attention to doors and windows), ventilation control, draughtproofing and the installation of heat recovery systems.

Heat supply

Space can be heated by low quality energy. This means that any source of heat can be used, but even though electricity might be preferred because it is clean, convenient and easily controlled, it is usually more expensive and requires more primary energy than coal, oil or gas burnt in an on-site boiler. Recent improvements to these include very efficient ($\approx$85 per cent) condensing boilers which recover latent heat from flue gases.

The reduced heat load resulting from improvements in insulation and other modifications may require the installation of a new heating system for the maximum benefit to be gained. Considerable savings may be made by monitoring conditions within the building and matching the heat supply to them, and the means to this end would include time switches, thermostats and the use of different temperatures in different zones. Small domestic systems need quite simple controls, but larger systems may need computerization. In the case of electricity, proper controls can ensure that it is used at the times when the rate is cheapest, but the price of gas varies, for large consumers, with the amount used and not with the time of the day.

Buildings are also heated incidentally by the occupants, by any appliances which use power (for example, lifts, computers, machines, cookers and lights) and by the sun. These sources help to maintain the internal temperature and, in a well-insulated building, they can be very significant. In large buildings with substantial areas of glazing, incidental solar heating during the summer may compel the use of power for cooling and ventilation. Optimizing the solar gains will reduce the power needed for both heating and cooling.

Efficiency in heat supplies would be considerably improved by the further commercial development, and the widespread adoption, of combined heat and power (CHP) powered by gas or oil, and of heat pumps powered by gas or electricity. CHP units range in size from 2 kW to several megawatts of electrical output and have overall efficiencies of about 80 per cent (25 per cent as electricity, 55 per cent as heat). Smaller units can be used for single buildings but the largest can supply factories, suburbs, small towns or even cities and they are best employed in meeting constant demand as when supplying electricity and hot water to places like hotels, leisure facilities, swimming pools or bottling plant. Heat pumps take heat from a low grade source, like the atmosphere, a stream or a well, and deliver it, wherever it is required, at a higher temperature. For each kWh of energy purchased as gas or electricity they can deliver two or three as heat. At present, heat pumps are available in a range of sizes but are expensive compared to conventional boilers.

Reducing losses

Ways of reducing the rate at which heat is lost from buildings are now widely known. Resistance to the flow of heat through the outer envelope of the building (the walls, floor, roof, doors and windows) can be increased by insulation, draughtproofing and double glazing. Porches at entrances and exits will also help. All these measures allow the internal conditions to be kept at a set level with a lower rate of heat supply and, hence, savings in fuel and cash. The extent to which these measures are employed usually depends on the cost of fuel and the cost of carrying them out, weighed against the benefits they bring to the installer.

Further fuel economies may be achieved in well-insulated buildings by sealing them and controlling their ventilation. A heat exchanger, which warms fresh, cool, incoming air by taking heat from stale, warm, outgoing air, can then be used. However, installation in existing buildings is often difficult because the ducting involved is quite large, but it can be successfully incorporated when large refurbishments are taking place, or in new buildings.

Water heating

Hot water may be supplied either by the same boiler as the space heating or by a separate appliance. Savings in fuel may be made by using less hot water, by using more efficient appliances to provide it, by reducing losses in the supply system, by lowering its temperature or by recovering heat from it after its use. Some heat lost from hot water systems contributes to 'free' heat gains in buildings.

Most savings can be made by reducing water use, for example by taking showers rather than baths. But the most cost-effective way of saving heat is to lower the temperature of the water. Point-of-use heaters are more fuel efficient than central hot water cylinders. It is technically possible to recover heat from waste water, but it is seldom done.

Lighting

Lighting is responsible for 10 per cent of the energy used in commercial and public sectors, and, for this purpose, electricity is essential. It is also a case where the conversion of energy to the desired output, an adequate approximation to daylight, is very inefficient. Common incandescent light bulbs in which a hot filament is the source of light have a typical efficiency of 5 per cent (long life bulbs, which operate at a lower temperature, produce even less light). But other kinds of lighting like halogen lamps and fluorescent fitments are from two to five times more efficient. The availability of compact fluorescent lamps which can directly replace conventional light fittings makes their adoption for domestic purposes much more convenient. The remaining energy given off by lighting can be used as 'free' heat.

Cooking

Sixty per cent of all cookers use gas and the other 40 per cent largely run on electricity (a small minority use solid fuel or liquified petroleum gas (LPG). Because most people prefer gas for cooking and use it wherever it is available, there is probably not much scope for fuel savings in replacing electricity with gas. Cookers can vary considerably and a wider use of the most efficient models would save fuel. However, further savings may be made by, for example, using microwave ovens for some cooking, or using toasters instead of grills, or using pans of a different design. But most of these would probably also involve revising cooking practices and, in some cases, the use of different materials like pre-prepared foods which only need reheating and not cooking.

Other appliances

Many other appliances and machines are found in buildings, ranging from lifts and computers in commercial buildings to TV and hi-fi, toys and electric drills in homes. Virtually all of these use electricity and most of the smaller appliances are only used intermittently. Improvement in fuel efficiency is only likely to come about as part of good engineering practice or as a by-product of some other technical change or cost reducing exercise in manufacture.

Refrigeration and freezing is one area where savings can be made. Use of this equipment is widespread and the efficiency of the available models varies widely. Better insulation and efficiency labelling could reduce fuel use.

Summary of total potential for reduction of energy use in buildings

It is difficult to be precise about the total potential for energy savings in buildings. The estimate will depend on the mix of end uses and on the mix of fuels which satisfies them. Different sources suggest that savings of up to 50 per cent may be possible in delivered energy, but savings in primary energy depend on the fuel mix. Most savings will be made in space heating (≈70 per cent) and lighting (≈10 per cent) followed by water heating (≈8–10 per cent) and cooking (≈4 per cent) (see also Appendix III).

Obstacles to energy efficiency

Obstacles to the adoption of energy saving appliances and practices fall into four broad categories: lack of information; inappropriate organizational arrangements; finance; and environmental and political factors.

Information

It is very difficult for consumers to find out about the energy performance of the appliances they buy, and their decisions are usually based on financial and aesthetic grounds. A cheaper appliance may cost more in fuel than a more expensive one, equally it may not, but unless information about fuel consumption is available the customer cannot know. An energy efficiency labelling scheme for all appliances is urgently required.

Consumers can seldom discover where the energy that they buy is used. Most of them, in both domestic and commercial premises, get single bills for either electricity or gas and cannot know whether cooking, heating, lighting or some other application used the most fuel. Indeed, in most premises there is no way of knowing which floor, or even which building, has used the most. To get this basic information

calls for more extensive metering, not necessarily so accurate as that which records consumption for billing, but adequate to call attention to the most important targets for improvements in efficiency.

The issue of the provision of information is a matter for both government and energy suppliers because most individual consumers do not have the means to deal with it themselves.

Inappropriate organizational arrangements

Organisational obstacles can stand in the way of saving fuel. One instance lies in the fact that it is seldom in the financial interest of the occupants of rented accommodation, whether public or private, to invest in energy saving measures. Another is in the direct legal responsibility of some organizations or companies to maximize their short term profits which may conflict with trying to save fuel. The old Central Electricity Generating Board (CEGB) was a case in point; it was obliged to produce cheap electricity rather than to increase the efficiency of its use of primary fuels. In this respect the structure of the privatized electricity industry is, if anything, worse – all sections of it must increase sales if they are to prosper. But a shift in perspective might help. If both electricity and gas companies saw themselves as selling services like light or comfortable living conditions rather than fuel, they might make more profit but sell rather less fuel.

Financial obstacles

As we saw in Chapter 2, accounting procedures may also get in the way. The distinction between capital and current spending often leads to the postponement of capital projects even though, in the longer run, the expenditure would reduce the running expenses.

We have already touched on the question of accounting procedures and spending by tenants, which is part of a more general difficulty presented by the time over which investment is required to make a return. Most investors, in whatever form, and whether private, public or corporate, want this to be short. Industry often wants a return within two years and people, on average, sell their houses every five to seven years. These times are too short for many energy efficiency measures to compensate their investors.

Pricing policies which impose standing charges on smaller consumers and decrease prices for larger consumers who sufficiently increase the amount of fuel that they use, do not encourage fuel savings. Tariffs which increase in stages as fuel consumption rises might be an improvement.

There is no doubt that money must be spent before fuel can be saved and this means that the poorest consumers, including pensioners, who most need to reduce their bills are the least likely to be able to make fuel saving modifications in their living conditions.

Another major financial problem arises in the policies of governments, both at home and abroad, which directly or indirectly subsidize one fuel industry as opposed to another and thus affect the market and, hence, the efficient use of energy. For example, in the UK the current non-fossil fuel levy favours renewable resources and the nuclear industry, whereas past policies encouraged the coal industry. Similarly, subsidies to help conservation in the UK have, in recent years, been steadily reduced or removed.

Environmental and political considerations

The environmental consequences of fuel use have been discussed at length in Chapter 2. If fuel prices were to include external costs, strong pressures for more effective use would emerge.

Significant reductions in fuel consumption would reduce the dependency of many developed countries on the Middle East and other suppliers. This would lead to changes in national balances of payments, and would affect the foreign and economic policies of both the fossil fuel rich and the importing nations.

CONCLUSION

This chapter has shown that various ways of maintaining services while reducing the amounts of fuel used are open to us. The need for government involvement has also been demonstrated: energy labelling, and standards and targets for appliances, vehicles and buildings are among the obvious areas in which government action is essential. The potential rewards of energy efficiency to consumers, humanity and the environment are so great that it must be pursued with urgency.

5

CONVENTIONAL FUELS

Most of the world's energy comes from fossil fuels. Carbon based fuels are stores of high quality solar energy accumulated over millions of years. Nuclear fuels, on the other hand, come from the concentration of elements present in geological formations since the earth was formed. In this chapter we shall discuss, briefly, the end-uses of these fuels, together with their composition, methods and places of occurrence, and their production both in the UK and throughout the world. We shall also look at their estimated lifetimes and at ultimate reserves. All uranium, much coal and some oil and gas are used to generate electricity, so electricity supply and generation will also be considered.

In the past wood, coal and oil have each, from time to time, and largely depending on relative cost and availability, dominated the fuel market. In 1989 38.7 per cent of the world's primary energy came from oil, 27.8 per cent from coal, 21.3 per cent from natural gas, 6.6 per cent from hydro-electricity and 5.6 per cent from nuclear power. These figures exclude the 20 per cent which comes from non-traded fuels used in the developing countries. In the immediate future, natural gas seems likely to become the most widely used and popular fuel. Large

reserves have recently been discovered, and its use reduces atmospheric pollution and releases less carbon dioxide than an equivalent amount of coal.

OIL

Occurrence

Crude oil is a mixture of liquid hydrocarbon compounds sometimes found permeating sedimentary rocks. Its elements are, by weight, carbon 82.2–87.1 per cent, hydrogen 11.7–14.7 per cent, oxygen 0.1–4.5 per cent, nitrogen 0.1–1.5 per cent and sulphur 0.1–5.5 per cent.

Different names, based on the number of carbon atoms in their compounds, are given to products derived from crude oil. They are called gasoline (C_4 to C_{10}), kerosine (C_{11} to C_{13}), diesel fuel (C_{14} to C_{18}), heavy gas oil (C_{19} to C_{25}), lubricating oil (C_{26} to C_{40}) and waxes (over C_{40}).

Oil is generated from organic matter in sedimentary rocks at depths of about 800–5000 m at temperatures between 66°C and 150°C. Its predominant source material is probably marine organisms. Three steps are involved in the conversion of organic matter to petroleum.

Diagenesis

In this stage, sedimentation is occurring, and as the organic rich sediment is buried and subjected to slightly increased temperatures and pressures the organic material is converted to an insoluble solid hydrocarbon called kerogen. This is finely dispersed and intermixed throughout the mineral matrix and is usually less than 2 per cent of the total rock mass. Some methane is generated anaerobically. Three types of kerogen have been identified with different ratios of carbon to hydrogen and carbon to oxygen reflecting their source materials. Type I results from marine algal material and eventually yields a light high quality oil; type II comes from a mixture of various marine organic materials and is the main source of crude oil and some gas, and type III, yielding mainly gas with some oil and waxes, derives from terrestrial material.

Catagenesis

This is the mature stage of the process where further ageing and sedimentation increases temperature and pressure to give a range of petroleum hydrocarbons by thermal cracking.

Metagenesis

Below 5000 m or so the increases in temperature and pressure are such as to convert the hydrocarbon material to methane and residual carbon. Oil is seldom found below this depth.

Sequential conditions

Four sequential conditions are necessary if an oil field is to form and to survive:

1   a source rock containing the necessary organic material must have been laid down in the right sort of environment and subsequently subjected to conditions leading to the formation of petroleum;
2   a permeable reservoir rock formation must be available, connected to the source rock by some sort of channel which allows the petroleum to migrate to a trap;
3   a closed trap where the petroleum can accumulate, like an inverted container, must have been formed;
4   the filled trap must have survived over long periods of geological time and still be present today.

In practice, source rocks are fairly common, reservoir rocks less so and traps rather rare. This suggests that the occurrence of all three in the correct combination may be infrequent.

Distribution

There are some 600 sedimentary basins in the world (see Figure 5.1). About 200 of them are unexplored for petroleum (because they are in the polar regions, deep water, the remote interior of continents or are restricted for political reasons); another 240 have been explored to some extent without making commercial discoveries and the remaining 160 are commercial producers.

Oil fields are classified in terms of their size as:

supergiants with 5×10^9 barrels, or more, of recoverable oil, and
giants (world class) with 5×10^8 to 5×10^9 barrels of recoverable oil

The remainder with less than 500 million barrels are just known as oil fields.

Fewer than 50 supergiant fields have been discovered and they contain around 50 per cent of all of the oil found so far. Of these nearly three-quarters are in the Persian Gulf, with a smaller number in the US, the former USSR, Mexico, Libya, Algeria, Venezuela and China. Around 300 world class giants have been found (the North Sea is one of them), and these and the supergiants account for 80 per cent of the world's known recoverable oil. In addition, there are about 1000 fields in the range of 50 to 500 million barrels capacity that account for a further 14–16 per cent of the known total. As around 30,000 oil fields have been discovered so far this means that 5 per cent of the known fields contain 95 per cent of the known oil reserves.

It is hard to escape the conclusion that oil will be very much harder to find in the future, as it seems unlikely that many supergiants remain undiscovered, and this implies higher exploration and production costs as the more marginal, or remote, sedimentary basins are explored and developed.

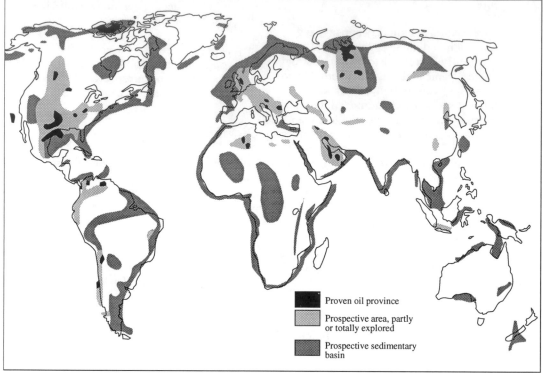

Source: D. Schumacher, 1985

Figure 5.1 *Sedimentary basins*

Oil supplies

UK

During the 1980s approximately 3 EJ (80 mtoe) of the UK's annual primary energy supply came from oil (except during the miners' strike of 1984–5 when there was a temporary increase in this rate). Table 5.1 shows where it was used.

In 1969 oil was discovered in the UK's North Sea continental shelf east of Aberdeen and the site was named the Montrose field. More fields were found (see Figure 5.2) and the rate of discovery increased until 1975, since when it has gradually decreased. UK production started with the Argyll field in 1975 and reached a peak level of around 127 million tonnes during 1985 and 1986 (see Figure 5.3). The North Sea's greatest output is thought to have been during that period and a decline in production will follow during the 1990s, perhaps dropping to between 40 and 70 million tonnes by the year 2000. Since 1980 consumption has varied between 70 and 90 million tonnes a year, and the UK has been an oil exporter.

By December 1993 it was estimated that there remained proven reserves of 605 million tonnes, probable reserves of 800 million tonnes and possible reserves of 690 million tonnes. By November 1993 cumulative production had reached ≈1659 million tonnes and is not included in these estimates (Department of Trade and Industry, 1994).

World

The UK provides only a small part of the global oil supply. Table 5.2 gives estimates, made in

Economic sector	1963	1973	1983	1989
Transport	43	43	63	74
Industry	39	38	21	17
Domestic	6	6	4	4
Other	12	13	11	6

Source: HMSO, annually

Table 5.1 *End-use of primary petroleum (per cent)*

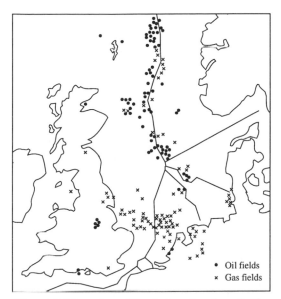

Figure 5.2 *Location of North Sea oil and gas fields*

Table 5.2 *Economically recoverable world oil reserves, 1989*

Region	Oil reserves	
	(10^9 tonnes)	% distribution
Western Europe	2.4	1.8
Eastern Europe	0.2	0.1
USSR	8.0	5.8
Africa	7.8	5.9
Middle East	89.3	65.2
USA	4.3	3.4
Canada	1.0	0.8
Central America	16.5	11.6
South America	1.1	0.9
P R China	3.2	2.3
Far East	2.8	2.2
Australia/ New Zealand	0.2	0.1
Total	136.8	100.0
(approx 1012 x10^9 barrels)		

Source: *BP Statistical Review of World Energy*, 1990

1990, of the amount of economically recoverable world oil reserves. In the late 1980s annual production averaged about 24 x 10^9 barrels/year. Dividing the estimated total recoverable oil in Table 5.2 by this figure indicates a 'lifetime' of 42.2 years.

Quoted estimates of the time remaining before 'the oil runs out' are often based on a method proposed by M King Hubbert in *Resources and Man* (1969). It is assumed that the life cycle of oil production has an initial exponential growth rate, later falling off as a maximum is reached. A symmetrical decline then follows. The differential equation for this growth cycle is:

$$dQ/dt = cQ(Q_f - Q)$$

where Q_f is the total available amount of the quantity involved. This has a solution:

$$Q/Q_f = 1/(1 + a \exp[-cQ_f t])$$

where a and c are constants. To draw the curves which might apply to oil supply, it is necessary to know the constants a, c and Q_f. Fitting the initial portion of the curve to the existing data, a and c can be found. However, Q_f must be estimated. Figure 5.4 shows King Hubbert's 1969 curves. They were produced by using the historical data to 1968 and values of Q_f of 1350 barrels and 2100 barrels. Note that these values of Q_f refer to estimates of probable resources as opposed to proven recoverable reserves. In 1968 the curves indicated that 80 per cent of oil reserves would be consumed by around the year 2025 if production rates continued to rise. The heavy curve in Figure 5.4 records data on oil production to 1991. Data accumulated since 1968 shows that the rise was steeper than predicted until the late 1970s, since when the trend in production rates has changed. If these lower rates persist, they will have the effect of prolonging the time that oil reserves will last. This

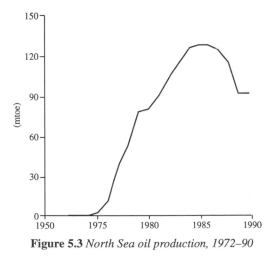

Figure 5.3 *North Sea oil production, 1972–90*

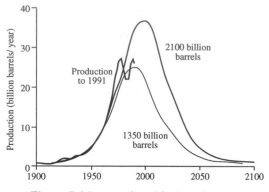

Figure 5.4 *Projected world oil production*

kind of analysis provides a tool for estimating the effects on oil reserves of rising and falling production rates.

For example, one-half of King Hubbert's estimate for Q_f of 1350 billion barrels can be seen to have been consumed. Estimation of Q_f is difficult and often controversial. Such uncertain factors as geology, extraction rate, new technological developments in exploration, drilling and extraction, lack of knowledge of some parts of the world, and whether 'total existing amount' or 'total recoverable amount' are being considered, need to be elucidated and estimated.

When trying to estimate the potential reserves in a given area, the following details may be taken into account:

- the size of the petroleum prospecting area;
- the density of past drilling;
- the amount of past drilling;
- the cumulative outcome of past exploration and development;
- the number of 'giant' fields discovered;
- the amount of petroleum found per unit of prospecting area;
- data extrapolated from certain 'benchmark' areas, such as the US or the Middle East and applied to geologically similar third world areas.

The most recent estimates of Q_f are not substantially different from those used by King Hubbert.

COAL

Occurrence and Distribution

Coal is a complex organic material consisting of fused carbon rings held together by assorted hydrocarbon and other atomic (O, N, S) linkages. Its average composition is something like $C_{10}H_8O$ (this ratio of 10 carbon atoms to 8 of hydrogen can be contrasted with the ratio of 10 carbons to 17.5 hydrogens in crude oil).

It is formed from dead plant material which has accumulated in swamps, usually in estuarine deltaic deposits, and then has been consolidated and altered by increasing temperature and pressure. In a similar evolutionary pattern to oil, the first stage in the conversion process is an anaerobic breakdown of the plant material which causes volatile products to be liberated and lost to give a compacted structureless mass of compounds enriched in carbon. The second stage is the process of coalification which proceeds through the ranks of peat, lignite, sub-bituminous coal, bituminous coal and anthracite to graphite. The proportion of carbon is gradually increased in this progression. Calorific values of the various ranks range from 15–26 kJ g^{-1} for low rank lignites, through 31–35 kJ g^{-1} for bituminous coals to 30–33 kJ g^{-1} for anthracite.

Coal deposits are not found before the lower Carboniferous age (about 400 million years ago), and the most important and widespread date from the Carboniferous to the early Triassic age (345 to 200 million years ago), and from the Jurassic to the early Tertiary age (150 to 50 million years ago). In general, the older coals have the highest rank but, depending on the geological history of the deposits, this is not necessarily so.

Although coal is widespread the major deposits are unevenly distributed (see Figure 5.5). Ten countries account for 92 per cent of the currently estimated reserves and resources. Three countries alone, the US, the former Soviet Union and China, have 83 per cent of the resources and 60 per cent of the reserves. All three could become exporters of coal and, in any case, compared with rates of use the total reserves are so large that the uneven spread does not, at the moment, mean supply difficulties.

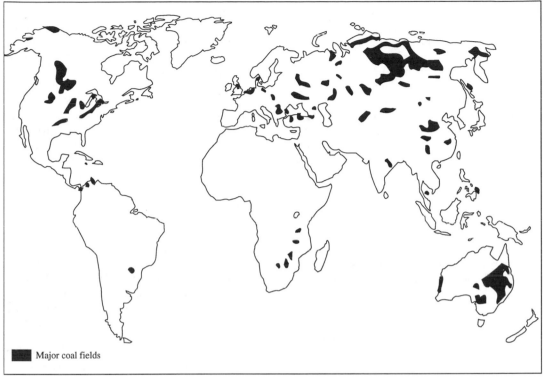

Source: G Brown and E Skipsey, 1986

Figure 5.5 *World distribution of coal*

Coal in the UK

Coal has been a major fuel in the UK for centuries. Figure 5.6 shows how the demand and the markets for coal changed in the years from 1960 to 1983 (the distortion shown in 1984–5 is due to the year-long miners' strike). It also shows that over this period coal consumption fell dramatically. Before 1960 the greatest output was in 1913 when it reached 287 million tonnes, but since 1953, as a consequence of the rise in popularity of oil and natural gas (see figure 1.8), the coal industry has been in almost continuous decline. The annual demand during the 1980s was around 3 EJ (110 mtoe), except in 1984 during the strike when it fell to 2.2 EJ (79 mtoe). In 1950 coal provided 90 per cent of the fuel used in the UK, but by 1982–3 this had declined to 35 per cent.

The end-uses of coal also changed during this period. It was once widely used throughout the economy, but 73 per cent is now used in the generation of electricity, which represents 75 per cent of the fuel used for the purpose (again excepting the year of the strike). Large modern power stations are often located on coal fields so as to minimize transport and other costs. A 1000 MWe power station will use about two million tonnes of coal each year.

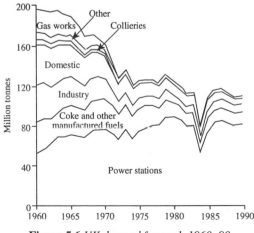

Figure 5.6 *UK demand for coal, 1960–90*

87

In industry coal is used both for high grade heat (temperatures above 200°C) in, for example, iron and steel making, brick making and cement manufacture, and for low grade heat (temperatures below 200°C) in space and process heating and in raising steam. About 60 per cent is used for producing low grade heat.

Running down the iron and steel industry has entailed the collapse of the market for coal and, with it, the South Wales coalfield. Since the Clean Air Act, which covers urban areas, was passed, the domestic demand for coal was substantially reduced; domestic users now burn naturally smokeless fuels, like anthracite, or manufactured fuels similar to coke. Most coking coal is now imported and manufactured smokeless fuels, principally for domestic use, are the biggest product of the coal conversion industry. The use of coal in transport has given way to oil and in heating systems for commercial premises to oil or to gas.

One of the key features of the UK coal industry is that its output is almost entirely of deep-mined coal. The costs of deep mining are higher than for open-cast mining and, although in recent years about 15 per cent of supplies have come from the latter, the thicker seams available in open-cast mines overseas means that prices are lower there than in the UK (see Table 5.3 for comparative costs).

In the economic and political climate following the 1979 election and the Coal Industry Act of 1980, which required the industry to 'break even' within three years, the industry found itself compelled to produce coal at a fixed price rather than to meet production targets regardless of the market. This, in the light of competition with 'clean fuels' and cheaper overseas production, has meant that rather than expanding the industry has had to struggle to maintain existing levels. In the aftermath of electricity privatization the industry's future is even more uncertain and it seems likely that it will shrink dramatically.

This picture is repeated throughout Europe: production in France fell from its 1952 level of 73 million tonnes to 12 million tonnes by 1985; and The Netherlands which, in 1950, produced 12 millions tonnes has now stopped mining altogether. Mainland Europe currently imports about 75 million tonnes and the UK's export of 2 million tonnes so far has little effect on this market.

It is important to remember that different types of coal are supplied to different consumers, for example, coking coal, anthracite and high rank coals are used in coke ovens and households, while lower grades, in smaller sizes and with a specified ash content, go to power stations. Premium markets are declining while the power station market was, until recently, increasing.

This pattern of demand determines which mines are closed and where new ones are opened up.

Coal supplies

UK

Published estimates of coal reserves are subject to wider variation than for other fossil fuels. They sometimes refer to 'coal in place', not all of which is recoverable; sometimes to 'economically workable reserves'; sometimes to 'recoverable reserves' and so on. Most are based on seams at least 60 cm thick and within 1220 m of the surface.

Various assessments for the UK give figures from:

190×10^9 tonnes of coal in place, to
45×10^9 tonnes of recoverable reserves, to
5×10^9 tonnes of operating reserves,

in increasing order of certainty of availability.

In any event, even the lowest figure is 50 times the current annual production and there is much more scope for exploration. It seems that supplies are assured at any practicable level of extraction for well into the next century.

Producing country	Deep mines	Opencast
UK	45–135	Average 38
West Germany	55	n/a
USA	20–35	8–18
Canada	n/a	15–20
Australia	15–25	12–20
South Africa	10–15	8–10

Source: G C Brown & E Skipsey, 1986

Table 5.3 *Comparative costs of mining coal, 1979 (US$/tonne)*

Country	Bituminous coal and anthracite (10^6 tonnes)	Lignite (10^6 tonnes)
Developed countries		
W Europe	218.2	232.3
USSR	497.7	164.7
E Europe less USSR	215.6	648.6
USA	608.0	283.8
Canada	39.1	31.7
Australia	149.3	48.3
Developing countries		
P R China	958.8	81.2
India	185.5	8.5
Rest of Asia	247.8	19.7
Latin America	38.5	–
Africa	186.7	–
Total	3197.1	1518.8

Source: *BP Statistical Review of World Energy*, 1990

Table 5.4 *World coal production, 1989*

Region	Total resources (10^9 tonnes)	Recoverable reserves (10^9 tonnes)
N America	2685	268
S America	35*	18*
W Europe	419	78
E Europe	170	90
USSR	4860	240
China	1438	167
India	57	62
S Africa	173	55
Australia	263	91
Other		14
World totals	10100	1083

* Almost certainly a very low estimate
Source: G C Brown & Skipsey, 1986 and *BP Statistical Review of World Energy*, 1990

Table 5.5 *World coal resources and reserves, 1988*

World

World coal production in 1989 is shown in Table 5.4. Difficulties in making estimates of world coal reserves are similar to those for the UK, with the added problem that many parts of the world are barely explored for coal, eg the interiors of Africa and South America (see Table 5.5). At the moment precision in estimates is not required as the global total of recoverable reserves (1083×10^9 tonnes) is over 150 times present world annual production.

The future of coal

Fuel futures

Assessments of the reserves of fossil fuels indicate that the present levels of production of oil and gas are likely to be maintained in the coming decades, but probably not at present prices. Coal, on the other hand, is available in quantities sufficient to satisfy any likely demand over the next century or so. Is coal therefore about to become the most widely used fuel? It has often been suggested that it could fill the 'energy gap' which may develop between demand and supply, but any discussion of its role must consider

carefully the end-uses to which fuels are put and then whether coal can fulfil all, or most, of them. The obstacles to its use must also be taken into account. For example, there are obvious questions about using coal for transport because this would certainly demand 'coal liquefaction'. While this is technically feasible and is used in South Africa at present, very large scale industries would be needed if it is to replace oil. Other sorts of obstacles include planning, transportation, pollution, international trade and possible production difficulties.

Pollution will be discussed briefly below (see also Chapter 2). The general technical and social problems associated with the wider adoption of coal as a fuel or as a substitute for other fuels indicate the need for caution.

Waste products and pollution attributable to coal

Tables 5.6, 5.7 and 5.8 list some of the relevant data. The figures give typical estimates and particular sources of coal may produce slightly different amounts.

The major effects that may be associated with these pollutants and effluents include:

- greenhouse effect (CO_2)
- acid rain (SO_2)
- chest complaints

- cancer
- ash (dirt)
- radioactivity

- heavy metal pollution
- heat pollution.

| Pollutant | Total annual emissions (per 1000 tons of fuel) | |
	Coal	Oil
Aldehydes	0.052	0.12
Carbon monoxide	0.52	0.0084
Hydrocarbons	0.21	0.67
Nitrogen oxides	21.0	22.0
Sulphur oxides	139.0	53.0
Particulates	4.5	0.7

Source: G Greenhalgh, 1980

Table 5.6 *Annual releases of chemical pollutants from 1000 MWe fossil fuelled power stations*

NATURAL GAS

Increasing interest is being shown in natural gas and there are two broad reasons for this. First, it has recently been realized that its resource base

	Coal	Oil
Annual consumption of fuel (tons)	2 300 000	1 300 000
Annual production of waste		
Bottom ash	50 000	
Fly ash retained	248 000	
Sulphur retained	46 000	
Annual discharges to atmosphere		
Carbon dioxide	6 000 000	4 500 000
Nitrogen oxides	27 000	22 000
Sulphur dioxide	24 000	21 000
Fly ash	1 000	150
Carbon monoxide	1 000	7 500
Mercury	5	
Arsenic	5	
Nickel	5	
Berylium	0.4	
Lead	0.2	
Cadmium	0.001	

Source: G Greenhalgh, 1980

Table 5.7 *Annual waste products (tons) produced by fossil fuels for a 1000 MWe plant at 75 per cent load factor*

| Metal | Range of values | |
	Coal	Oil
Arsenic**	1–15	0.02–0.06
Cadmium*	0.01–2	<0.01
Cobalt	1–40	0.2–0.5
Chromium**	2–50	0.02–0.09
Copper**	0.4–40	0.1–0.3
Mercury**	0.07–1.5	0.002
Manganese	25–100	0.03–0.1
Molybdenum	7–20	0.07–0.3
Nickel**	4–60	6–23
Lead*	2–30	0.07–2
Vanadium	5–35	11–90
Zinc	5–100	0.3–1
Uranium**	0.4–3.7	
Thorium**	0.3–3.6	

* = toxic
** = Carcinogenic
Source: G Greenhalgh, 1980

Table 5.8 *Metals in fossil fuels (ppm)*

is much larger than had previously been thought. Second, it is environmentally more benign than other fuels, particularly coal. Generating electricity from advanced turbines, using natural gas instead of coal, can reduce carbon emissions by 50 per cent for each unit of production and by a further 20 per cent because of their increased efficiency. However, it would be important to ensure that such machinery was largely proof against leaks because the reductions in greenhouse gas emissions could be wiped out, even if only 3 to 4 per cent of the methane finds its way into the atmosphere (methane is 30 times more powerful as a greenhouse absorber than CO_2). Burning methane does not release SO_2, because the source of sulphur, H_2S, is removed before the gas is distributed.

Occurrence and global distribution of gas

Natural gas consists of hydrocarbons with from one to five carbon atoms, together with small amounts of other gases as impurities. Table 5.9 shows the percentage composition by volume of natural gas from four different sources. It was formed under essentially the same kind of condi-

	North Sea (Leman Bank)	The Netherlands (Groningen)	Libya	Algeria
Methane	94.8	81.7	71.4	86.5
Ethane	3.0	2.7	16.0	9.4
Propane	0.6	0.4	7.9	2.6
Butanes	0.2	0.1	3.4	1.1
Pentanes	0.2	1.1	1.3	0.1
Nitrogen	1.2	14.0	–	0.3

Source: E N Tiratsoo, 1979

Table 5.9 *Composition of some commercial natural gases (per cent)*

Region	Ultimate gas reserves		
	Number	10^{12} m³	% of total
USSR	40	28.5	49.7
N America	17	4.7	8.2
Middle East	11	15.2	26.6
W Europe	10	3.4	6.0
Australia	5	0.7	1.2
N Africa	4	2.7	4.8
Far East	4	0.9	1.6
Others	5	1.1	1.9
Total	96	567.2	100.0

Source: E N Tiratsoo, 1979

Table 5.10 *Non-associated supergiant and giant gas fields, 1977*

tions as oil, anaerobic decomposition of organic matter under heat and pressure assisted by bacteria. Marine organisms are the primary source material for oil, but natural gas can be formed both from land plants and from marine organic material. Gas can be formed in very young deposits as, for example, marsh gas in swamps; it can also be formed in association with coal deposits, particularly those of the Permo-Carboniferous, with crude oil and as 'thermal' gas below the oil window. Therefore the depths and areas of sedimentary basins which may hold gas far exceed those of oil. Gas fields, like oil fields, are not distributed uniformly, and differ in size and geographical concentration, but because of its more diverse origins gas is more widespread.

Gas, found on its own in 'dry' wells, is called 'non-associated gas'. It is also found dissolved under pressure in oil in a reservoir or as a 'gas cap' over an oil pool; in these cases it is called 'associated gas'. It has been estimated that about 72 per cent of world reserves are non-associated, 17 per cent are dissolved and 11 per cent are gas caps.

Natural gas fields are classified in terms of their size as supergiants with 10×10^{12} ft³, (2.83×10^9 m³), or more, of recoverable gas, and giant (world class) gas fields with between 3×10^{12} ft³ (8.5×10^{10} m³) and 10×10^{12} ft³ (2.8×10^{11} m³) of recoverable gas.

Non-associated gas fields

Table 5.10 lists the giant and supergiant gas fields that had been discovered by 1977. There are now 125 gas fields in these two categories. In the UK sector of the North Sea, the Leman

Bank and Frigg gas fields are giants, and The Netherlands and Norway sectors each have one.

Associated gas fields

Every oil field is also a gas field. Tiratsoo assumes an average ratio of gas to oil of about 750–800 ft³/barrel and so oil fields with capacities of over 5×10^9 barrels may be thought of as at least 'giant' gas fields. There are between 30 and 40 such fields, and their total of gas is around 400×10^{12} ft³. Less than 1 per cent of the world's gas fields are giants or supergiants, but they contain, along with the associated gas in giant oil fields, 80 per cent of the world's proven and produced reserves; four-fifths of these are in the supergiants.

Natural gas use in the UK

In 1960 natural gas consumption in the UK was negligible, and most of it came from seepages from coal mines, and as by-products of other industries and processes. Since then it has increased to more than 2 EJ (70 mtoe), drawn from the North Sea gas fields.

With the increase in supply has come an increase in demand, mainly in the domestic and industrial sectors of the economy. Domestic use accounts for about 57 per cent, industry for 26 per cent, iron and steel making for 3 per cent, and services for 14 per cent.

Domestic gas, derived from coal at a gas works, was a common fuel for cooking and room heating from the middle of the 1800s until after the Second World War. The discovery of North Sea gas involved the complete replacement, between 1965 and 1975, of the country's supply infrastructure and it also meant modifying domestic appliances so that they could burn it. Since about 1977 all domestic supplies have been of natural gas. Its market expanded rapidly as it became increasingly available at a price lower than competing fuels and as automatic controls for gas heating equipment were developed. This has been particularly obvious in the increase in the number of households with gas fired central heating systems. While, in most cases, it is still probably the cheapest domestic heating fuel, its price, since government intervention to bring it more into line with its competitors, is much closer to the price of solid fuel and electricity.

In the industrial sector there has been a similar switch from town to natural gas and an increase in its use. Industrial fuel use can conveniently be grouped in three categories, non-premium or bulk heat commonly used for steam based operations; premium heat, where fuel is used directly as in kilns; processes specifically involving the use of electricity. In the last 30 years there has been a transition from non-premium to premium heat as 'clean' fuels, oil, LPG, gas and electricity have been used directly. This has led to greater efficiencies because losses involved in steam generation and distribution have been eliminated. In 1976 24 per cent of the gas was used in CHP, 34 per cent for steam raising, 40 per cent for direct heat and 2 per cent for other uses.

In 1990 the chemical industry and its allied trades were the largest industrial users of gas (173 PJ), they were followed by engineering, vehicles and non-ferrous metals (116 PJ), food, drink and tobacco (71 PJ), building materials (68 PJ), iron and steel (49 PJ), paper making, printing and stationery (42 PJ), textiles, leather and clothing (21 PJ), electricity generation and other energy industries (13 PJ), all other trades accounted for 40 PJ.

Until recently most commentators expected the UK production of natural gas to remain near the 1992 level for about a decade. This was to be followed because of falling North Sea production, higher costs and increased efficiency in use, by a slow decline to the year 2030, to about 60 per cent of present consumption. The privati-

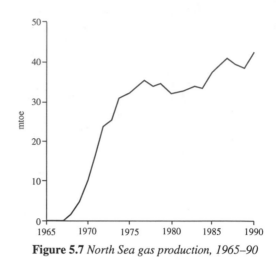

Figure 5.7 *North Sea gas production, 1965–90*

zation of the electricity industry in 1990 has been followed by the decision to build several combined cycle gas fired power stations, which will lead to an unforeseen increase in consumption. It will be some while before the impact of this can be assessed.

Gas supplies

North Sea

Gas was discovered in 1965 in the West Sole field situated in the southern sector of the North Sea and it began to come onshore in 1967. More was found in association with the oil fields in the northern sector and production increased rapidly (see Figure 5.7). The locations of significant North Sea finds are shown in Figure 5.2. Pipelines have been laid to bring the gas onshore from the southern sector to terminals at Bacton, Theddlethorpe and Easington, and from the northern sector at St Fergus. Distribution throughout the UK is achieved through the natural gas grid, a series of interconnected steel pipes up to 1.08 m in diameter and operating at pressures up to 75 bar (about 1100 psi)

In 1993 estimated proven reserves were 630 $\times 10^9 m^3$; probable reserves were 805 $\times 10^9 m^3$; possible reserves were 480 $\times 10^9 m^3$. Cumulative production to the end of November 1993 was 918 $\times 10^9 m^3$. The figures for remaining reserves do not include production to date and annual production is ≈50 $\times 10^9$ m (Department of Trade and Industry, 1994).

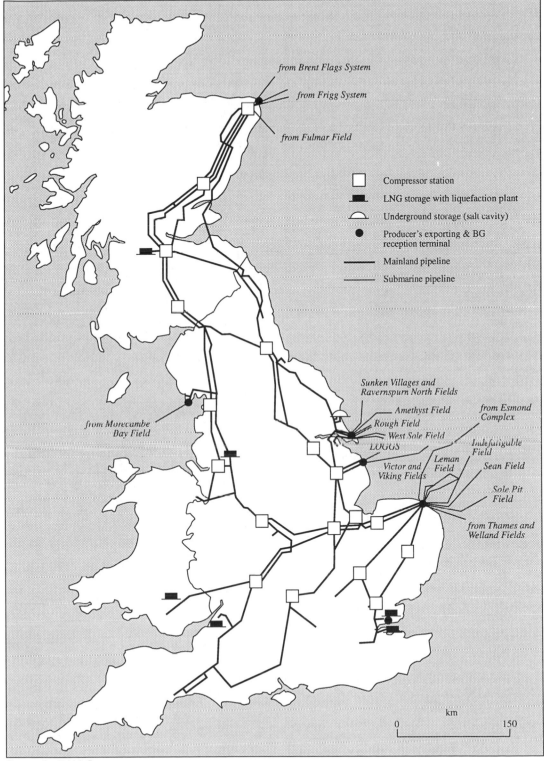

Figure 5.8 *UK natural gas grid*

93

World

Table 5.11 shows an estimate made in 1989 of the amount of economically recoverable world gas reserves.

At present rates of production the ratio of reserves to production is about 56. It is thought likely that more gas will be discovered and, because of the difficulties of delivery, no real crisis in supply is imminent.

Region	Gas reserves	
	10^{12} m^3	% total
W Europe	5.4	4.9
E Europe	0.8	0.7
USSR	42.5	37.6
Africa	7.5	6.7
Middle East	34.7	30.7
USA	4.7	4.1
Canada	2.7	2.4
C America	5.4	4.6
S America	1.3	1.2
P R China	1.0	0.9
Far East	6.4	5.7
Australia/New Zealand	0.6	0.5
Total	113.0	100.0

Source: *BP Statistical Review of World Energy*, 1990

Table 5.11 *Economically recoverable world gas reserves*

Future availability of natural gas

The 113 x 10^{12} m³ of recoverable reserves of natural gas has an energy value equivalent to about 103 x 10^{10} tonnes of oil, and so the published figures for the reserves of each are about the same. In trying to estimate the future position, there is much more uncertainty in the case of gas than of oil.

The reasons include the following

- Less exploration specifically for non-associated gas and when dry gas wells have been found in oil areas they have not always been included in the totals.
- Gas can only be used conveniently by countries within pipeline range of deposits. It is not easily transported in bulk by other

means, for example as liquid methane in refrigerated containers.
- Deep drilling for gas alone is in its infancy.
- New kinds of reserves, like hydrate deposits in which the gas is held in an ice-like solid buried beneath permafrost and in the sediments of continental shelves, and tight sands, are not yet being exploited.
- Giant gas fields, which affect the totals substantially, are still being discovered.

Given the known reserves and the rates of consumption, it seems certain that gas will be available for the next hundred years. The former Soviet Union alone had reserves which could meet its own needs and those of Europe for that period.

URANIUM

Uranium, in a variety of reservoirs with widely differing concentrations, occurs extensively in the earth's crust, with an average presence of about 2 ppm. Granites contain up to 20 ppm, currently exploited ores typically have over 350 ppm, coals commonly have around 20 ppm (some are known with 500–2000 ppm). Sea water contains 0.0005 ppm. The estimate for the earth's crust as a whole is 2.5 x 10^{13} tonnes.

Uranium increases in quantity as the ore grade decreases, thus every tenfold decrease in ore grade leads to a three-hundredfold increase in the recoverable amount. The grade of ore mined at any particular time is determined by the price on the open market. At present the price is low because, following the world-wide slow down in nuclear power plant construction, there is very little demand for it.

World distribution of uranium ore

Primary uranium ores are derived from Precambrian sources which have been buried and submitted to high temperatures and pressures. This results in the creation of uranium rich magmas, or uranium rich solutions, which give rise to the primary ore bodies. These, in addition to magmatic deposits, comprise pegmatites, vein deposits and veins associated with unconformities. Secondary ore bodies are derived from primary ores by sedimentary processes. Most of them are to be found in sandstones, conglomerate placers, phosphates and shales. Many more deposits must exist in numerous unexplored areas, particularly in remote shield regions.

Primary uranium deposits

The European deposits, of which those in Cornwall form a part, are vein deposits in fractures in rocks above major granite emplacements, the granite being derived from much older basement rocks.

Rossing in Namibia is the largest known deposit and is composed of granites and pegmatites. It has a relatively low grade of around 0.035 per cent but can be worked cheaply on a large scale. Similar deposits occur at Bancroft in Canada. Magmatic syenites are responsible for the deposits in Greenland and Brazil. The Cornish deposits are no longer economic but those in France, Spain, Portugal and Czechoslovakia are worked.

Some of the richest known ore bodies are related to veins accumulated below unconformities. At Cigar Lake in northern Canada deposits with a grade of around 5 per cent are found and at Key Lake, further south, the average grade is around 1.95 per cent with some veins yielding 30 per cent. The Alligator River, near the Gulf of Carpentaria, Australia is also a rich area.

Secondary uranium deposits

Generally speaking, these have lower grades than primary deposits, typically below 500 ppm

and they are often mined for uranium in conjunction with other elements, for example, the deep gold mines of the Witwatersrand basin near Johannesburg yield 2–5 ppm of gold and around 150 ppm of uranium. The sandstones of the Colorado basin are won from low cost drift mines, which are, at times, economic, although the grade is about 140 ppm of uranium.

Reserves and availability

Economic finds have been made in both primary and secondary ore deposits, and Table 5.12 shows how resources are distributed among them.

Although the production and availability of oil, natural gas and coal are all dependent to some extent on prevailing prices, uranium production reflects price changes much more strongly. 'Reasonably assured reserves' are also price dependent and at higher prices it becomes economic to exploit a wider resource base.

Deposits which are expensive to mine must have a higher grade of ore in order to produce uranium at a common price. In other words, if deep mined uranium ore is twice as expensive to mine as that from an open-cast source, it must yield twice as much uranium per tonne to remain competitive.

The price of uranium is affected principally by fluctuating demand, but the discovery and development of a new, high grade, accessible ore body can also cause the world market price to fall. Long term supply contracts tend to have a stabilizing effect on the price.

Uranium mining saw a boom following the 1974 'oil crisis' when it was thought that

Type	Uranium Grade (%)	Largest known deposit (tonnes of uranium)	% of reasonably assured world resources
Pegmatite and magmatic	0.03–0.13	100 000	14.0
Vein/fissures	0.1–2.0	20 000	5.5
Vein/unconformity	0.4–4.0	200 000	16.0
Sandstones	0.05–0.5	40 000	39.0
Placer	0.01–0.1	15 000	16.5
Other	0.001–0.3	500 000 at lowest concentration	9.0

Source: G C Brown & F. Skipsey, 1986

Table 5.12 *Uranium deposits*

nuclear power might expand rapidly. The price reached a peak of about $120/kg in 1979 after starting in 1974 at $20/kg, but had fallen back to about $40/kg by 1984 and $21/kg in 1991. It also suffers from short term fluctuations.

Annual global production during the same period rose from around 20,000 tonnes in the early 1970s to a peak of 45,000 tonnes in 1980, but slumped in the early 1980s to below 40,000 tonnes.

Against this kind of background, it is usual to estimate available reserves in terms of postulated price levels. Table 5.13 shows reserves and cumulative production from principal non-Communist uranium producing countries before 1984 (the units are thousands of tonnes of uranium metal).

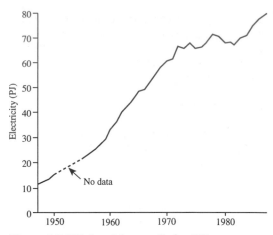

Figure 5.9 *UK electricity supplied to UK consumers, 1947–88*

ELECTRICITY

Crude oil, coal, natural gas and uranium are all primary raw materials which need processing before they can be used as fuels. Once processed they can be used for further energy conversions and all uranium, most coal, some oil and an increasing amount of natural gas is used to provide electricity. The proportion of energy supplied to consumers as electricity has increased rapidly over the past few decades and Figure 5.9 shows how total demand fluctuated from 1947 to 1988. Demand rose slowly at an average rate of around 2.3 GWh/yr which is about 1 per cent of present demand. It has premium uses, as in electric motors, lighting, arc furnaces, electronic equipment and eddy current heating, but much of it is used for low grade heat particularly in the domestic, public administration and miscellaneous sectors.

Electricity is generated in power stations as alternating current. Heat supplied by the fuel is used to provide mechanical energy of rotation which turns electrical generators. The second law transition of heat to work means that electricity generation is inherently inefficient in its use of primary energy. From the power station electricity is distributed through the electricity grid.

Country	Pre-1984 production	Resonably assured reserves		Estimated additional reserves	
		<$80/kg	$80–$130/kg	<$80/kg	$80–$130/kg
Brazil	1	163	0	92	0
USA	300	131	276	30	52
Canada	162	176	9	181	48
France	56	75	16	28	15
S Africa	111	191	122	99	48
Namibia	25	119	16	30	23
Niger	30	160	0	53	0
Australia	22	314	22	369	25
Others	33	139	114	32	97
Totals	740	1468	575	914	308

Source: G C Brown and E Skipsey, 1984

Table 5.13 *Reserves and cumulative production from non-Communist uranium producing countries, before 1984*

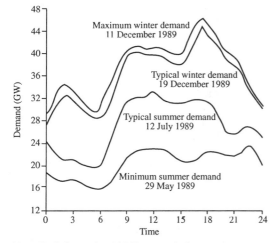

Note: Peak demand on NGC's transmission system was 46,763 MW at 1700 hours on Monday 11 December 1989. This compares with peak demand of 46,875 MW on 22 November 1988, and the highest peak demand ever recorded on the transmission system of 47,925 MW which occurred on 12 January 1987.

Source: National Grid Company Annual Report, 1989–90

Figure 5.10 *Daily electricity demand variations, 1984*

Electricity is unique among fuels in that it cannot be stored in other than minute quantities and then only as direct current. A typical 90 ampere-hour car battery, fully charged, stores 1080 Wh which is only just over 1 'unit' of electricity. AC cannot be stored at all (but see below). This means that electricity has to be generated as it is required and that the mains electricity supply must be designed and operated so that it can meet any instantaneous demand which might be placed upon it. Figure 5.10 shows how demand varies daily in winter and summer.

Final user	TWh	%
Iron and steel	7.87	3.0
Industry	82.98	31.3
Railways	5.22	2.0
Domestic	93.79	35.4
Public administration	19.32	7.3
Agriculture	3.88	1.5
Miscellaneous	51.63	19.5
Total	264.69	

Source: *Digest of UK Energy Statistics 1990*, 1991

Table 5.14 *End-uses of electricity, 1990*

Type of fuel	1970	1980	1990
Coal	44.7	52.7	48.6
Oil	12.4	6.6	6.7
Natural gas	0.1	0.4	0.2
Nuclear	5.5	7.8	14.2
Hydro	1.4	1.3	1.6
Other	–	0.1	–
Total	64.1	68.7	71.2

Source: *Digest of UK Energy Statistics 1991*

Table 5.15 *Fuel used for generation (million tonnes of oil equivalent)*

End-uses of electricity

Table 5.14 shows where the electricity sold in the UK has been used.

Electricity generation

The amount of electricity produced by different types of power station is shown in Table 5.16 and the fuel inputs to the system in Table 5.15.

Energy is fed into the grid by power stations. In 1989 there were 80 (17 of these are 1000 MW or greater) of them in England and Wales, and 87 in Scotland, see also Table 5.17.

The power stations installed in Great Britain in 1986 were capable of a combined output of 62.9 GW, of which 9.56 GW was generated in Scotland, and 53.4 GW in England and Wales. The maximum instantaneous load in 1986 was 54 GW, of which approximately 48 GW was in England and Wales, and 6 GW in Scotland. This load came close to 86 per cent of the total capacity of the system and left little margin for breakdowns, refuelling or maintenance (although the last two are normally scheduled for the summer when demand is low). The average demand on the system in 1986 was 27.6 GW (that is, 241.4 x 10^{12} Wh/24 x 365 h). By 1990 it had risen to 30.2 GW.

Efficiency of stations

Turbine generator sets for the present family of power stations have a capacity of 660 MWe and a power station will probably have two or three of them driven by steam from its fossil fuel or

Power station	1970	1980	1990
Conventional steam stations	89.2	87.0	78.9
Nuclear	9.1	11.8	19.8
Hydro	1.8	1.3	1.6
Pumped storage	0.5	0.5	0.7

Source: *Digest of UK Energy Statistics 1991*

Table 5.16 *Electricity supplied by each type of power station (per cent of total)*

Coal fired	35
Coal/gas fired	1
Coal/oil fired	4
Oil fired	5
Nuclear (Magnox)	10
Nuclear (AGR)	6
Gas turbines	10
Hydro electric	7
Pumped storage	2

Table 5.17 *CEGB power stations in 1989*

nuclear furnace. The average thermal efficiency of fossil fuelled steam power stations has, in recent years, been around 33 per cent. One of the most recent coal fired plants, Drax, achieves an overall thermal efficiency of 37 per cent. The thermal efficiency of nuclear plant is similar, Heysham 2 AGR was scheduled to achieve 40 per cent, the Sizewell PWR 34.3 per cent and the Dungeness B Magnox reactor returns 32.7 per cent.

Pumped storage

Energy produced by the electricity system can be stored if it is first converted to another form, for example, rotational kinetic energy of a fly-wheel, potential energy of an elevated mass of water or pressure in a volume of gas. Pumped storage schemes are used at present. Within this system two reservoirs, separated in height, are connected by a tunnel. Water may be pumped from the lower to the higher, or may flow from the higher to the lower. Electricity from the grid is used by the pumps at times of low demand and at times of high demand, the flow of water is used to drive hydro-electric generators. In practice, combined pump/turbine sets are used.

Dinorwic scheme

One such scheme is located at Dinorwic in North Wales and details of it are given below.

Dimensions
The vertical distance between the reservoirs is 530 m and they are separated by 2 km horizontally. A 10 m diameter tunnel links them.

Pump/turbines
Six 300 MW machines each consume 292 MW while pumping and can generate a maximum of 313 MW. They are constrained to 300 MW when all six are operating because the line to the site has only 1800 MW capacity.

Response times
It takes six hours to fill the upper reservoir and five hours to empty it at an average output of 1681 MW. This gives 80 per cent efficiency. The station can reach 1320 MW within 10 seconds of start-up and 1860 MW in about 15 seconds.

Economics
The CEGB calculated that £40 million per annum would be saved at a cost of £400 million.

Electricity grid

Electricity is supplied throughout the UK mainland on the National Grid network (see Figures 5.11 and 5.12). This is a system of transmission lines which carry power at high voltages. The bulk of it is transmitted at 400 kV, with 275 kV linkages, and 132 kV links and spurs to those regions needing smaller amounts of power. Power is taken from the grid through transformers which reduce the voltage in steps, first from 132 kV to 33 kV for local distribution or to supply large industrial consumers, then from 33 kV to 11 kV to supply light industries and areas of towns or villages, and, finally, from 11 kV to 415 V three phase and 240 V single phase for supplies to individual customers. Before privatization the grid was operated by the CEGB, and in England and Wales the Area Electricity

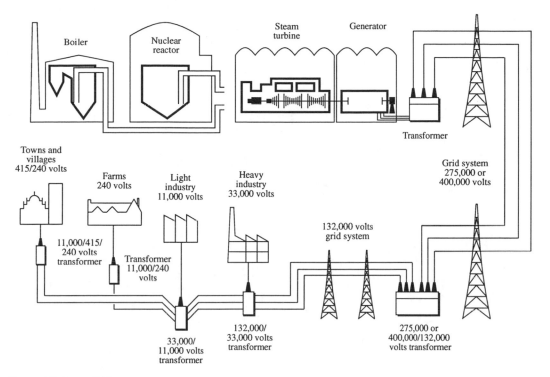

Source: R Cochrane, 1985

Figure 5.11 *Electricity distribution*

Boards took supplies from the grid to consumers. It is now run by the National Grid Company which transmits power to the Regional Electricity Companies. In Scotland the SSEB and NS Hydro Board are responsible for electricity supplies.

High voltage transmission is necessary for economic reasons. At any particular amount of transmitted power an economic balance must be sought between the costs of conductors (which will be greater for large currents and low voltages) and the costs of insulators (which will be greater for high voltages and low currents). The higher the voltage the more power a line can carry. A 400 kV line can transmit 1800 MW, a 275 kV line can transmit 430 MW and a 132 kV line can transmit 100 MW. Therefore, for 1800 MW one 400 kV pylon is needed rather than 4 275 kV pylons, or 18 at 132 kV. If these factors are evaluated carefully, a particular voltage yields a minimum cost when a particular amount of power is to be transmitted.

Structure of the UK industry after privatization

On 31 March 1990 the electricity industry in the UK was 'privatized' and restructured. Before that date, the CEGB had been responsible for power generation and the national grid in England and Wales. It had supplied electricity to the area boards, which then sold it on to the consumer. Generation, distribution and retailing were separated in the restructuring, and a number of other changes were made. All this was rationalized as an attempt to increase competition.

Electricity generation is now dominated by two private companies, National Power and Powergen. Nuclear power remains in the public sector and has been consolidated into one company, Nuclear Electric. Power is also supplied to the system by two more privatized companies, Scottish Power and Scottish Hydro-electric, by Scottish Nuclear which is still in the public sector, by some independent generators (whose numbers are likely to increase) and by France

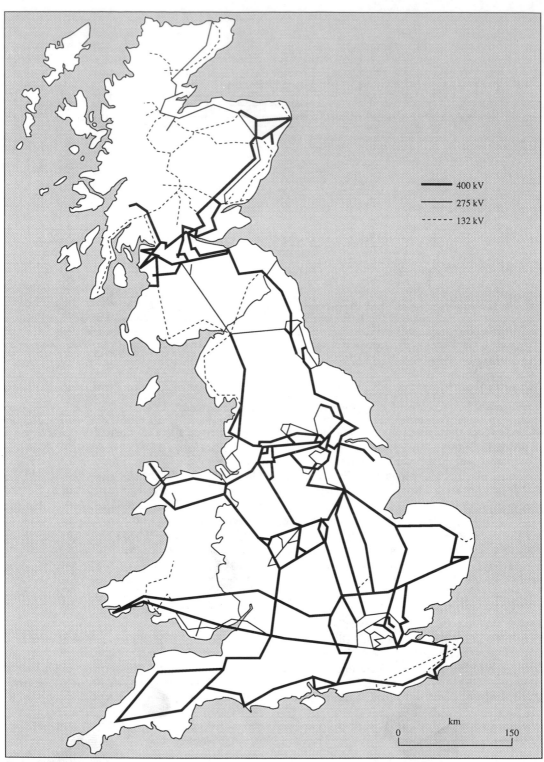

Source: R Cochrane, 1985

Figure 5.12 *Electricity grid*

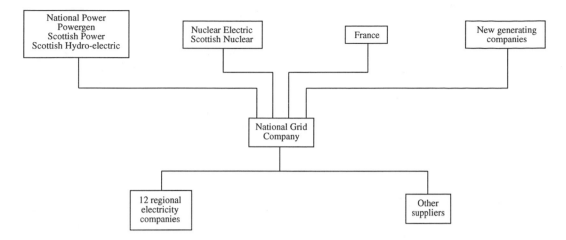

Figure 5.13 *Structure of UK electricity supply industry*

through the cross-Channel link (see Figure 5.13).

The principal customers for this power are the 12 regional electricity companies (RECs) which now sell to the consumer. There are also some large customers (>1 MW) who are supplied directly by individual generating companies.

The national supergrid transmission system which links the generators to the RECs' local networks is run by the National Grid Company, which is owned jointly by the RECs.

Operation of the system

The grid is managed to provide power when it is needed. There are a number of standards which it has to meet, for example, the voltage and frequency for consumers must be kept within certain limits, and power stations are connected to and disconnected from the grid to achieve this.

Before privatization, when the CEGB managed the national grid, power stations were connected to it in an order determined by their costs, the merit order. The stations supplying the cheapest electricity were connected first and then, as more power was required, progressively more expensive stations were added. In broad terms, nuclear stations are cheapest to operate, followed by newer coal plant, and then by older coal plant and other stations. Because they were first in the merit order, nuclear stations often achieved an availability of over 80 per cent, although their average load factor is around 60 per cent, whereas for the coal fired plant, which

includes some small older stations late in the merit order, it was around 50 per cent.

This method of operation is no longer possible because the National Grid Company does not control the generators. The key concept of the new system is the 'pool'. This is a trading market similar in operation to a spot market and is run by the National Grid Company. Demand and supply in any electricity supply system must always be balanced. Every day the generating companies provide the grid with a list of generators which will be available the following day and offer a price on a half-hourly basis for the power each generates. On receiving the offers, the grid ranks the stations according to price and then produces its schedules to meet expected demand, starting with the cheapest plant. In any particular half-hour through the day, the price paid for electricity is that charged by the most expensive station. This is known as the 'system marginal price' for that period. In addition to this price, the generating companies receive a 'capacity' charge which is related to the ability of the grid to balance supply and demand. If available plant exceeds demand, the capacity charge is very low, but if there is a possibility of demand outstripping supply the capacity charge is high. This mechanism is intended to encourage generators to make supply available when it is required. These two payments comprise the pool input price. A final pool output price includes an additional element for any further services provided. The retail price includes REC costs, charges for transmission and distribution,

Voltage (kV)	Ratio of cost of UG cable/ cost of OH line
400	18 (23 for heavy duty)
275	13 (17 for heavy duty)
132	8
66	7
33	5
11	3
415	2 or less

Source: S Y King and N A Halfter, 1982

Table 5.18 *Comparison of costs of overhead lines and underground cables*

and the non-fossil fuel levy of 11 per cent which subsidizes nuclear power and renewables.

A number of interim proposals, intended to aid the transition to a market based electricity system, were contained in the Act of Parliament authorizing privatization. They include such things as restrictions on the size (at present only loads above 1 MW, falling to 100 kW in 1994 and, by 1998, to any load) and number of customers that may be supplied directly by generating companies, the adjustment of pricing with the RECs until 1993, and targets for new suppliers and targets for non-fossil fuel supplies.

Efficiency of the system

The efficiency rating of the total system must take into account the losses in distribution. These are about 8 per cent of the power leaving the station, half of which occur as corona losses in silent electrical discharges over insulators and half in i^2R losses. If the power station is 30 per cent efficient, then the overall efficiency of supply is $0.3 \times 0.92 = 0.27$ or 27 per cent.

Overhead versus underground transmission

Table 5.18 shows why overhead lines are preferred in all except the most environmentally sensitive locations: they are so much cheaper. The costs arise from insulating and cooling, and from the large wayleaves necessary for high power underground lines. Cables are laid in special trenches with joint bays every 300 m. Twelve such cables in four trenches are needed to replace a double circuit overhead line. Each trench is 1 m wide by 1 m deep and separated from its neighbour by 4 m. Therefore, a width of 16 m is needed, about the same as a three lane motorway. New developments envisage the water or oil cooling of cables which would call for pumps and heat exchangers every 3 km. Maintenance and fault finding are also more difficult and expensive on underground cables.

6

NUCLEAR ENERGY

Of all of the present ways of generating electricity nuclear power is the most discussed and the most feared. The purpose of this chapter is to provide an outline of the scientific background to nuclear power generation, and therefore enable informed discussion concerning the costs, safety and disposal of this energy technology.

RADIATION AND RADIOACTIVITY

The atomic nucleus

For present purposes the nucleus of an atom may be considered as a spherical agglomeration of nuclear particles, or nucleons. The particles involved are of two types, protons and neutrons. They have approximately equal mass and the protons have a positive electric charge while the neutrons are uncharged. For the nucleus to be stable, ie for the collection of nucleons to remain bound together, the balance of forces between the particles must be such that they attract each other. Because there is a force of repulsion between the protons, as they have the same charge, an attractive force of some sort must

also be present and all nucleons are thought to interact over short distances with the strongly-attracting nuclear force. This is also known as the strong force and is one of only four known types of force. Both protons and neutrons contribute to the attractive force of the total nucleus, but the protons also contribute a repulsive force. As nuclei become larger, when the numbers of nucleons increase, the repulsive force increases and to counterbalance this the strong forces must be increased accordingly. The number of neutrons associated with the protons therefore increases and the ratio of neutrons to protons gradually rises from 1 for light nuclei to more than 1.5 for the heaviest nuclei. In some of these heavy nuclei the forces are only just about balanced and sometimes disintegration occurs. In the process of disintegration, or decay, a particle is emitted and the element which decays is said to be an unstable radioactive element.

- The number of protons in a nucleus is called its atomic number and is given the symbol Z. This is also equal to the number of electrons belonging to the atom of that element.
- The total number of nucleons in a nucleus is its mass number and is given the symbol A.

- The number of neutrons is the difference between the mass number and the atomic number, ie (A − Z).
- The mass can be expressed, approximately, in kg by multiplying A, which is in mass units (u), by 1.66×10^{-27}, which is the mass in kg of one mass unit.
- Avogadro's number, 6×10^{23}, is the number of atoms (and therefore nuclei), in 1 gram atomic weight of an element.

It is possible for some elements to have different sorts of nuclei where different numbers of neutrons are associated with the Z protons. These nuclei which have identical Z but different A are called isotopes of the element. The chemical symbol for the element is used to identify its nucleus, and A and Z are added to it as below to indicate the number of nucleons and protons:

eg $^{235}_{92}U$ $\quad$ $^{238}_{92}U$ $\quad$ $^{14}_{6}C$ $\quad$ $^{90}_{38}Sr$

The atomic number Z is the subscript and the mass number A the superscript. Two isotopes of uranium are shown, with mass numbers 235 and 238 and atomic number 92. (Natural uranium has 0.7% ^{235}U and 99.3% ^{238}U.) The other two isotopes in the list are carbon-14 and strontium-90.

Atoms typically have dimensions of the order of 10^{-10} m, whereas nuclei are 100,000 times smaller, ie with a diameter of the order of 10^{-15} m. For a nucleus with a mass number A the radius is given by:

Radius = $1.3 \times A^{1/3} \times 10^{-15}$ m.

Radiation

The nuclei of some naturally occurring heavy elements are unstable and break down by emitting nuclear particles. They are said to be radioactive. It is the emitted particles which may cause genetic and somatic effects if they strike, and damage, molecules of living matter. The particles involved are alpha particles (which are the nuclei of helium), beta particles (which are electrons) and gamma rays (which are quanta of electromagnetic radiation). X-rays, protons and neutrons can cause similar effects, and are generated in nuclear reactions, and in laboratories and medical facilities. See Table 6.1 for details of some of their properties.

Name	Formula represent-ation	Common represent-ation	Rest mass(u)	Charge (e)
Electron				
Beta particle	e^-	ß	0.0005486	−1
Neutron	^1_0n	n	1.008665	0
Proton	^1_1H	p	1.007277	+1
Alpha	^4_2He	α	4.001506	+2

Table 6.1 *Properties of some nuclear particles*

Radioactivity

All nuclei which have values of Z greater than 82 are radioactive. Examples of the radioactive decay of nuclei are:

$$^{203}_{83}Bi \rightarrow ^{199}_{81}Tl + alpha\ (^4_2He)$$

$$^{238}_{92}U \rightarrow ^{234}_{90}Th + alpha\ (^4_2He)$$

$$^{234}_{90}Th \rightarrow ^{234}_{91}Pa + ß\ (e^-)$$

Notice that in the process of radioactive decay the original element changes into a new one.

A gramme of uranium-238 contains approximately 2.5×10^{21} atoms and in 1 second approximately 12,000 of these decay to thorium-234. However at any particular time any nucleus has an equal probability of being the one to decay and it is not possible to identify which will be the next to change. The process is truly random and it is only possible to discuss it in terms of the probability that a nucleus has of decaying in one second. In the case of the ^{238}U to ^{234}Th transition this probability is 4.9×10^{-18} s^{-1}.

It is more usual to talk in terms of the half-life of a particular reaction. The half-life,

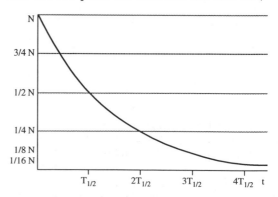

Figure 6.1 *Number of atoms remaining after a time, t*

$T_{1/2}$, is the time taken for one half of the nuclei that are originally present in a sample to decay. This is related to the probability mentioned above as follows:

Half-life = 0.693/probability of decay

Figure 6.1 shows how the number of atoms of a radioactive element change with time. The half-life, $T_{1/2}$, is the time taken for one-half of the original nuclei to decay. As can be seen from Figure 6.1 after a time equal to one half-life the number of atoms present is halved, no matter how many are present initially. Table 6.2 lists some radioactive nuclei of importance in the environment and nuclear power, together with their half-lives. Nuclides with long half-life undergo comparatively few decays per second, whereas those with short half-life have many decays. The activity (number of nuclei decaying per second) is therefore much higher for short half-life nuclides than for those with long half-life. Most of the naturally occurring radioactive materials have long half-lives. In the time since the earth was formed those with short half-lives have decayed to become stable iso-topes of new elements. There are exceptions, notably carbon-14 which is constantly renewed by cosmic ray bombardment and has a half-life of 5568 years.

Background radiation

Radioactivity is a phenomenon which occurs widely, at low levels, in nature. Soil is radioactive, houses are radioactive, people are radioactive, food is radioactive. Cereals have a comparatively high radioactive content, as do Brazil nuts; whereas milk, fruit and vegetables have a low content. Evolution has occurred in the presence of this background of radiation. In addition to the natural background human activity has introduced more radiation, principally due to the diagnostic use of X-rays and the use of radionuclides in the treatment of cancer. Table 6.3 lists some of the sources of radiation which contribute to the background. The two sets of units used are millirems and microsieverts. As will be explained later sieverts have been adopted as the modern standard but the old units of rems are still in common use.

The values presented in Table 6.3 are averages and include some which are estimates, but the orders of magnitude are probably correct. For different individuals and different areas the levels will vary significantly. Those living in brick houses in areas of sedimentary geology who do not travel by air or ski in the Alps will encounter much less background radiation than those living in granite houses in areas with igneous geology who travel by air to the Himalayas and return requiring extensive X-rays to allow their fractures to be set.

Biological effects of radiation

Concern about the use of nuclear power arises from the knowledge that nuclear radiation can harm living tissue. The effects are usually considered in two categories, somatic and genetic effects. Somatic effects are those which occur in the radiated individual, while genetic effects appear in any progeny. It may also be useful to divide effects into acute (due to large amounts of radiation received in one dose) and chronic (due to receiving repeated small amounts of radiation over a long period of time). Of these categories the acute effects are comparatively straightfor

Isotope	Decay particle	Half-life (years)
Primeval radionuclides		
$^{238}_{92}$U (Uranium 238)	α	4.50×10^9
$^{232}_{90}$Th(Thorium 232)	α, γ	1.39×10^{10}
$^{40}_{19}$K (Potassium 40)	β, γ	1.28×10^9
$^{8}_{37}$Rb(Rubidium 87)	β	4.70×10^{10}
$^{235}_{92}$U (Uranium 235)	α	7.13×10^8
Radionuclides produced by cosmic rays		
$^{14}_{6}$C (Carbon 14)	α	5568
$^{3}_{1}$H (Tritium)	α	12.35
$^{7}_{4}$Be(Beryllium 7)	γ	53 days
Radionuclides from human activities		
$^{239}_{92}$Pu (Plutonium 239)	α	2.41×10^4
$^{3}_{1}$H(Tritium)	β	12.35
$^{90}_{38}$Sr(Strontium 90)	β	29
$^{131}_{53}$I (Iodine 131)	α	8.04 days
$^{137}_{55}$Cs(Caesium 137)	α	30.17
$^{85}_{36}$Kr(Krypton 85)	β	10.72

Table 6.2 *Some radionuclides found in the environment*

Natural	mrem	msv
In the body		
Radium in bones	6	0.06
Carbon-14 in body	2	0.02
Potassium-40 in body	20	0.2
Potassium-40 from nearby persons	2	0.02
External		
Cosmic rays (sea level)	25	0.25
Gamma rays from ground and building materials	35	0.35
Radon in the air	117.5	1.175
Thoron in the air	10	0.1
Total (sea level)	187.5	1.875
Other		
Medical, diagnostic X-ray ⎫		
Medical, radiotherapy ⎬	30	0.3
Medical, radio-isotope use ⎭		
Nuclear fallout	1	0.01
Industrial/occupational	0.5	0.005
Air travel (cosmic rays above sea level)	1	0.01
Consumer products	0.2	0.002
Nuclear wastes	0.2	0.002
Nuclear reactors	0.01	0.0001
TOTAL BACKGROUND	250	2.5

Principal source: NRPB, 1989

Table 6.3 *Average annual whole-body equivalent doses received in the UK from natural and other sources of radiation*

ward to describe and there is a large measure of consensus about them. The effects of long term exposure to low levels of radiation are not well known and there is some controversy about whether there are such effects, what they might be, and whether or not they can be distinguished among the mass of similar, or identical, outcomes due to other causes.

Radiation affects the human body through its action on cells. The amount of energy deposited in tissue is too small to cause significant rises in temperature and the only other damage mechanism is that of direct impact on the cell or its nucleus with consequent rupture of some of its structures. This damage may be large scale, with immediately recognizable effects, or it may be more localized on a smaller scale, per-

haps causing a cell to grow in an abnormal manner eventually being manifest as cancer, or if damage is caused to chromosomes it may lead to mutations which eventually propagate into the population.

To be able to discuss the possible biological effects of exposure to radiation we need a suitable system of measurement units and it is desirable that the units are proportional to the amount of any biological damage caused. This damage is likely to be dependent on the type of radiation, its energy, the number of particles and the type of tissue absorbing the particles. A related set of units is used for these factors as seen in Table 6.4.

Activity is the measured count rate, and depends on the amount of material present and its half-life. Exposure relates to the amount of ionization produced in air by a radioactive source and is an approximate measure of the amount of ionization produced in tissue. Neither of these quantities is a good universal measure of the biological effects of radiation because neither incorporates the amount of energy absorbed by the tissue. The absorbed dose, which is the amount of energy absorbed per kg, indicates this directly and is a more appropriate measure, because tissue which is exposed to radiation of a particular activity or exposure does not necessarily absorb all of this radiation. It is also unlikely, even if the same dose is absorbed, that different types of particles will cause identical amounts of damage. They differ in mass and charge, and different particles of the

Property	New unit (Old unit)	Definition
Activity	Becquerel (Bq) (Curie)	1 disintegration/sec 3.7×10^{10} disint/sec
Exposure	Coulomb/kg (Roentgen)	2.58×10^{-4} C/kg
Absorbed dose	Gray (Gy) (Rad)	1 J/kg 0.01 J/kg
Dose equivalent	Sievert (Sv) (Rem)	D x Q x N D x Q x N

(Where D is Gy or Rad, Q relates to the particle and N the tissue)

Table 6.4 *Radiation units*

Particle	Q
β	1
X-ray	1
γ	1
α	10–20
Neutrons	5–10

Table 6.5 *Quality factors*

same type may well have different kinetic energy. To account for this the relative biological efficiency, RBE, or Q factor is introduced, see Table 6.5. Different types of tissue have different susceptibility to damage by radiation and a biological weighting factor, N, is assigned to different tissue types, see Table 6.6. The dose equivalent incorporates the absorbed dose and these two further factors to arrive at a measure of the likely biological effect on any tissue or organ by a particular type of radiation.

Much of the existing literature is written in terms of the old units, rads and rems, but grays and seiverts are beginning to find more common use. When discussing the biological effects resulting from exposure to radiation the absorbed dose, or dose equivalent as appropriate, is used to compare or predict likely outcomes.

Acute effects of exposure to radiation are fairly well known from the victims of the bombs dropped on Japan in the Second World War and from accidents associated with the use of radiation in weapons testing, power generation, medicine or industry.

Doses larger than 100 grays (10,000 rads) result in damage to the central nervous system and death usually occurs within one to two days. A dose between 10 and 100 grays (1000 to 10,000 rads) has its major effect on the gastro-intestinal tract, producing symptoms such as vomiting, fever and dehydration, and death is likely within one or two weeks. In the dose range 3 to 10 grays (300 to 1000 rads) blood cells and blood formation are the worst affected, and haemorrhaging, pallor, loss of hair and diarrhoea are some of the symptoms; leading to death in three to six weeks for most victims. For doses below 3 grays, and certainly below 0.5 grays, the percentage of exposed persons who die within 30 days is very small. There may be symptoms including loss of hair, loss of appetite, sore throat, pallor, diarrhoea. There is also an increased risk of leukaemia and other cancers, as well as other diseases, developing from one to ten or more years later.

These effects of large doses have been confirmed by experiments on insect populations and it has also been found that mutagenic effects are proportional to dose rate down to about 1 gray. The rule of thumb is that about 100 cancers per million people will result per 0.01 gray (1 rad) dose of radiation. The question, and source of controversy, is whether or not this holds down to very small doses (remember that the background radiation is about 0.002 gray (0.2 rad)).

It has often been argued that a threshold for radiation damage exists. The evidence for this is based on experiments comparing the effect of delivering the same total dose of radiation either as a single large dose or as the accumulation of many separate smaller doses. It has been shown that the single larger dose may be fatal whereas the several smaller doses seem to have little effect. This seems to imply that a somatic or genetic repair mechanism exists for small amounts of damage. But it is also clear from long term observation of the recipients of the smaller doses that the repair is not permanent because the life expectancy of this group is less than that of a control group.

There is no evidence for an increased rate of damage at low irradiation levels and so it is generally assumed that extending the linear damage/dose relationship to low dose rates is a reasonable, if not conservative, assumption. Standards for radiation exposure are produced on this assumption. Table 6.7 summarizes the recommendations of the International Committee on Radiation Protection (ICRP) for the maximum levels of radiation to which people should be exposed

Organ	N
Whole body	1
Gonads	4
Breast	7
Red marrow	8
Lung	8
Thyroid	33
Bone	33

Table 6.6 *Biological weighting factors*

Identification of effect of exposure to low level radiation

It is possible from the postulated relationship between damage and radiation dose discussed above to estimate the likely effects on a population of its exposure to a source of radiation. But it is very difficult to detect any effects due to this one event against the background of similar effects due to a wide range of unknown 'natural' causes. Just over 20 per cent of deaths in Britain each year are attributed to cancer, the number being around 130,000. For comparison the estimated somatic effect of a radiation dose of 0.0025 sieverts (doubling the average background radiation) on the UK population of 55 million is an additional 550 cancer cases.

For the radiation released to the atmosphere at Chernobyl in the former Soviet Union the range of effects is from 800 possible additional deaths to the 30,000 expected for the population within 30 km of the reactor, to perhaps an additional 40,000 deaths in 500 million for the world population. The 800 among the local population might be detectable, but the 40,000 in the global population would not.

NUCLEAR ENERGY AND NUCLEAR REACTIONS

When coal, oil and natural gas are burned their hydrocarbons react with the oxygen in air to yield carbon dioxide and water. In the process energy is released. The source of this energy is the rearrangement of the chemical bonds of the various compounds involved in the reactions. Chemical bonds involve the outermost electrons of atoms. Nuclear energy results from rearrangements of the components of the nuclei of atoms, and because the forces between these are very much greater than those between the outer electrons of the atom, the energy released in nuclear reactions is very much greater than that in chemical reactions. Typically 100 million times more energy is released in a nuclear reaction than in a chemical reaction. The following sections provide an introduction to nuclear reactions and their role in nuclear reactors.

Binding energy and mass defect

Nucleons stay together as a nucleus because the nuclear strong force of attraction is dominant in stable nuclei. Therefore, to dismember a nucleus into separate protons and neutrons work has to be done against this force. The amount of work that is necessary is called the binding energy of the nucleus. An alternative way of looking at this is to say that the total energy of a group of nucleons bound together as a nucleus is less than their total energy when they are separated. A mechanical analogy might compare the nucleons in the nucleus with marbles in the bottom of a bowl. The marbles remain together in the bowl unless kinetic energy is supplied to them, by stirring for example, when they may be able, while moving around, to fall over the upper edge of the bowl. In the same way, energy supplied to nucleons may cause the nucleus to disrupt.

Exposed part of body	Registered worker	Member of public
Whole body; blood forming organs; gonads	50 mGy/yr (5 Rads/yr) 30 mGy/quarter	5 mGy/yr (0.5 Rads/yr)
Skin; thyroid	150 mGy/quarter 300 mGy/yr	30 mGy/quarter
Limited exposure of single organs other than those above	80 mGy/quarter 150 mGy/yr	15 mGy/yr
Hands, forearms, feet, ankles	400 mGy/quarter 750 mGy/yr	75mGy/yr

In addition the ICRP recommends that radiation doses should be subject to an overall criterion of being kept 'as low as reasonably achievable', known as ALARA

Table 6.7 *ICRP maximum permissible levels of radiation*

Energy and mass are known to be related by the formula:

$$E = mc^2,$$

where E is the energy, m is the mass and c is the velocity of light,

and so it follows that the mass of a nucleus will be less than the mass of its separated constituent parts because it has been necessary to supply energy to the complete nucleus to break it up.

The mass defect of a nucleus is the difference in mass between its separated components and its own mass. If Δm denotes the mass defect,

$$\Delta m = (A - Z)m_n + Zm_p - M$$

where M is the mass of the nucleus, m_n the mass of a neutron and m_p the mass of a proton, expressed in mass units.

When $E = mc^2$ is used to convert the mass defect into an equivalent amount of energy, the energy is the binding energy of the nucleus and will be given by

$$BE \text{ (Joules)} = \Delta m\, c^2$$
$$= [(A - Z)m_n + Zm_p - M]u\, c^2$$

(u is the unified mass unit = 1.66×10^{-27} kg). Or, it can be expressed in MeV using

$$BE \text{ (MeV)} = 931\, [(A - Z)m_n + Zm_p - M]$$

Binding energies have been measured for nuclei over the whole range of the elements and it is found that different nuclei have different binding energies. It is common to present the results of these experiments in terms of the average binding energy per nucleon, that is BE/A, which is a measure of how tightly each nucleon is bound to the rest, and Figure 6.2 shows how this varies with the mass of a nucleus.

As an example, consider the $_3^7$Li atom. It has a mass of 7.016u, and has 3 protons and three electrons, (ie three hydrogen atoms, mass 1.007825u), and three neutrons, mass 1.008665u.

The combined mass of these constituents is 7.058135u, and so the mass defect is (7.058135 − 7.016) = 0.042135u.

The binding energy of $_3^7$Li is 0.042135 × 931 = 39.23 MeV

or 39.23/7 = 5.6 MeV per nucleon.

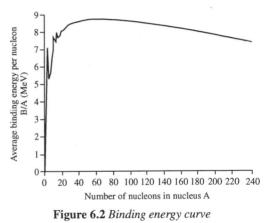

Figure 6.2 *Binding energy curve*

In joules the binding energy is

$$0.042135 \times 1.66 \times 10^{-27} \times (3 \times 10^8)^2$$
$$= 6.3 \times 10^{-12} \text{J}$$

Fission and fusion

The binding energy curve, Figure 6.2, has a flattish maximum over the range of mass numbers from about 50 to 80. This means that these nuclei are the most stable, because the largest amount of energy was released, or the most mass lost, when they were formed. It also indicates the two possible ways of releasing energy from the nucleus.

1 **By fission** – whereby a nucleus with A greater than 120 is split into two nuclei which have A around 60 and, because the new nuclei have greater binding energies, energy must be released in the process.

2 **By fusion** – whereby two light nuclei (A below about 20) fuse together to form a nucleus with A up to around 60. As the binding energy curve is much steeper for nuclei with low values of A than for those with values of A above 120 the energy released in the process of fusing together two light nuclei is much greater than that in the fissioning of a heavy nucleus.

Energy released in the fission process

From the curve in Figure 6.2 a nucleus with a mass number of 220 can be seen to have nucleons with an average binding energy of 7.8 MeV, while one with a mass number of 110 has an average binding energy per nucleon of 8.6 MeV.

If the heavy nucleus is split so that two of the lighter nuclei are produced the average binding energy of the nucleons increases and there is an energy release of:

$$(8.6 - 7.8) \times 220 = 176 \text{ MeV}$$

Obviously the exact amount of energy released, which is predominantly the kinetic energy of the two lighter nuclei, depends on the mass of the nucleus which is fissioned and the masses of the nuclei which result. A figure of:

200 MeV per fission

is often used as a rough order of magnitude when estimating the energy released in fissioning a large mass of material. This amount of energy is equivalent to a mass loss of about:

0.2 mass units per fission.

We can estimate the energy released when 1 kg of ^{235}U is fissioned as follows:

Avogadro's number, 6×10^{23}, is the number of nuclei in 1 gram atomic weight of an element and so the number of nuclei in 1 kg of ^{235}U is

$$(6 \times 10^{23}) \times 1000/235$$

In their fission

$$(6 \times 10^{23}) \times 1000/235 \times 200 \text{ MeV , or}$$

$$(6 \times 10^{23}) \times 1000/235 \times 200 \times 10^6 \times 1.6 \times 10^{-19} \text{ joules, ie}$$

$$(6 \times 2 \times 1.6)/235 \times 10^{15} = 8.2 \times 10^{13} \text{ joules}$$
of energy is released. This amount of energy could be used to operate a 1000 MW power station, which can convert thermal energy to electrical energy with an efficiency of 33 per cent, for

$$(6 \times 2 \times 1.6 \times 10^{15})/(235 \times 3 \times 1000 \times 10^6 \times 60 \times 60 \times 24) \text{days} = 0.35 \text{ days}$$

The amount of ^{235}U used when the power station is run continuously for a year is therefore 1158 kg (ie approximately 1.2 tonnes). For comparison, a coal fired power station of similar output might need to burn 2.5 million tonnes of coal.

Nuclear reactions relevant to nuclear power

In the previous section the energy released in fission was discussed but no means were suggested for bringing fission about. Interactions between nuclei are discussed in terms of nuclear reactions, which play an analogous role in nuclear physics to that played by chemical reactions in chemistry. For there to be any chance of a reaction between nuclei the interacting particles must be brought together and the achievement of this is one of the major preoccupations of nuclear physicists. Nuclei are positively charged and, if a reaction is to occur between two of them, their mutual repulsive force must be overcome. Because this force is inversely proportional to the square of the distance separating the nuclei, and because they must approach each other to within about 10^{-15}m to be able to react together, ie for their constituent nucleons to be capable of rearrangement, it is a very large force. The usual way in which this force is overcome is to accelerate one of the nuclei to a very high velocity so that its kinetic energy is sufficient for it to reach the other 'target' nucleus.

There is one group of nuclear reactions for which the problem of repulsion does not exist, and these are the reactions between nuclei and neutrons. Because the neutron has no electric charge, it does not experience the repulsive force and can contact a nucleus more easily. Fission reactions, and indeed all of the major processes which need to be considered to understand nuclear reactors, involve the interaction of neutrons with nuclei. In essence the conditions inside a reactor need to ensure a supply of neutrons of the optimum kinetic energy for the fission of ^{235}U to take place at a reasonable rate. It must also be possible to maintain control of the reactor by reducing or increasing the availability of neutrons as necessary.

When neutrons are incident on a material a large number of different reactions can occur. Their relative probabilities of occurrence are known as their reaction cross-sections. The probability of interaction of a nucleus and a neutron is known as the microscopic cross-section (denoted by σ) and if a beam of neutrons interacts with 1 m^3 of material (with n atoms/m^3) the probable number of interactions is $n\sigma$, called Σ,

Cross-section (in barns)	Fast neutrons (2 MeV energy or 2 x 10⁷ m/s)	Slow neutrons (0.025 eV energy or 2200 m/s)
σ_s	5.0	10
σ_c	0.25	107
σ_f	1.27	580

Table 6.8 ^{235}U *cross-sections*

the macroscopic cross-section. Because many types of reaction can occur the probability of a reaction of some kind happening, the total cross-section, σ_T, is the sum of several individual cross-sections

$$\sigma_T = \sigma_s + \sigma_c + \sigma_f + \ldots..$$

where σ_s is the cross-section for scattering a neutron, σ_c that for capturing (or absorbing) a neutron, σ_f that for a fission reaction and so on.

Cross-sections are quoted in the units of barns, where 1 barn is 1×10^{-28} m^2.

For pure ^{235}U some reaction cross-sections are listed in Table 6.8, which illustrates that the probability of a particular reaction occurring is different for different values of the kinetic energy of the neutrons.

For each type of neutron reaction the cross-section will vary with the energy of the neutron involved and, because it is possible for any or all of these reactions to occur when a beam of neutrons interacts with bulk material, the number of reactions of each type which actu-

ally occur depends on the reaction's cross-section and how the cross-section varies with the neutron's energy.

Figures 6.3, 6.4 and 6.5 show some typical neutron reaction cross-sections and how they vary with the energy of the incident neutron. Neutron energies of around 0.01 eV are referred to as thermal energies, because this energy corresponds to that which a particle would acquire if it was in collision with particles with velocities typical of those possessed by gas molecules at room temperature. Neutrons with this amount of energy are known as thermal or slow neutrons.

The ^{235}U Fission Reaction

Figure 6.4 shows the variation in the cross-section of the ^{235}U fission reaction. This reaction is one possible outcome when ^{235}U absorbs a neutron. When a fission reaction does result there are many ways in which the ^{235}U can split up, yielding a variety of nuclei with masses in the range 70 to 160, depending on which particular reaction happens to occur.

For example, three ways in which the ^{235}U nucleus breaks up are shown below :

1   $^{235}_{92}U + ^{1}_{0}n \rightarrow (^{236}_{92}U) \rightarrow ^{141}_{56}Ba + ^{92}_{36}Kr + 3^{1}_{0}n$

2   $^{235}_{92}U + ^{1}_{0}n \rightarrow (^{236}_{92}U) \rightarrow ^{143}_{55}Cs + ^{90}_{37}Rb + 3^{1}_{0}n$

3   $^{235}_{92}U + ^{1}_{0}n \rightarrow (^{236}_{92}U) \rightarrow ^{149}_{60}Nd + ^{87}_{35}Br + 3\beta$

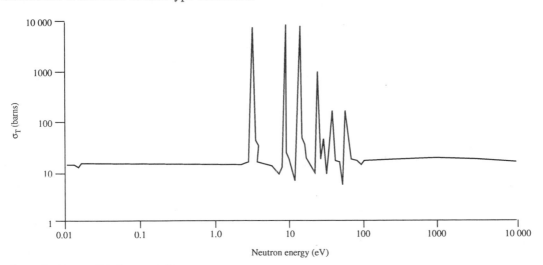

Source: D J Bennet and J R Thomson, 1989

Figure 6.3 *The total cross-section of* ^{238}*uranium*

111

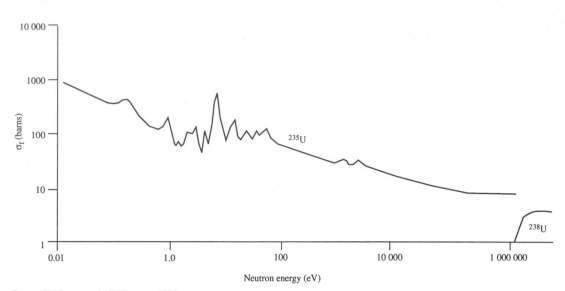

Source: D J Bennet and J R Thomson, 1989

Figure 6.4 *The fission cross-sections of ^{235}U and ^{238}U*

In reactions 1 and 2 the neutrons resulting from the fission, the fission neutrons, are known as prompt neutrons, because they are emitted within less than 10^{-15}s of the incident neutron being absorbed. In fact 99.24 per cent of neutrons resulting from ^{235}U fission fall into this category.

However, in reaction 3 the bromine-87 decays to krypton-86 as follows:

$$^{87}_{35}Br \rightarrow {}^{87}_{36}Kr + \beta \rightarrow {}^{86}_{36}Kr + {}^{1}_{0}n$$

The bromine-87 to krypton-87 transition, involving the emission of a beta particle, has a half-life of 55.6 s. The krypton-87 then immediately emits a neutron and becomes krypton-86. The net effect of this sequence of reactions is a delay of 55.6 s between the ^{235}U fission occurring and a neutron being emitted.

This neutron is known as a delayed neutron and 0.76 per cent of the neutrons produced in fission reactions are delayed for times ranging from 55.6 s to 0.05 s, depending on the particular reaction. The average delay is about 12 seconds. It is the existence of this group of delayed neutrons which allows the control of the power output of nuclear reactors, because it means that for some reactions there is time to monitor what is occurring and, if necessary, take action to control subsequent events.

In two of these examples of fission three neutrons result, while one results from the other.

Different reactions yield different numbers of neutrons and when all the reactions are taken into account the average yield is 2.4 neutrons per fission. Uranium-235 is the only natural isotope that can be made to fission with thermal neutrons. Three artificial isotopes, plutonium-239, plutonium-240 and uranium-233 also behave in this way. The most common of these, plutonium-239, yields 2.9 neutrons per fission.

The nuclei with masses approximately half that of uranium are known as the fission fragments, or fission products, and the resulting neutrons as fission neutrons.

About 200 MeV of energy is released in each fission event. The distribution of this energy is as in Table 6.9.

Inspection of Figure 6.4 shows that the cross-section for the fission reaction is approximately 1000 barns at low neutron energies and that it decreases erratically to approximately 1

Kinetic energy of fission products	168 MeV
Kinetic energy of fission neutrons	5 MeV
Prompt gamma radiation	7 MeV
Fission product radioactive decay	
Beta radiation	8 MeV
Gamma radiation	12 MeV

Source: D J Bennet and J R Thomson, 1989

Table 6.9 *Distribution of energy released in ^{235}U fission*

barn at high neutron energies. The 1 barn cross-section is for neutrons with kinetic energies of 1 or 2 MeV and, as can be seen in Table 6.9, this corresponds to the energy of the fission neutrons. Therefore fissions are 1000 times more likely to be induced by thermal (slow) neutrons than by fission (fast) neutrons.

Chain reactions and criticality

If it is possible to use the fission neutrons to initiate further fission reactions with new nuclei of ^{235}U, a growing number of nuclei will be involved as time goes on. This situation is referred to as a chain reaction. Chain reactions would not be achievable if, on average, one or fewer fission neutrons was produced per fission because inevitably some of them would not interact with further ^{235}U nuclei. The fission neutrons can take part in all types of neutron reactions. In broad terms these neutrons are involved in three kinds of process. They either leak out of the fissionable material and escape, are absorbed by it or surrounding material to react in ways other than fission, or are absorbed by ^{235}U and provoke further fissions. If, on average, one of the fission neutrons produces a further fission the reaction is self-sustaining, if more than one produces a further fission the number of fissions increases with time and if less than one produces a further fission the number of fissions gradually decreases with time. These three possibilities are described by a factor, k, the reaction multiplication constant. If:

k > 1 the reaction is supercritical and the number of fissions increases with time;

k = 1 the reaction is critical and the reaction rate is constant; and

k < 1 the reaction is subcritical and the number of fissions decreases with time.

To produce a working, controllable nuclear reactor it must be possible to initiate a chain reaction, allow the number of nuclei involved per second to increase gradually until the fission rate is sufficient to generate the required power level and then to maintain this rate steady. In the event of wanting to close down the reactor, eg for refuelling or to repair a fault, it must be possible to decrease the reaction rate in a controlled fashion. Control of the reactor is achieved by

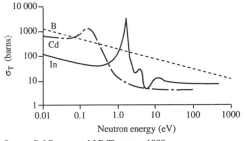

Source: D J Bennet and J R Thomson, 1989

Figure 6.5 *The total cross-section of Cd, In and B*

controlling the number of neutrons which are present in the core.

Thermal reactor cores are designed so that they are subcritical when only the prompt neutrons are considered. The 0.76 per cent of delayed neutrons therefore are crucial for the reaction rate to grow, and because they are delayed on average by about 12 seconds there is time for neutron absorbing materials to be introduced or withdrawn from the core to control, whether or not the delayed neutrons participate in the chain reaction.

The essential parts of a reactor core

From the discussion in the previous sections it is clear that a number of conditions must be satisfied if a stable nuclear reactor is to be built. These are are follows.

1 The core must contain sufficient fissionable material for a chain reaction of the required magnitude to be maintained

This depends on the amount of ^{235}U, the configuration of the core, the moderator (see below) and the coolant (see below). Some reactors, for example, the Magnox and Candu types, use natural uranium as a fuel, others, for example, advanced gas cooled reactors (AGRs) and pressurized water reactors (PWRs), use enriched uranium as a fuel. In enriched uranium the proportion of ^{235}U is increased to around 3 per cent.

As the life of a fuel load progresses some of the neutrons are absorbed by ^{238}U in reactions which produce plutonium. ^{238}U may also fission occasionally. Over the lifetime of a fuel load the energy generating reactions occur in roughly the following proportions:

60% in ^{235}U

31% in ^{239}Pu

4% in ^{241}Pu

5% in ^{238}U

At the beginning of a fuel load ^{235}U produces most energy, while at the end of the load most comes from ^{239}Pu.

2 At least one fission neutron from each fission event must produce a further fission

This depends on the factors mentioned in 1 and also on the reaction cross-section of ^{235}U, which is higher for thermal neutrons than for high energy neutrons. Because the fission neutrons have an average energy of about 2 MeV they must be slowed down if their chance of inducing further fissions is to be enhanced. The moderator material does this. It is a material that has a cross-section which is approximately constant for collisions over a range from MeV to eV, see Figure 6.6. In this case the fast neutrons colliding with its nuclei lose energy in each collision and are slowed down to thermal speeds. Moderator materials must have a low mass number and low neutron absorption. Table 6.10 lists the relevant properties of some important moderators.

Magnox and AGR reactors use a graphite moderator, PWR reactors use water and Candu reactors heavy water.

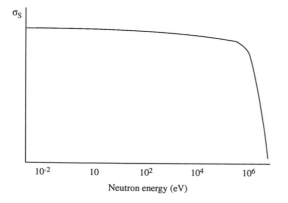

Figure 6.6 *Scattering cross-section of a typical moderator*

Property	Water (H_2O)	Heavy water (D_2O)	Graphite (C)
σ_a (barns)	0.66	0.001	0.0045
σ_s (barns)	approx 50	10.6	4.7
No of collisions to thermalize fission neutrons	20	36	115

Source: D J Bennet and J R Thomson, 1989

Table 6.10 *Properties of moderators*

3 An uncontrolled supercritical chain reaction must not be possible

Control rods made of materials which strongly absorb neutrons are provided for the purpose of constraining the number of neutrons in the core to the required operating levels. Additional control rods are incorporated for use in emergency. The materials which are suitable for this purpose include steel with cadmium, boron or indium dispersed through it. Figure 6.5 shows the cross-sections for these strong neutron absorbers.

4 The heat which is generated must be removed to prevent the core overheating

A coolant which is compatible with the moderator must be used. In Magnox and AGR reactors carbon dioxide gas is the coolant, whereas in PWRs water is both the coolant and the moderator. The coolant is circulated through a heat exchanger and there produces steam for the steam turbines of the electricity generators.

5 Radiation must be contained

Containment is incorporated at various levels. The fuel is sealed within cylindrical tubes of an appropriate metal, eg magnox, zircalloy or stainless steel, so that the fission products are not in contact with the coolant. The core and coolant are contained in a sealed system and the whole of this system is encased in reinforced concrete which serves as a biological shield. There are numerous radiation detectors at critical parts of the system looking for leaks. Any containment must also be effective under fault conditions. Overheating and partial melting of the core due to failure of cooling systems is the condition most likely to lead to a serious release of radioactivity from the core and the containment arrangements must prevent radioactivity from reaching the environment.

NUCLEAR POWER STATIONS

Nuclear power stations differ from conventional power stations only by using the heat from a nuclear reactor to raise steam for their steam turbines. Their steam turbines and electrical generating sets are identical with those of conventional coal, oil or gas fired stations.

Thermal reactors

The current generation of commercial nuclear reactors are all thermal reactors. That is to say the fission reactions in the core of the reactor are initiated by thermal neutrons with kinetic energies of around 0.025 eV. The high energy fission neutrons are 'thermalized' by repeated collisions with the moderator of the reactor. Power reactors can be classified according to various characteristics, including the type of fuel they use, the moderator involved and the coolant employed. Details of an example of each of the common types of reactor are included below.

Magnox

Figure 6.7 shows the layout of a typical Magnox reactor. The core is contained within a pressure vessel which is either spherical or a short vertical cylinder with hemi-spherical end caps. Natural uranium metal, encased in magnox fuel cans, is used for the fuel and the moderator is graphite. CO_2 coolant is blown through the core and then passes to heat exchangers which are used to raise steam for the turbines. These reactors are conservatively designed, with a low power density in the core. A typical early Magnox station has two reactors and Table 6.11 gives some details of the reactors at Bradwell Nuclear Power Station.

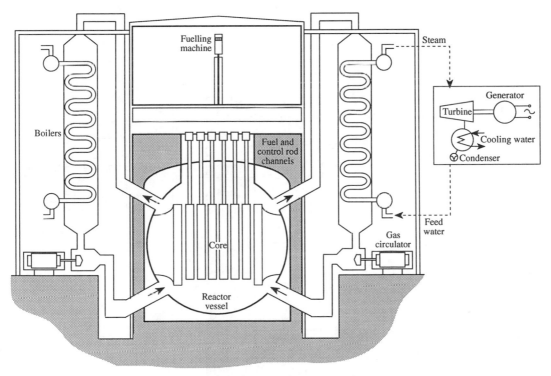

Source: S Rippon, 1984

Figure 6.7 *Magnox reactor*

Electrical output of the power station	300 MWe
Efficiency	28.2%
Each reactor has:	
Heat output	531 MWt
Fuel	Natural uranium metal, in 'Magnox' alloy fuel cans
Weight of fuel	239 tonnes
Fuel burn-up	3000 MW-days/tonne
Moderator	Graphite
Core dimensions	12.2m diam x 7.9 m high
Power density	0.57 kW/litre
Coolant	Carbon dioxide gas
Colant pressure	8.9 atmospheres
Coolant outlet temperature	390°C
Pressure vessel	Welded steel, 10.2 cm thick
Refuelling	On load

Table 6.11 *Details of the Bradwell magnox reactor*

Advanced gas cooled reactor (AGR)

AGRs are second generation graphite moderated, gas cooled nuclear reactors. Building on the experience gained with the Magnox type it was hoped to achieve higher thermal and fuel efficiency. The higher operating temperature and power density require uranium oxide fuel, slightly enriched in ^{235}U, encased in stainless steel fuel cans. The reactor core and heat exchangers are contained within a prestressed concrete pressure vessel. Figure 6.8 shows an AGR reactor and Table 6.12 gives some details of a late model AGR, such as that at Torness. There are two reactors at each station with a combined thermal output of 3100 MW and an electrical output of 1235 MW.

Pressurized water reactor (PWR)

Most of the nuclear power stations world wide use this type of reactor and Figure 6.9 shows its

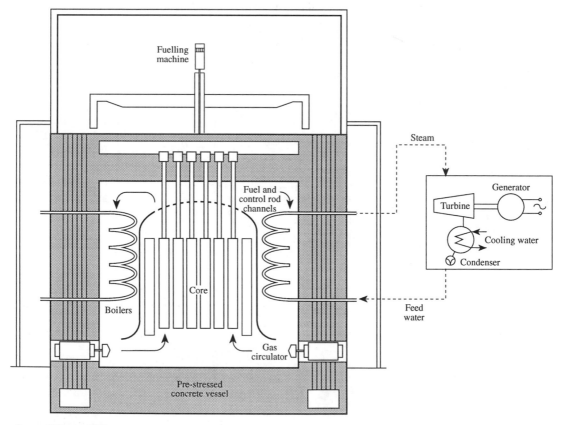

Source: S Rippon, 1984

Figure 6.8 *AGR reactor*

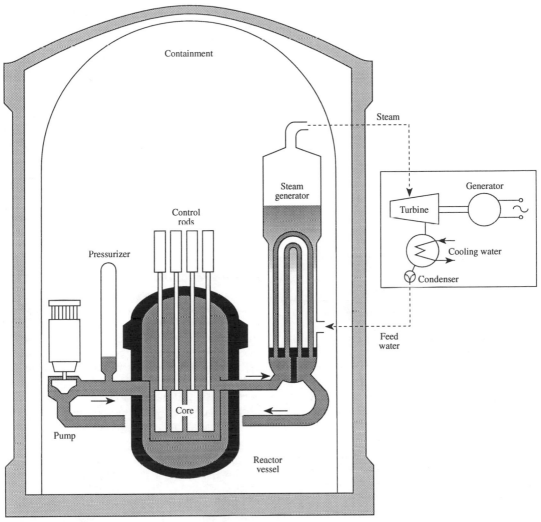

Source: S Rippon, 1984

Figure 6.9 *PWR reactor*

construction. It uses a uranium oxide fuel, enriched to around 3 per cent, encased in zirconium alloy fuel cans. Water is used as a moderator and coolant. Britain's first PWR reactor is under construction at Sizewell and details of its design are given in Table 6.13.

The power station has a single reactor serving two turbine generators.

Fast breeder reactor

If uranium-238 absorbs a neutron it can react in the following way:

$$\ce{^{238}_{92}U} + \ce{^{1}_{0}n} \rightarrow \ce{^{239}_{92}U} \rightarrow \ce{^{239}_{93}Np} + \beta^- \rightarrow \ce{^{239}_{94}Pu} + \beta^-$$

Plutonium-239 can undergo fission reactions of the form,

$$\ce{^{239}_{94}Pu} + \ce{^{1}_{0}n} \rightarrow \ce{^{137}_{55}Cs} + \ce{^{100}_{46}Pd} + 3\ce{^{1}_{0}n} + 7\beta^-$$

The first reaction is referred to as a breeding reaction, because ^{238}U is bred into a fissionable fuel. Some of the power output from thermal reactors, as pointed out earlier, results from the fission of plutonium produced in this way. This sort of reaction makes it possible to envisage using all of the 99.3 per cent of natural uranium present as the uranium-238 isotope for energy production by converting it to fissionable plutonium isotopes.

117

Electrical output of the	
power station	1235 MWe
Efficiency	40%
Each reactor has:	
Heat output	1550 MWt
Fuel	Uranium oxide, 2% enriched, in stainless steel fuel cans
Moderator	Graphite
Core dimensions	10m diameter x 8.5m high
Power density	2.4 kW/litre
Coolant	Carbon dioxide gas
Colant pressure	42 atmospheres
Coolant outlet temperature	635°C
Pressure vessel	Prestressed concrete 5.7m thick
Refuelling	On load

Table 6.12 *Details of a recent AGR reactor*

In order to do this at least one of the fission neutrons is needed for breeding, while another will be needed for further fissions. An average fission neutron production of 2.4 to 2.9 per fission from thermal reactions cannot achieve this. However, Figure 6.10 shows that although the fission cross-section for fast neutrons is lower than for thermal, a higher yield of fission neutrons is achieved from fast fission reactions. A reactor operating with neutrons at these energies can maintain a chain reaction and breed plutonium from uranium-238.

Because the cross-section for fast fission is so low such a reactor must not have any moderating material present in the core and must have a very small core of enriched fuel to maintain a high density of neutrons. It will also need a very efficient coolant which has a low neutron absorption cross-section. Liquid metal coolants, sodium or potassium, best meet this criterion and sodium is usually chosen.

Prototype reactors have been built in the UK, US, France and the former USSR. At present research into this type of reactor has slowed down. The availability of cheap uranium and the glut of fossil fuel has led most governments to give breeder reactors a low priority and reduced funding levels. The UK government will close down the prototype fast reactor at Dounreay in 1994 and has recently announced that it will withdraw from the European Fast Reactor Programme. Figure 6.11 shows the construction of a fast breeder reactor.

No commercial fast breeder is yet in routine operation, although the Superphénix reactor at Creys-Malville on the Rhone in France was completed in 1986. It has only been operating for about one-third of the time since it came into service, and rarely at full output. In July 1990 it was shut down due to fouling of its primary coolant and the French prime minister announced in June 1992 that a number of conditions would need to be met before a new licence for its operation could be issued. There is to be a public hearing before any restart. Table 6.14 gives details of its design.

Fusion reaction

In contrast with nuclear fission, which can be initiated in ^{235}U by thermal neutrons, nuclear fusion requires two light nuclei to be brought into contact. As both of these nuclei are electrically charged this is very difficult to achieve and a large amount of energy must be used to accomplish it. If the fusion process is to be a net producer of energy, the energy released by the fusion reaction has to be greater than the energy

Electrical output of the	
power station	1110 MWe
Efficiency	32.5%
The reactor has:	
Heat output	3411 MWt
Fuel	Uranium oxide, 3.2% enriched, in zircalloy 4 fuel cans
Weight of fuel	101 tonnes
Moderator	Water (light water)
Core dimensions	3.37 m diam x 3.66 m high
Power density	105 kW/litre
Coolant	Water (light water)
Coolant pressure	158 atmospheres
Coolant outlet temperature	325°C
Pressure vessel	Welded steel, 21.5 cm thick
Refuelling	Off load

Table 6.13 *Details of the Sizewell PWR reactor*

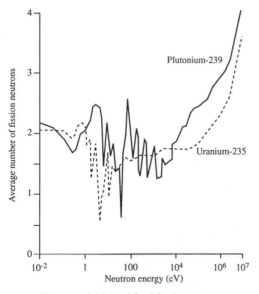

Figure 6.10 *Yield of fission neutrons*

Heat output	2990 MWt
Electrical output	1200 Mwe
Efficiency	40.1%
Fuel	Mixed uranium and plutonium oxides. ≈20% effective enrichment, in stainless steel fuel cans
Weight of fuel	6.7 tonnes
Fuel burn-up	100,000 MW-days/ tonne
Moderator	None
Core dimensions	3.7m diam x 1m high
Power density	277 kW/litre
Coolant	Liquid sodium
Coolant pressure	1 atmosphere
Coolant outlet temperature	545°C
Vessel	Cylindrical stainless steel pot, 20m diameter x 17m high
Refuelling	Off load

Table 6.14 *Details of the Superphènix fast breeder reactor*

used to bring it about. As yet there is no theoretical proof that this positive energy balance is possible. Some researchers are pessimistic about ever generating energy from fusion, but most do expect that it is possible. Contrast this with nuclear fission, where the theoretical justification for the energy-producing potential of the process was clearly demonstrated before fission was achieved.

Research into nuclear fusion has been progressing for a number of years and at present the European effort in this area is undertaken with the Joint European Torus (JET) machine sited at Culham in Berkshire. This is designed to try to achieve and investigate physical conditions close to, but less than, those thought to be necessary for positive energy production from fusion. Three variables must be optimized in these experiments. The temperature of the plasma containing the interacting nuclei must be around 100 million degrees kelvin; the density of the plasma must be high enough for one nucleus to be able to interact with another in the short time for which the plasma is established; and the confinement time of the plasma (its lifetime) must be long enough for the energy produced by fusion reactions to be large enough to balance the energy lost by radiation and other cooling mechanisms.

The JET programme started in 1983 and has gradually moved towards acceptable values of these parameters using fusion reactions between deuterium nuclei. In November 1991 mixed deuterium–tritium fuel with 10–15 per cent of tritium was used for the first time. It was heated to ≈200 million degrees kelvin and the fusion of deuterium and tritium nuclei generated about 2 MW of peak power in a pulse lasting two seconds. This was some 20 times greater than the power produced in the deuterium–deuterium reactions. A mixture containing 50 per cent tritium–50 per cent deuterium should increase the energy output by another 10 times to 200 times that of the deuterium–deuterium mixture.

Experiments are continuing at JET and if funding can be maintained hopes are high that the first use of a mixture containing 50 per cent tritium will take place in 1995–6. It is possible that at this stage 'breakeven', the point where energy input to the machine equals energy released in the reaction, might be achieved.

NUCLEAR FUEL CYCLE

It is often argued that nuclear fuels are cheaper for the generation of electricity than fossil fuels, and there is justification for this in terms of the

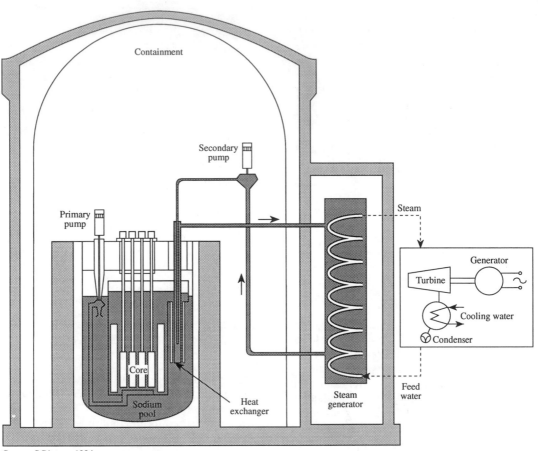

Containment

Secondary
pump

Primary
pump

Steam

Generator

Turbine

Cooling water

Condenser

Core

Sodium
pool

Heat
exchanger

Steam
generator

Feed
water

Source: S Rippon, 1984

Figure 6.11 *Liquid metal fast breeder reactor*

small amounts of fuel needed (a few kilograms a
day of ^{235}U for a 1000 Mwe station) and the current price of uranium. There are a number of
issues which are at present unresolved which
could contribute substantially to the costs however. This section will discuss the fuel cycle and
point out some of these areas. Mining, processing, enrichment and fuel rod fabrication are
well-established technologies, as are many
aspects of the reprocessing of spent fuel (magnox fuel has been reprocessed for many years at
Sellafield, formerly Windscale), but the management and disposal of radioactive wastes,
particularly intermediate and high level wastes,
and the cancer hazards associated with mining
and milling have yet to be successfully resolved.

Mining, processing and fuel rod fabrication

Over 70 per cent of the Western nations' uranium comes from the US, Canada, Australia and
South Africa. It is also available from many
other countries including the former USSR,
Niger, Zaire and Gabon. The end product of the
milling and extraction processes is 'yellow-
cake', which is fairly pure U_3O_8. These
processes vary with the particular orebody that
is involved but in essence the crushed ore is
leached with either an acidic or a basic solution,
depending on the ore. Uranium is then extracted
from this solution either by solvent extraction or
ion-exchange to give a product with 70–80 per
cent U_3O_8.

This process is not without hazards.
Radium, thorium and their daughter products

120

are found with the uranium, and radon gas is a daughter decay product of all of these. Daughter products of radon itself may be absorbed on to dust particles and inhaled and deposited on the surface of the lungs. Mine tailings, ie the remains of the ore after the uranium has been extracted and often dumped on open mine heaps, can have a high thorium concentration and again this leads to high radon emissions.

For AGR and PWR reactors the fuel needs to be enriched to a concentration of 2–3 per cent ^{235}U. Various processes are available to do this and they all need to find a way to sort out the slightly lighter ^{235}U compounds from the ^{238}U equivalents. Gaseous diffusion, atomic centrifuges, mass spectrometers and laser based processes have all been used. The uranium is converted to UF_6, a gaseous form, for the diffusion and centrifuge processes.

Reprocessing

Spent fuel rods are removed from the reactor when so much of their ^{235}U has been used that neutron absorption is increased and the power output of the reactor cannot be maintained. At first the rods are stored at the reactor site in tanks of water until their radioactivity falls to a defined level. Large amounts of heat are generated, while the proportion of the fission products which have very short half-lives decay and the fuel rods are cooled as well as shielded by the water. After a period of weeks to months the fuel rods are loaded into shielded containers for transport to the reprocessing plant at Sellafield in Cumbria.

Here, again under water, they are stored and eventually moved to shielded 'cells' where the magnox fuel cans are stripped from the fuel and separated from it. The fuel cans, which are weakly radioactive due to neutron absorption, are removed for disposal. By the time the fuel is processed 99 per cent of its activity has decayed. The fuel is sheared into small fragments and dropped into a nitric acid bath, where it dissolves. Organic solvent extraction is used to leach uranium and plutonium salts out of the acid solution, leaving this solution containing the fission products and other radioactive isotopes formed in the fuel to be neutralized and stored prior to disposal. Uranium and plutonium

from the process are then available for use in new fuel rods. The liquid containing the unwanted radioactive isotopes is usually referred to as high level radioactive waste.

Radioactive waste management

Three categories of radioactive waste materials are recognized, low, intermediate and high level wastes.

Low level wastes

These comprise detritus from laboratories and plant, for example, clothing, some laboratory equipment, dust swept from laboratories, gases from fume cupboards and fuel cladding stripping, liquids from cleaning etc. All wastes in this category are low activity alpha, beta and gamma emitters generating little heat.

Disposal policy is based on dilution and dispersion. Gaseous products are vented to the atmosphere, low activity liquids piped out to sea and low activity solids buried. The burial site is at Drigg, near Sellafield, and the wastes are now compacted and placed in containers which are stored in concrete vaults.

Intermediate level wastes

These are low level, long half-life wastes, for example, fuel cladding, some process stream liquids, reactor and laboratory equipment etc.

At present they are stored on site at Sellafield and at other nuclear sites. UK Nirex Ltd was set up in 1982 to select a site and build a repository for intermediate level wastes. Since then progress has been made in the packaging of the wastes for storage and disposal, and in the design and assessment of safety requirements for a repository. It is proposed that the repository will be at least 300 m underground and the geophysical requirements, particularly with regard to groundwater movement and chemistry, of the host rock are thought to be well understood. Nirex is investigating two sites, at Sellafield and Dounreay, for its repository. It is involved in seeking permission to drill exploratory boreholes near Sellafield. Similar repositories have been built in other countries, for example, Finland and Germany.

Nuclide	Half-life	Activity at time of discharge (Curies)
Group 1 (Half-life < 10 yr)		
Iodine-131	8 d	1.7×10^7
Cerium-141	32.5 d	3.0×10^7
Zirconium-95	65 d	3.1×10^7
Cerium-143	284 d	2.5×10^7
Ruthenium-106	1 yr	1.0×10^7
Caesium-134	2.1 yr	3.3×10^6
Promethium-147	2.6 yr	4.9×10^6
Europium-154	8.6 yr	1.1×10^3
Group 2 (Half-life 10–30 yr)		
Krypton-85	10.8 yr	2.8×10^5
Tritium	12.3 yr	1.3×10^3
Strontium-90	29 yr	2.3×10^6
Caesium-137	30 yr	2.8×10^6
Group 3 (Half-life > 100,000)		
Technetium-99	2×10^5 yr	3.9×10^2
Zirconium-93	1.5×10^6 yr	8.3×10
Caesium-135	2.3×10^6 yr	1.2×10
Iodine-129	1.7×10^7 yr	7.4×10^{-1}

Source: British Nuclear Energy Society, 1981

Table 6.15 *Output of fission products from AGR (for 1 GWyr of electricity)*

High level wastes

When nuclear wastes are discussed it is usually this category of waste which is viewed as presenting the most difficulties. About 30 tonnes of spent fuel are removed from a 1000 MWe reactor each year and the high level wastes constitute about 1 tonne of this. The total volume of material is small but it consists of high activity, high heat output isotopes. These result from the irradiation of the fuel itself and fall into two broad groups, the fission products and the actinides (the heavy elements formed in the fuel by various neutron capture and radioactive decay reactions). Tables 6.15 and 6.16 list some of the important fission products and actinides produced by an AGR. It is possible to calculate the composition of the waste and the way its activity changes as time goes on. The calculations assume that 99.9 per cent of the uranium and plutonium are recovered. It is found that the activity is dominated for the first 300 years by the beta decay of the caesium-137 and strontium-90 isotopes with half-lives of around 30 years and from 300 to 3000 years by americium-241, which is an alpha emitter, and then neptunium-237 (the daughter nuclide of americium-241). After a few thousand years the activity of the waste has fallen below that of uranium ores.

At present the highly active liquid resulting from reprocessing at Sellafield is kept there in cooled, double walled, stainless steel tanks.

Following years of research at Sellafield a process has been developed which can incorporate the high level wastes into a solid glassy material. The large glass blocks are sealed into stainless steel cylinders which can be handled and stored easily. This process immobilizes and isolates the waste much more effectively than storing it as a liquid. Recently a commercial facility to carry out this process has been commissioned and work has started on vitrifying the 1300 m^3 of liquids resulting from the magnox reprocessing programme. The encapsulated glass blocks are being stored in a convection cooled store at Sellafield and will remain there for 50 years.

Each 400 kg glass block initially produces 2 kW of heat, which will fall to 1 kW while it is in the Sellafield store. It is expected that they will eventually be placed permanently in an

Nuclide	Half-life AGR(a)	Activity (Curies)
Uranium-235	7.1×10^8 yr	–
Uranium-238	4.5×10^9 yr	–
Neptunium-237	2.1×10^6 yr	4.6
Plutonium-238	87 yr	2.9×10^4
Plutonium-239	2.4×10^4 yr	1.0×10^4
Plutonium-240	6.6×10^3 yr	1.9×10^4
Plutonium-241	15 yr	3.1×10^6
Plutonium-242	3.9×10^5 yr	3.6×10
Americium-241	433 yr	3.9×10^3
Americium-243	7.4×10^3 yr	1.7×10^2
Curium-242	163 d	8.2×10^5
Curium-244	18 yr	1.0×10^4

(a)Irradiation time 1370 days, mean burn-up 17,250 MWd/t
Source: British Nuclear Energy Society, 1981

Table 6.16 *Output of actinides from AGR (for 1 GWyr of electricity)*

underground repository, but there are as yet no plans for it. Experience gained from the proposed repository for intermediate level wastes will have a direct influence on what happens to the vitrified high level wastes.

COSTS OF NUCLEAR POWER

For most of their history nuclear power stations have been seen by their operators as providing electricity more cheaply than stations fuelled by coal, oil and gas. Recently the claims have been reversed. This has been particularly so in the UK in the build up to and aftermath of electricity privatization. The reversal is partly due to changes in the accounting practices and procedures used, partly to the increased cost of constructing modern nuclear reactors to standards which satisfy the latest regulations, and partly to the recognition of higher 'downstream' costs associated with fuel reprocessing, decommissioning and management of radioactive wastes (see also Chapter 2).

The economics of power generation

In the planning of any revenue earning project, such as a power station, estimates have to be made of the costs that will be involved and the amount of income that the project can produce during its existence. In principle a decision can be made as to the viability of the project by comparing the costs and earnings. However, in practice it is not so easy to be certain of the outcome because the construction and operation of the project extend over many years, decades in the case of power stations, and the calculations necessarily involve assumptions about future economic conditions and about the performance of the plant.

In addition to the fuel costs there are three main parameters which contribute to the calculation of the likely cost of electricity production, usually expressed in p/kWh, for a new project. The discount rate applied to the capital invested in the project, the capital costs of construction and the performance expected of the station when it is in operation. The discount rate is a parameter used in financial calculations to account for the cost of borrowing or investing

money in the project (see Chapter 2). Estimates and assumptions must have been made for these items in the planning and evaluation of the project, and in any comparisons made between it and any alternative means of achieving the same electricity production. The calculations are very sensitive to these assumptions and changing them yields different values for the cost of the electricity from the power station. For example, in 1990 the cost of electricity from the Sizewell B PWR power station was put at 3.7 pence/kWh using a 5 per cent discount rate, 5.2 pence/kWh using an 8 per cent discount rate and at 2.6 pence/kWh on an avoidable cost basis at an 8 per cent discount rate (with, in all cases, a 40-year life and a 75 per cent availability). Different costs would have resulted if the figures chosen for lifetime and availability had been different.

Fuel costs for nuclear power are a small part of the final cost of the electricity produced. Comparison of the cost of electricity from various sources also requires estimates of their future fuel costs. Renewable sources will have no fuel costs, whereas coal, oil and natural gas prices will change as time goes on, and will be subject to the influence of the policies of governments in many countries.

As emphasized in Chapter 2, this discussion is as relevant to coal fired power stations, wind generators and combined cycle gas plant as to nuclear power. The final costs will also be influenced by any government subsidies or tax regimes which apply to the projects. With all of this room for adjustment it is not possible to arrive at a 'true' or 'real' cost. In effect the cost of power is determined by political considerations rather than economics or technology. The next section looks in more detail at the ways in which some of these considerations have affected the quoted costs of nuclear power.

Costs of nuclear power in the UK

As we saw in Chapter 2, both capital and running costs influence the final cost of any power produced. For example a change in the discount rate from 10 per cent to 11 per cent increases generating costs by 12 per cent, an increase of 10 per cent in capital costs increases generating costs by around 9 per cent, and an improvement in the load factor from 60 per cent to 66 per cent reduces generating costs by 10 per cent.

Political control of the nationalized fuel industries in the UK resulted over the years in changes in the financial targets and procedures. A test discount rate (TDR) of 10 per cent was set in 1969 for individual capital projects, and a typical amortization period was 40 years. This was replaced in 1978 by the establishment of a real rate of return (RRR) on capital for investment in the industry as a whole of 5 per cent. British Gas and British Coal used a TDR of 10 per cent on revenue earning projects to subsidize safety and infrastructure investment, while maintaining a RRR for their industries of 5 per cent. The CEGB used a TDR of 5 per cent, arguing that because most of their investment was revenue earning a RRR of 5 per cent would result. In April 1989 the RRR was raised to 8 per cent for nationalized industries. Private industry generally requires a quicker return on capital, and uses a higher TDR and shorter amortization time, typically 20 years for large capital projects.

Throughout the world the capital cost of nuclear reactors has increased, both during the construction phase and from one reactor to the next. The initial estimate for the cost of the Sizewell B PWR reactor was £1.896 billion in 1982, but a revised estimate in June 1991 was £2.648 billion. With the project due for completion in 1995 it is likely that further increases will occur. Capital costs contributed 1.35 pence/kWh to the generating costs of an early AGR, Hunterston B, but are estimated to be 3.02 pence/kWh for the latest AGR at Torness. Other countries have a similar experience. Hoped for economies of scale in moving from small to large reactors, and reductions in costs by manufacturing series of substantially identical reactors, have not been realized.

The performance record of the nuclear industry in the UK has not been good. Some Magnox reactors have never achieved their design output and a reduced level of power output means that the revenue earned during their lifetime is not as high as that assumed when costing the project. Their average lifetime load factor is about 60 per cent. Most AGRs have performed badly, with an average lifetime load factor of around 41 per cent. At present performance is improving and operating costs of reactors are tending to reduce. Load factors are increasing with better reliability and shorter down-time for refuelling and maintenance.

Downstream costs have recently assumed a much higher profile than previously. These are the costs of reprocessing spent nuclear fuel, or of storing it without reprocessing, of dealing with nuclear wastes, and of decommissioning reactors and other facilities at the end of their productive lives. Most Magnox reactors are approaching the end of their life and the industry faces their decommissioning costs. British Nuclear Fuel's (BNFL) assessment of decommissioning liabilities went from £0.438 billion in 1988 to £4.605 billion in 1989, because their operation was to be changed from a 'cost plus' basis to fixed price contracting on privatization. Similarly CEGB's nuclear provisions increased from £3.1 billion in 1988 to £6.9 billion in 1989. Of this £3.1 billion was the cost of decommissioning BNFL plants and £0.9 billion that of CEGB plants. For comparison the turnover of the CEGB was £8.9 billion in 1989.

The proposal to privatize the electricity industry led both the industry and analysts in the financial institutions to reappraise nuclear power using commercial criteria, as opposed to those applied to nationalized industries. This reappraisal was also applied by BNFL to its charges for waste processing and decommissioning. Following these exercises it was soon appreciated by the industry, and later recognized by the government, that nuclear power could not be privatized; the electricity produced would be too expensive and the unknown 'downstream' costs, particularly the decommissioning of the Magnox reactors, represented too high a risk.

Nuclear power was removed from the privatization sale, but provisions were made to help it survive, at least until a major review proposed for 1994. The RECs are obliged under the non-fossil fuel obligation (NFFO) to purchase electricity from sources which do not use fossil fuels. A fossil fuel levy on consumers' bills will pay for this. Currently the levy amounts to about 10 per cent and raises £1.25 billion, of which 98 per cent goes to nuclear power to establish a fund to contribute to future decommissioning. The remaining 2 per cent is allocated to other projects using renewable sources of energy. An additional sum of £2.5 billion was also set aside to pay towards decommissioning costs.

Other factors influencing the decision to build large power stations

Further considerations involve the diversification of fuel types and the diversification of reactor types. Each of the factors will tend to increase the stability of the grid to external or internal contingencies.

At the moment over 80 per cent of the fuel used to produce electricity is coal. An increase in the proportion of nuclear power would tend to make it easier for the industry to cope with strikes or other causes of fuel restriction.

A set of a few PWR reactors would also mean that the nuclear part of the grid would be less vulnerable to the discovery of a common fault in all of its reactors which would necessitate them all being taken out of service to rectify it.

THE FUTURE OF NUCLEAR POWER

Nuclear power made a very confident entrance into the arena of electricity production. Talk was rife of the electricity they would produce being too cheap to be worth metering. For many years, although the electricity was charged for as usual, nuclear power was a non-controversial contributor to electricity generation throughout the world. Gradually, however, with growing environmental awareness and changing public attitudes to science and technology, concern has grown. It is most evident in the areas of safety, the possible long term consequences of exposure to increased levels of background radiation and what is to be done about high level radioactive wastes. Additional concerns are voiced about plutonium production and accumulation, the spread of nuclear power to countries which may not be sufficiently technically advanced to cope with its management, and the political and

ethical problems associated with providing security for nuclear plant. The cost of electricity produced by nuclear power has also been queried and the claim that it is cheaper than that produced by its competitors has been contested for some years.

These changing attitudes have had a widespread influence. They have also been gained support in the wake of the accidents involving the nuclear power stations at Three Mile Island in the US and at Chernobyl in the Ukraine. In much of the world construction of nuclear plant has slowed down or been halted. Exceptions to this are France and Japan, both of which are poor in fossil fuel resources and have embarked upon extensive programmes of nuclear power.

Recent designs for nuclear reactors reflect public concerns about safety and incorporate many features to make the reactors safer. Test facilities are also being developed where fault conditions can be initiated, the results monitored and procedures developed to eliminate or contain the faults. As far as the disposal of nuclear wastes is concerned the industry feels that the technical aspects have been adequately addressed and that the remaining obstacle is public acceptability. The industry also feels and expects that nuclear power has a role to play in reducing the emission of greenhouse gases from electricity production.

Nuclear power is at a crossroads at the present time. It is able to become one of the least polluting producers of electricity, but it has to overcome a legacy of distrust in a sceptical public. For there to be a resurgence in its fortunes it must re-establish its credibility. Any new major accident to an existing reactor would make this very difficult, whereas serious power shortages or large price rises due to the implementation of expensive pollution control procedures with fossil fuel plants would enhance its prospects.

7

ALTERNATIVE ENERGY RESOURCES

S o much progress in the technologies for producing energy from renewable sources has been made over the past ten years that some of them can now compete with traditional energy technologies and others are coming close to doing so. The potential, over the next 20 to 30 years (that is, within the lifetime of any electricity generating station now being built), for the use of renewable resources is considerable. However, creating the necessary infrastructure and building enough plant to exploit our renewable resources fully could take 40 to 50 years unless, for environmental reasons, the government decides to mount an expensive crash programme to replace fossil and nuclear plant.

If the full range of energy efficiency measures were introduced then renewables could supply all the energy needed. Wind, water, photovoltaics and biogas could fuel electricity production, and solar energy, biogas and solar hydrogen could meet all other energy requirements. Neither the lack of technology nor costs stand in the way – the means of achieving low enough costs and sufficiently high efficiency rates are well understood. Moreover, if the external costs of using fossil and nuclear fuel were internalized, then the case for turning to renewable energy resources by early in the next century would be overwhelming.

In this chapter we will describe, briefly, those renewable energy technologies which could make a major contribution to the energy supplies of the world. Almost all renewable resources derive their power, directly or indirectly, from the sun, so we must also consider solar radiation and the technologies for converting it into socially useful forms of energy.

Solar radiation means the light and heat received by the earth from the sun which emits radiation because its surface is hot – just as an electric fire emits light and heat when the element is hot. Radiant energy is emitted in a range of colours (wavelengths) which, together with the amount emitted by any object, depends on its temperature. The sun is very large and very hot, and so emits enormous amounts of energy in the visible spectrum.

Only a tiny fraction of the sun's energy (about two parts in one billion) arrives on earth; most of it misses the earth and other planets and disappears into space. Of the energy received by earth nearly one-third is reflected back into space by the clouds, ice and the oceans etc. The other two-thirds keeps the earth warm, drives the weather, makes crops grow and powers most of the world's natural processes.

The average temperature of the earth's surface, night and day throughout the year, remains

THE SUN'S VITAL STATISTICS

Distance from Earth	150,000,000 km (93,000,000 mi)	Corona	1,000,000°C
		Pressure – Central	68,000,000,000 atm
Rotation period	Equator 26 d Poles 38 d	Composition (% mass) Hydrogen	~ 75
Revolution period (around galaxy)	225,000 y	Helium Oxygen	~ 23 1
Diameter	1,392,000 km (864,000 mi)	Carbon Iron Silicon	0.4 0.16 0.1
Angular diameter	32 minutes of arc	Nitrogen	0.1
Mass	2×10^{33} g (10^{27}t)	Magnesium Neon	0.09 0.07
Density Average Central	1.41 g/cm^3 150 g/cm^3	Other elements Power output	traces 3.8×10^{20} MW
Surface	(13 x density of lead) 10^{-7}g/cm^3 (0.0001 x density of air)	Solar Constant	1.353 kW/m^2
Magnetic field Surface average Disturbed areas Sunspots	1 gauss hundreds of gauss thousands of gauss	Energy source – fusion of hydrogen nuclei into helium Rate of mass loss through conversion to energy	$4H \rightarrow HE + 2e^+ + 2v + y$ 4,500.00 t/sec
Temperature Surface Central Sunspots	5700°C 16,000,000°C 4200°C	Life expectancy Present age	10,000,000,000 y 5,000,000,000 y

remarkably constant. If it were to drop by only a few degrees centigrade, then we should have a new ice age, and if it were to rise by a similar amount then the polar ice caps would melt and large areas of the world would be flooded. To keep the temperature at its present average, the earth must radiate into space as much energy as it gets from the sun. During the day the earth gets more energy from the sun than it can radiate and thus the temperature rises, but at night it radiates more than it gets and so the temperature falls again. As clouds can reflect some of this energy back to the earth, cloudy nights are not as cold as clear nights.

Solar radiation reaching the earth varies in a complex way. It is at its maximum during the day but is zero at night and it is less in winter than in summer. In the winter not only is the sun lower in the sky than in the summer so that its power (energy/second) is less, but the day is also shorter. In the high latitudes, where the UK is to

be found, sunshine varies from day to day because of the cloud cover. If the best use is to be made of solar energy we need to know the average amount available and how reliable it is.

Figure 7.1 is a flow diagram of the energy balance of the earth. The major sources are the sun and tides, and the energy from nuclear, thermal and gravitational forces within the earth itself. More than 99 per cent of incoming energy is solar radiation. The input solar energy is either directly reflected from the atmosphere (short wave radiation) or radiated into space (long wave radiation). Tidal energy and geothermal energy inputs are much less than solar.

SOLAR RADIATION

Annual average power

The simplest way of thinking about solar energy

127

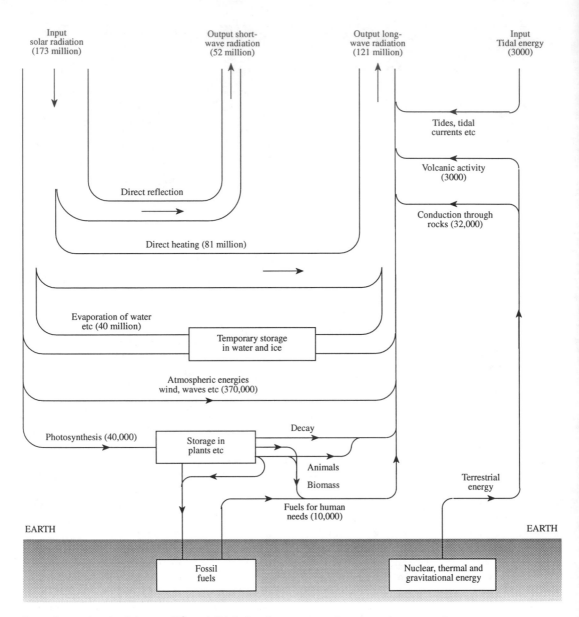

Energy flows are in units of gigawatts (10^9 watts). This is about the power output of a coal or nuclear power station.

Figure 7.1 *Energy flows of the planet earth (units gigawatts)*

is to think about the average power which falls on the earth. If we divide the total solar energy falling on 1 m² in one year by the number of seconds in a year, we get the average power (see Figure 7.2 for the world-wide variations). The averages shown on the map include both day and night, so that daytime radiation is always much higher than the average.

Solar insolation

Solar insolation is a measure of the energy received on 1 m² of horizontal surface in one day. It differs in different places and varies with the seasons. In Figure 7.3 there is also a map of the annual average of received energy. The maps in Figure 7.4 show the insolation in kWh/m² in the UK for the months of March, June, September and December.

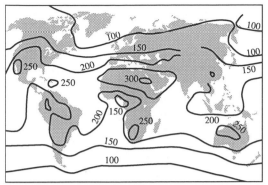

Source: Commission of the EC, 1979

Figure 7.2 *Annual average solar power (watts/m²)*

As the sun is never directly overhead in Europe it always strikes a horizontal surface at an angle. The power density (watts/m²) received by this surface is always less than the density of the sunlight (see the account of the laws of radiation, below). Solar cells with their surfaces facing the sun will receive the full density, therefore in the UK, where the sun is usually about 60° from the vertical, it is important to mount them at an angle about equal to the angle of latitude. This would mean that the power density falling on them would be roughly twice that falling on a horizontal surface.

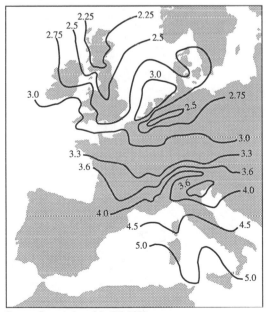

Source: Commission of the EC, 1979

Figure 7.3 *Annual average irradiance (kWh m⁻²/day)*

Variability of solar radiation

The data in the maps in Figures 7.3 and 7.4 are for all days in the specified months averaged over many years. But the energy received in any given month in one year will be different from that received in the same month in any other year. For instance, the summer of 1976 was hot and sunny, while the summer of 1986 was cold and wet. So it is usual to take the maximum and minimum radiation expected in one year in ten as the extremes. Figures 7.5 (a) and (b) show these maximum and minimum rates of insolation for June and Figures 7.5 (c) and (d) for December. In June in the UK the range runs from 8 kWh/m² to 2 kWh/m² and in December that range is reduced by a factor of about ten. However, maxima and minima taken from 1 year in 10 will conceal the greater variations that would be experienced by someone living for, say, 70 years.

To deal with these greater variations it is necessary to consider the number of occasions in 100 years when the average energy received will be less than a certain value. This is known as the 'cumulative frequency distribution' and, in Figure 7.6, it is given for the months of June and December. Not only is the average energy much lower in December than in June, but the variability is much greater. However, it is important to remember that months vary from fortnight to fortnight, week to week, even day to day. It is also possible to plot a century long cumulative frequency distribution for fortnights and weeks, which could be a useful guide to the chances of a sunny or a wet summer holiday.

Solar energy varies in intensity during the day and these variations, measured by the amount of energy falling on a horizontal surface of 1 m², is shown, in Figure 7.7, for daytimes in June and December. The graphs give averages for the best and worst days in every 50 and the absolute average.

Spectral dependence of solar radiation

Light from the sun ranges in colour from ultraviolet through the visible spectrum to infrared. Extreme ultraviolet burns the skin and can cause skin cancer, near ultraviolet tans the skin and infrared simply makes us feel hot. Energy in sunlight is at its strongest around the yellow part

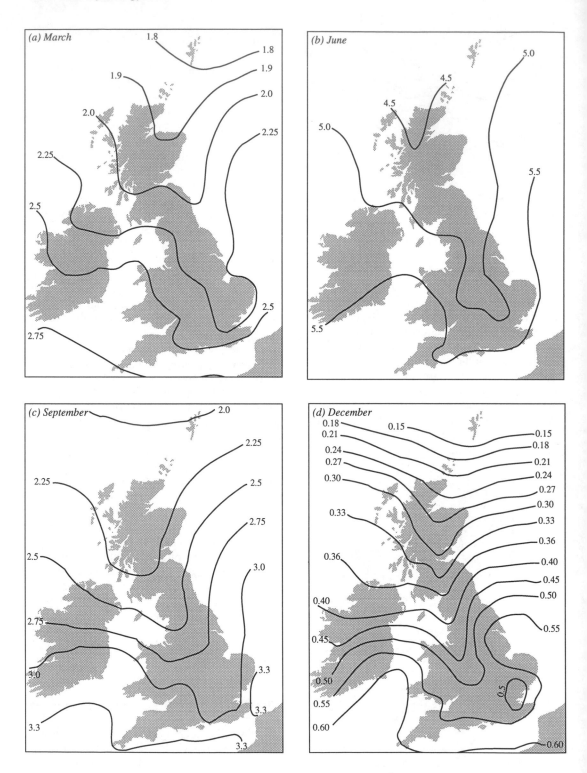

Figure 7.4 *Average insolation (kWh m⁻²/day)*

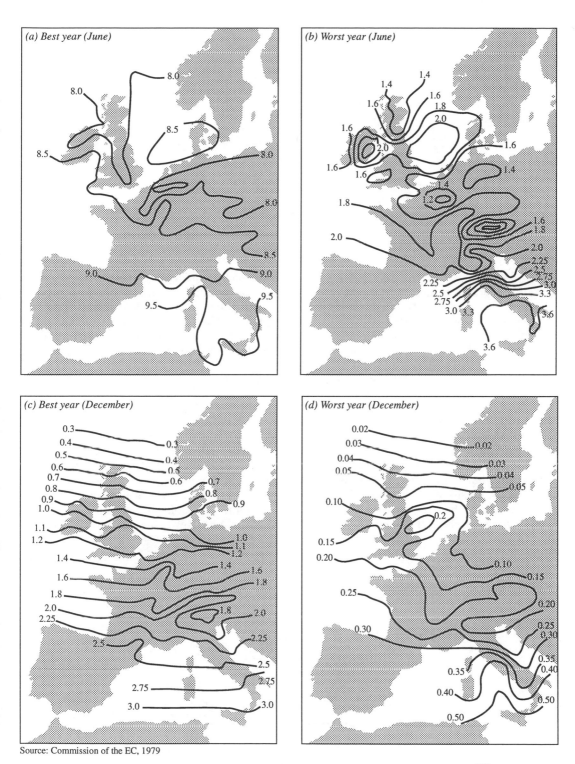

Source: Commission of the EC, 1979

Figure 7.5 *Solar insolation for best/worst year in ten (kWh m⁻²/day)*

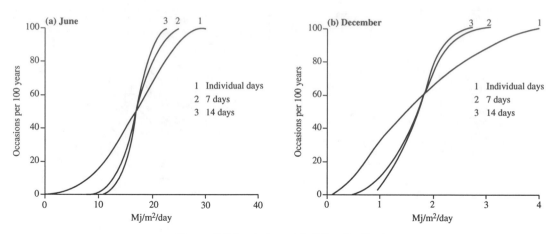

Figure 7.6 *Insolation probability distribution*

of the visible spectrum, the part to which the eyes of living creatures are most sensitive. The way in which the power of sunlight varies with wavelength is shown in Figure 7.8.

Direct sunlight

Outside the earth's atmosphere the spectral distribution of sunlight is very like that from a black body with a surface temperature of 5800° Kelvin (see 'Laws of radiation' below). The carbon dioxide and water vapour in the earth's atmosphere absorb some wavelengths of sunlight more than others. The distance through the atmosphere that sunlight must travel is determined by the height of the sun in the sky. If it is directly overhead then the light travels vertically through the atmosphere. If the sun's elevation is less than 90°, the light travels through a longer path in the atmosphere, so more absorption occurs. The length of this light path is described by the Air Mass Number – AM0 for sunlight in space, AM1 for a vertical path, AM2 for a solar elevation of 60° for example.

Diffused sunlight

Much of the sunlight that we get in the UK is not direct but diffused, scattered by water droplets and dust particles in the atmosphere. Scattered sunlight is less intense than direct sunlight and also has more blue radiation. This can be seen on a clear day because blue light is scattered eight times more efficiently than red and so makes the sky look blue. On the other hand when the sun is low in the sky, either at dawn or

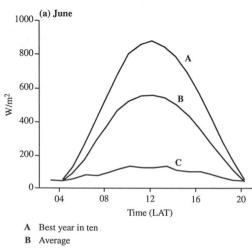

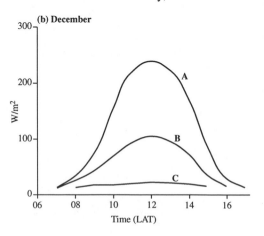

A   Best year in ten
B   Average
C   Worst year in ten

Figure 7.7 *Variation of solar incidence with time*

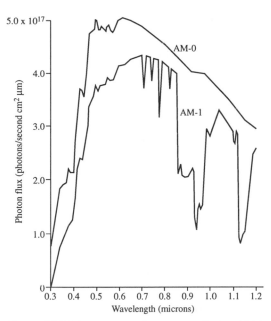

Figure 7.8 *Solar spectrum for space radiation AM-0 Sahara Desert summer noon AM-1*

at dusk, it looks very red because the blue light has been completely scattered.

Most solar energy equipment responds well to both direct and diffused radiation, and so will still work in cloudy conditions.

LAWS OF RADIATION

Kirchoff's laws

An object which is perfectly black absorbs all radiation which falls on it, so no real object can absorb more radiation than a 'black body' of the same size. The absorptance (α) is the ratio of the radiation absorbed by a surface to the radiation falling on the surface, and for a black body α = 1. for any other object α is between 0 and 1.

Kirchoff also showed that no real object can emit more radiation than a similar black body at the same temperature. The emittance (ε) of a surface is the ratio of the radiation emitted from the surface and that emitted by a similar black body at the same temperature. For a black body ε = 1, while for any other object ε is between 0 and 1.

For radiation of any given wavelength (λ), the absorptance of a surface for the monochro-

matic radiation is equal to its emittance. This result is true for all surfaces when the emittance and absorptance are measured at the same surface temperature.

Planck's radiation law

The power per unit wavelength radiated by unit area of a black body at temperature T (K) is given by

$$P = \frac{C_1}{\lambda^5 \, [\exp{(C_2/T)} - 1]}$$

where $C_1 = 3.74 \times 10^{-16}$ Wm^2 and $C_2 = 0.0144$ mK

If we plot the power density as a function of wavelength, we see a very characteristic curve (see Figure 7.9).

In deriving his radiation law, Max Planck had to make the assumption that radiant energy occurred in tiny discrete chunks called 'quanta'. He thus founded quantum theory which underlies all of modern electronic technology.

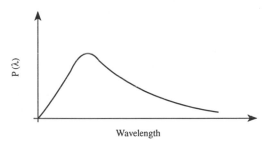

Figure 7.9 *Power output per unit wavelength versus wavelength for a black body*

Wein's law

Wein discovered a relationship between the temperatures of a surface and the wavelength (λ_{max}) (see Figure 7.10) at which the power per unit wavelength is a maximum. Wein's Law states that

$$\lambda_{max} T = \text{constant} = 2898 \times 10^{-6} \text{ mK}$$

For the sun, where T = 5800K, $\lambda_{max} = 0.5$ µm yellow light

For the earth, where T~280K, $\lambda_{max} = 10$ µm infrared light

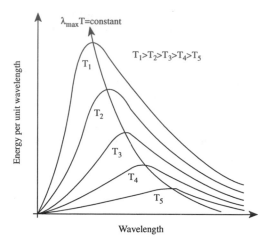

Figure 7.10 *Variation in black body radiation with temperature*

The infra-red radiation which the Earth radiates into space can be absorbed by carbon dioxide in the atmosphere. This can cause the so-called 'Greenhouse Effect' and raises the temperature of the Earth.

Cosine law of radiation (Lambert's law)

If a rectangular beam of light (1 m x 1 m, say) falls at an angle on to a surface, the beam will cover an area of that surface which is greater than 1 m². If the beam falls at an angle θ to the normal to the surface, then the beam will cover an area of surface equal to $(1 \times 1/\cos\theta)$m². If the power density of the beam is P watts/m², then this power P is now spread over $(1/\cos\theta)$m² of the surface. The power density received by the surface is therefore $P/(1/\cos\theta) = P\cos\theta$ Watts/m².

On a clear day in the UK, the power density

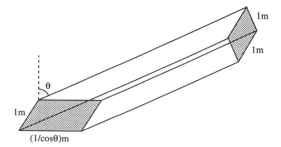

Figure 7.11 *Representation of decrease in irradiance with incidence angle*

in sunlight may be 900 watts/m². In June at midday the sun is (latitude – 22°) from the vertical, ie about 30°, so the power density falling on the ground is 900 cos 30 = 900 x 0.866 = 780 watts/m². In December at midday the sun is (latitude + 22°) from the vertical, ie about 75°, so the power density falling on flat ground is 900 cos 75 = 900 x 0.259 = 233 watts/m².

Stefan's law

The power per unit area of radiation emitted from a black surface at temperature T (K) is given by Stefan's Law as

$$P = \sigma T^4$$

where σ = Stefan's constant = $5.67 \times 10^{-8} \mathrm{Wm^{-2}K^{-4}}$

For a surface with an emittance ε

$$P = \varepsilon \sigma T^4$$

The sun behaves rather like a black body with surface temperature of 5800 K so:

$$P = 5.67 \times 10^{-8} (5800)^4 = 64 \text{ MW m}^{-2}$$

The earth's surface has many different colours and therefore many different values of emittance, for different areas: sand, sea, forest etc. Taking an average emittance of 0.7 and an average surface temperature of 280 K,

$$P = (0.7)\ 5.67 \times 10^{-8} (280)^4 = 240 \text{ Wm}^{-2}$$

PHOTOVOLTAICS

Solar cells

A solar cell converts light to electricity. The cells produce both electric current and voltage by the 'photovoltaic effect', and the technology is often given the name 'photovoltaics'. Solar cells are electronic devices made from semiconductors such as silicon, usually in the form of thin slices (wafers) about $\frac{1}{4}$mm thick. The positive contact is a layer of metal on the back of the wafer, while the negative contact on top of the cell must collect the current but also allow as much light as possible to enter the device. The top contact is usually made in the form of a grid, as shown in Figure 7.12

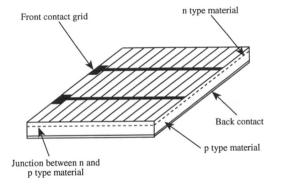

Figure 7.12 *Schematic diagram of a solar cell*

The process by which the absorption of light in a solar cell can produce DC electrical power is represented by Figure 7.13 below. Note that a cell must produce both current and voltage to generate power, since power = current x voltage.

In bright sunlight, a 10 cm square cell will give an output of about $\frac{1}{2}$ volt and 3 amps, about $1\frac{1}{2}$ watts of power. Manufacturers quote the output of their cells for a sunlight intensity of 1 kilowatt per square metre (similar to that of the Sahara Desert at noon). This standard output is labelled 'peak watts' or 'W_p' and is measured at a standard temperature of 25°C.

The power output of a solar cell varies with the intensity of light. If the light is halved, then the current output will also halve but the voltage will drop by only a few per cent. The voltage also depends on the temperature of the cell and decreases by about 0.5 per cent for every one degree rise above 25°C.

PHOTOVOLTAIC MODULES AND ARRAYS

Single solar cells give only small amounts of power and are commonly assembled in modules, each containing 30–36 cells. The top contact of each cell in the module is connected to the back contact of the one which precedes it (a 'series' connection). This ensures that the output will exceed 12 volts, even in moderate sunlight and, hence, will charge a 12 volt battery.

The module must be strong enough to withstand the elements, and to protect the cells and their electrical contacts from attacks by moisture and atmospheric pollutants throughout their 20-year lifetime. Cell temperatures can vary from –20°C on a cold night to +60°C on a hot day, so the thermal contraction and expansion of the cells must be allowed for. The string of interconnected cells is usually surrounded by a layer of soft plastic with an upper layer of glass to let in the light and with a protective layer of plastic, metal or glass at the back. A metal frame round the edges gives added strength and the means of attaching the module to a structure.

One module will typically give a power output of 40–60 Wp and when more is required they can be connected together either in series (positive to negative), which will increase the voltage, or in parallel (negative to negative, positive to positive), which will increase the current. 'Arrays' of modules, fastened to a secure structure, can either be fixed in the best position to receive the greatest amount of sunlight or they can be driven so that they follow the changing position of the sun. These arrays can vary in size from just a few modules, for purposes like telecommunications, to hundreds of thousands for large supplies to grid-connected utilities.

Photovoltaic systems

A photovoltaic (PV) module, or array of modules, generates DC electricity. To provide a

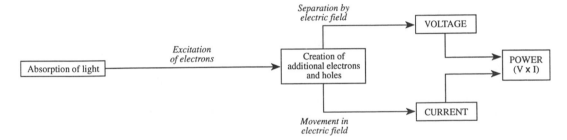

Figure 7.13 *Conversion of light to electricity by the photovoltaic effect*

135

useful service it must be incorporated into a system and these vary in complexity depending on their purpose. For instance a water pump working only in daylight could adequately be powered by a direct coupled system (see Figure 7.14a) in which the DC load is the motor of the pump. On the other hand lights are mostly used at night so a lighting system would have to include battery storage which would be charged during the day and would power the lights at night (see Figure 7.14b). For higher power PV systems, a charge controller becomes necessary (see Figure 7.14c). This provides a controlled charge into the batteries and will also prevent the batteries from discharging themselves. Trickle charged systems designed to produce smaller amounts of power do not need controllers because there is little or no chance of overcharging their batteries.

Figure 7.14d shows the sort of system needed to run a house on solar energy. Lights and small electrical appliances like hair-dryers can run off DC power, but the addition of a DC to AC inverter allows electrical equipment designed for use with AC mains electricity, like microwave ovens, washing machines, fridges etc, to be run from PV power. Throughout Europe there are thousands of holiday homes powered entirely by PV systems like this.

Production of single crystal silicon cells

Most solar cells now produced in volume are made from silicon, a plentiful natural resource making up more than a fifth of the earth's crust and the chief component of ordinary sand. Silicon used in solar cells must be purified to a very high degree and for this the silicon oxide (sand) is first heated to the point where the oxygen is driven off, leaving impure silicon. This is reacted with hydrogen chloride to give a liquid silicon compound which, in turn, is purified by fractional distillation. The resulting ultra-pure trichlorosilane is then heated until it dissociates, leaving lumps of silicon which have a purity of about one part per billion. These lumps of silicon are then grown, in a furnace, into a large crystal. If a small amount of boron is added to the molten silicon, this makes the silicon electrically conducting through positive mobile charges. The boron-doped silicon is referred to as 'P' type sili-

(a) Direct coupled DC load

(b) DC load coupled through battery

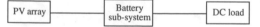

(c) DC load coupled to array and batteries via charge controller

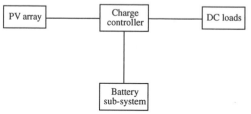

(d) PV system supplying both AC and DC loads

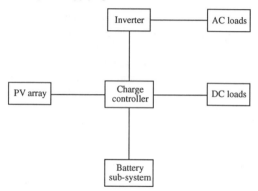

Figure 7.14 *Photovoltaic systems*

con and is used to form the base of the cell.

A single crystal of silicon is called a 'boule' and is usually about 12–15 cm in diameter and about 1 m long. To make solar cells, or any other electronic device such as silicon chips, the boule is cut, usually by a diamond impregnated wire, into very thin slices called 'wafers'. These are then polished to about 0.25 mm thick and, with one face covered, are put into a furnace containing a vaporized phosphorus compound which diffuses into the exposed surface of the wafer to a depth of about 1/1000 mm. This phosphorus doping gives mobile negative charges and the resulting surface is called 'N' type silicon and the wafer is now a semiconductor diode. The junction between 'P' and 'N' silicon creates an electric field. Contacts are screen printed, covering the whole area, on to the back of the cell, and in a grid formation, allowing in as much light as possible, on to the front. The top silicon surface is then coated with a transparent layer to reduce the amount of light reflected from the surface of the cell. All the cells are then tested to see that they reach their specifications and are then sorted into groups depending on their quality. Figure 7.15 provides a flow chart of the stages in production of a photovoltaic module of silicon cells from the raw materials.

Production of modules

The first step in manufacturing modules is called 'tabbing' and is the process of connecting the cells together. They must then be laid out in the formation required by the panel manufacturer, usually either 3 rows by 12 or 4 rows by 9. The connected cells are then placed in their soft plastic protection and a sandwich of the cells is then made under a glass front layer, with soft plastic in the middle and a waterproof backing plate. An aluminium frame is put round the assembly to give it extra strength and stability, and it is sealed with a plastic, waterproof sealant. Electrical contacts are then connected to the tabs of the outermost cells and the contact

boxes are weatherproofed. As solar panels or modules are often used in hot countries, allowance must be made for thermal expansion. Once all this has been done the panel is ready for use anywhere in the world.

Amorphous silicon cells

There is another type of solar cell in common use, particularly for things like calculators, which is also based on silicon. In these the silicon is not crystalline but amorphous, that is the atoms are arranged randomly. Although, like crystalline silicon, the material is a semiconductor, it responds better to blue light. Extremely thin cells of 1/1000 mm are made with it which call for much less material. Very pure silicon, which has been turned into a very poisonous and very explosive gas called silane (SiH_4), is used to make them; great care must be taken.

Silane is introduced into a vacuum chamber at low pressure, and is broken down by the action of high frequency electrical fields into silicon and hydrogen. The silicon condenses on to plates of glass until it forms a very thin film. As the film starts to form, tiny amounts of a boron compound are added to the silane to make the

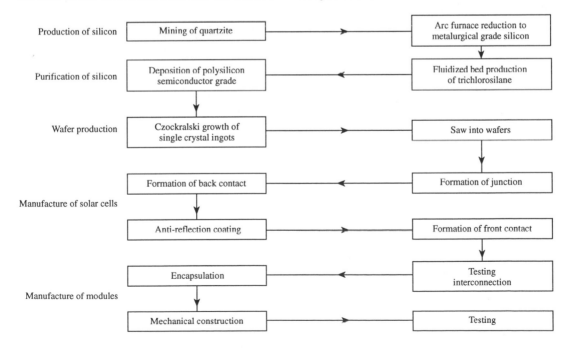

Figure 7.15 *Manufacturing sequence of crystalline silicon modules*

silicon into the 'P' type. This first layer has a thickness of only 1/10,000 mm. The next layer has no dopant and is known as the 'intrinsic', I, layer. It has a thickness of 1/1000 mm. The final 'N' layer is deposited by adding phosphorus compounds to the silane and has a thickness of about 1/10,000 mm. This PIN junction is what creates the electric field and makes the solar cell work (see Figure 7.16).

The contacts on the cell are also very thin and that to the 'P' layer is a transparent but electrically conducting layer which was deposited on the glass plate before it went into the chamber. The contact to the 'N' layer is usually a thin film of aluminium vaporized over the completed cell.

Complete modules can be made in this way if the silicon layer is scribed to separate the individual cells (see Figure 7.17). This allows amorphous silicon modules to be produced much more cheaply than modules of silicon wafers. Amorphous silicon cells are more efficient than most wafer silicon cells in the low levels of light of the kind found in houses and schools, so this makes them eminently suitable for things like calculators and toys.

The prospects for those materials which are in commercial production or pre-commercial development at the moment are listed in Table 7.1 (see page 140).

Uses of photovoltaics

Photovoltaic cells have no moving parts and no fuel costs, and they can be designed to supply power ranging from less than 1 watt to many megawatts. There are many kinds of use for them and we list some of the more important below.

Space

Photovoltaics were first used extensively in space and it is to a solar array that space engineers first turn for the power supplies of almost all satellites. Power output ranges from a few hundred to a few thousand watts.

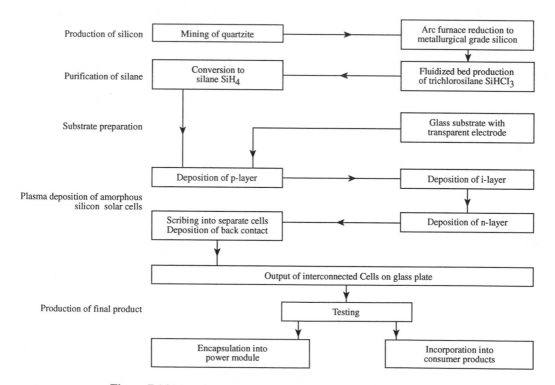

Figure 7.16 *Manufacturing sequence of amorphous silicon modules*

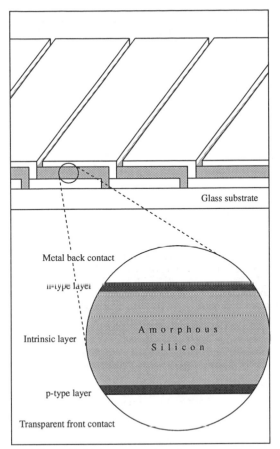

Glass substrate

Metal back contact

n-type layer

Intrinsic layer

Amorphous
Silicon

p-type layer

Transparent front contact

Figure 7.17 *Representation of an integrally
interconnected module*

Consumer products

The range of products with built-in photovoltaic
power supplies, which includes things like calculators, watches and clocks and so on, is
constantly expanding. They account for more
than a quarter of the world-wide annual output
of photovoltaics and the market is dominated, at
present, by the Japanese.

Stand-alone terrestrial appliances

There is a wide range of stand-alone photovoltaic devices with output levels from around
30–40 W to several kW. They can be used to
charge batteries in, for example, the leisure and
military markets, and to supply power for
houses not connected to the national grid.
Because they are so reliable and need so little
maintenance, they are now the first choice for

some purposes, as in the cases of tele-communi-
cations and cathodic protection against rust.

Grids and public utilities

Photovoltaics can be used to supply the grid, but
it is not yet economically worth while unless the
peak demand for electricity coincides with the
peak in the intensity of sunlight. This happens in
the south-western part of the US where the use
of PV to support the distribution grid network is
cost-effective in some instances. Utilities in
southern EU countries are exploring the possibility of supplying mountain or island
communities, particularly those with large holiday populations, with power generated by
photovoltaics.

Photovoltaics in developing countries

Most developing countries lie between the latitudes 40° N and 40° S and, therefore, enjoy not
only more solar radiation than countries like the
UK but, because of a much smaller variation
between winter and summer, have it available
for use throughout the year.

Energy, including electricity, is crucial for
social and economic development, and developing countries all have problems which arise
from the very restricted spread of electricity distribution systems, the absence of rapid
communications and the acute shortage of
skilled maintenance engineers. In most villages
and in many towns electricity generated by central power stations is unavailable and, at the
same time, poor distribution and the lack of
maintenance makes diesel generation both
expensive and unreliable. The latter can cost
more than £1 per kW and is often broken down
for more than half the time. Photovoltaic generators not only produce electricity more cheaply,
but are also more reliable. It can often be
cheaper to install a photovoltaic generator in a
small village than to connect it to a grid.

There are several uses for which photovoltaic systems have, in many circumstances,
proved to be the best choice in developing countries on both engineering and economic grounds
(see Figure 7.18). In telecommunications their
reliability and low maintenance needs not only
reduce costs but also increase revenue because

Cell material	η_c	η_m	Module Costs ($£Wp^{-1}$)		
			$1\,MW_p\,p\,a$	$10\,MW_p\,p\,a$	$100\,MW_p\,p\,a$
Silicon					
Single crystal	23	14	3	1.5	1.0
Polycrystalline	18	12	3	1.2	0.8
1 *Amorphous*	14	6	2	1	0.4
2 *Copper indium diselenide*	17	>10	2	1	0.4
3 *Cadmium telluride*	15	>10	2	1	0.4
4 *Concentrator cells*					
Silicon	27	15–19	4	1.5	0.8
Gallium Arsenide	29	-	3	1.2	0.7
Multi-junction	37	-	4	1.0	0.5

η_c = Best cell efficiency achieved in research laboratories
η_m = Standard commercial module efficiencies
1   Amorphous silicon is a thin film material. The entire module is deposited, cells and interconnects, in one continuous process. The initial efficiency of a-Si modules is about 8 per cent and they degrade over a few months to about 4–6 per cent where they are stable for years.
2   Copper indium diselenide is a thin film material. It is at a pre-commercial stage, with a commercial product expected in 1995 from one or more of three manufacturers. The stability appears to be excellent and 1 ft x 1 ft modules with over 11 per cent efficiency have been produced.
3   Cadmium telluride is the third thin film material, also at pre-commercial development stage, with commercially available modules expected in 1995. It shows excellent stability and module efficiencies over 10 per cent.
4   Concentrator systems use lenses or mirrors to concentrate sunlight, typically by a factor of 50–100, on to a small solar cell. Only silicon concentrators are commercially available in quantity at present. These cells need 2-axis tracking to ensure that the concentrated sunlight always falls on the cell, and will collect only the direct beam component of sunlight. The estimates of production costs are FOB for quantity purchase. The data for the commercially available modules is compiled from US DOE and industry figures. The data for CIS and CdTe are from the author's own calculations on CEC contract. The estimates for concentrator cells are based on US DOE data.

Table 7.1 *Materials and efficiencies of devices available through the 1990s, with module costs estimated for different annual production rates*

people can be sure that telephones will work when they want them. Lighting homes, shops, clinics, hospitals, communal buildings or camps not connected to the grid, reliably and cost-effectively, using high efficiency DC lamps powered by photovoltaic systems is perfectly possible. Many thousands of photovoltaically powered water pumps, both for drinking water and for irrigation, are already in use. At the end of the cold chain small but reliable refrigerators are needed for keeping vaccines. Photovoltaically powered refrigerators cost more than those powered by kerosene or similar fuels, but because they are so reliable the cost per effective dose is significantly lower.

The main obstacle to the widespread use of photovoltaic systems for purposes like these is financial. Although the lifetime costs are lower than for diesel systems, the initial capital cost is beyond the reach of villagers in developing countries. One solution, possibly with the help of agricultural banks, would be to develop a financing system that would transform the capital into a recurrent cost (effectively some form of hire purchase) to allow the system to be bought from income rather than from capital. Photovoltaic systems, by supplying electricity to many remote villages, could make a major contribution to development and to the quality of life in developing countries.

Market readiness of photovoltaics

In 1993 the world-wide shipment of photovoltaic modules was around 60 MW_p. These were worth more than £250 million and the associated batteries, control systems and so on matched or exceeded this figure. Sales of cells and modules for consumer goods and leisure

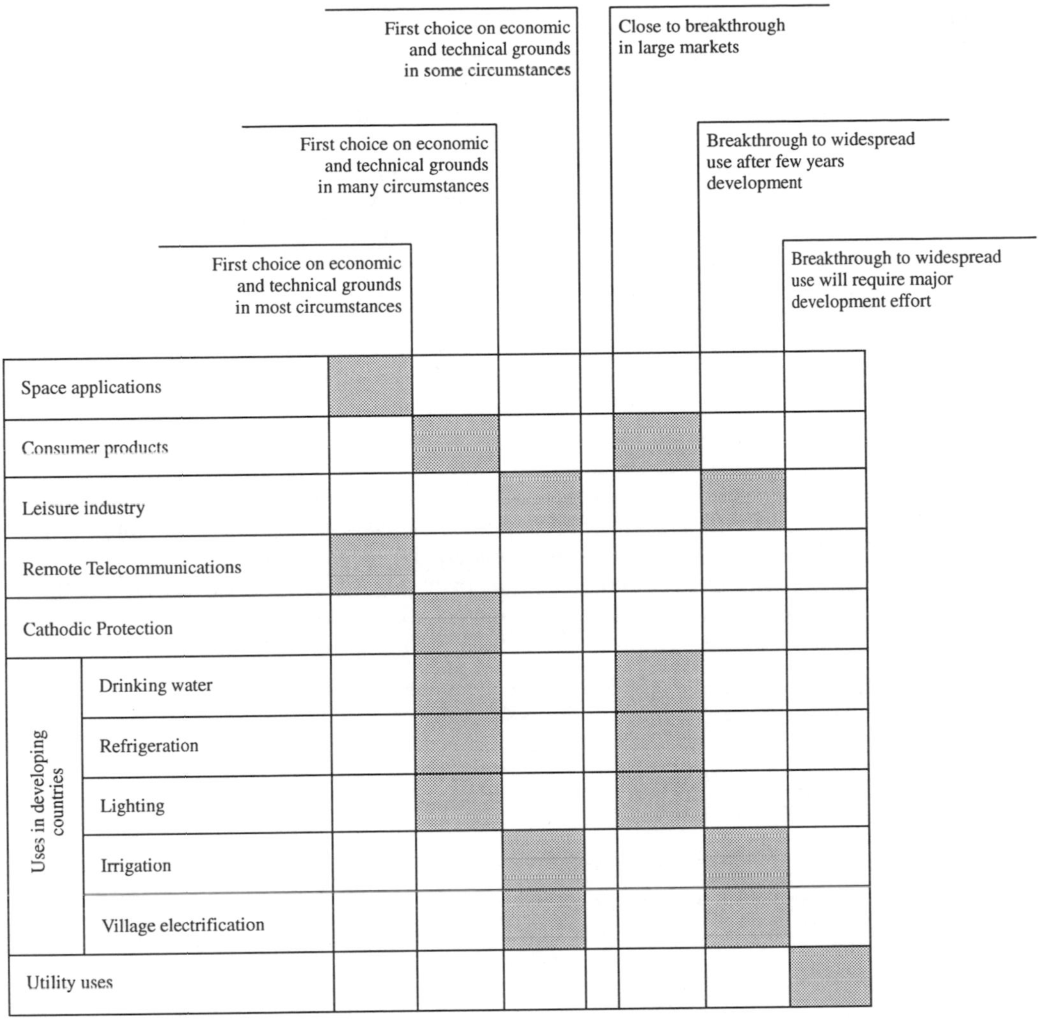

Uses	First choice on economic and technical grounds in most circumstances	First choice on economic and technical grounds in many circumstances	First choice on economic and technical grounds in some circumstances	Close to breakthrough in large markets	Breakthrough to widespread use after few years development	Breakthrough to widespread use will require major development effort
Space applications	▓					
Consumer products		▓		▓		
Leisure industry			▓		▓	
Remote Telecommunications	▓					
Cathodic Protection		▓				
Uses in developing countries — Drinking water		▓				
Uses in developing countries — Refrigeration		▓				
Uses in developing countries — Lighting		▓				
Uses in developing countries — Irrigation			▓		▓	
Uses in developing countries — Village electrification			▓			
Utility uses						▓

Figure 7.18 *Uses for photovoltaic systems*

applications are increasing rapidly, and the installation of systems for medical refrigeration, lighting and the provision of drinking water in the remote areas of developing countries is also growing. The use of photovoltaic power generation for remote telecommunications and the cathodic protection of pipelines etc is now standard in many parts of the world. The market is expected to grow to over 200 MW_p a year by the turn of the century, and to continue to grow thereafter, eventually to many GW pa.

Photovoltaics in the UK

The use of PV is surprisingly widespread in the UK at the present time. There are many hundeds of small systems providing power for monitoring and control devices for the gas, electricity and water industries, for meteorological stations, for most small lights on buoys in estuaries and at sea, lighting for caravans and in other remote sites, and of course, millions of solar calculators.

A few larger (few kilowatt) systems are in operation providing power for houses and farms, and a 40 kW_p system has been installed as a cladding on the South facade of a building at the University of Northumbria (see cover).

A study of the potential resource of PV clad buildings in the UK showed that the annual electrical energy generated could be comparable to the annual UK demand, if all suitable roofs and walls were clad. However the most sensible use of PV cladding would be on commercial buildings, where the energy demand is mainly during working hours, rather than houses which use most electricity during winter nights. Much of the electricity demand of commercial buildings could be met by the electricity generated by cladding their South-facing walls with PV. The cost-effectiveness of this is enhanced for three main reasons: the demand occurs when sunlight is available, the electricity is used within the building, replacing electricity purchased at retail price, rather than feeding into the National Grid in competition with electricity from coal or gas power stations, and thirdly becauses the conventional cladding of commercial buildings is expensive. PV cladding presently costs about £800m^{-2}. Marble cladding costs around £1000m^{-2}, granite cladding £800m^{-2}. Even cheap cladding systems for offices might cost £100m^{-2}. For prestige office blocks, PV cladding gives the high status and high tech image at lower cost than marble. Even for ordinary office blocks it is only the difference between the cost of PV cladding and that of ordinary cladding which counts towards the cost of the PV-generated electricity. Early in the next century, as PV costs are reduced by large scale manufacture, the cost of electricity from PV clad commercial buildings will be lower than the retail price. It will thus be economically viable for electricity companies to install PV facades and sell the electricity to the building users at retail price, or for the building owners to install the facades and enjoy the lower costs themselves. Around one quarter or one fifth of the UK electricity demand could be met in this way by the year 2030 or so.

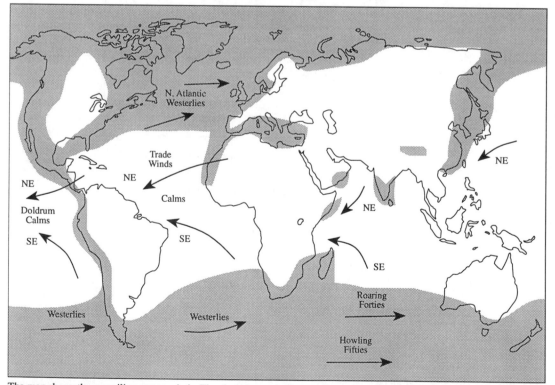

The map shows the prevailing strong winds. The shaded areas indicate regions where the wind energy is attractive for power generation with average wind speeds over 5ms^{-1}, and average generation over 33% of rated power. Note the importance of marine situations, and beware of non-site-related generalizations.

Source: J Twidell and A D Weir, 1986

Figure 7.19 *Prevailing strong winds*

WIND ENERGY

Solar radiation over the Equator heats up the air which rises as the cold Polar air sinks. This sets up the basic pattern of wind circulation (see Figure 7.19). An average of 300,000 nuclear power stations would be needed to generate power equal to that in the wind around the world. Not only is wind power enormous, but it is pollution free and the turbines need far less maintenance than conventional power stations, all of which makes it an attractive form of power production. The UK has some of the best wind conditions in the world and, as the wind blows more strongly in the winter than the summer, the demand for extra energy can be matched by the extra supply. Wind generators have been tested in Britain for some years and supply an increasing amount of electricity to the grid.

Siting a wind generator

Windmills have existed for between one and two millennia, and although modern turbines bear as little relation to them as Concorde does to a coracle, what they do have in common is that the amount of energy either of them produces is heavily dependent on where they are sited. Placing a wind generator at the foot of a hill would be pointless, but if it is placed at the top where the wind has been forced to accelerate by the rise in the ground, it will work very successfully (see Figure 7.20).

Ground drag also makes a large difference, as the less there is the faster is the wind. A wind generator sited on a sheet of ice or concrete will produce its expected output, but put behind a forest it will not. We may notice that concrete council estates are windy while forests are calm. By the same token, wind generators are built quite tall – 50 m above the ground is usually high enough to escape the drag factor.

Wind energy converters

Wind energy converters (WECs) convert the energy of the wind into socially useful energy, usually electricity, and they come in many shapes and kinds. For machines with a horizontal axis (see Figure 7.21) the dominant force is lift and the rotor blades may be in front of (upwind) or behind the tower (downwind). Upwind turbines need a tail or some other mechanism to point them into the wind. Downwind turbines may be quite seriously affected by the tower, which can produce wind shadow and turbulence

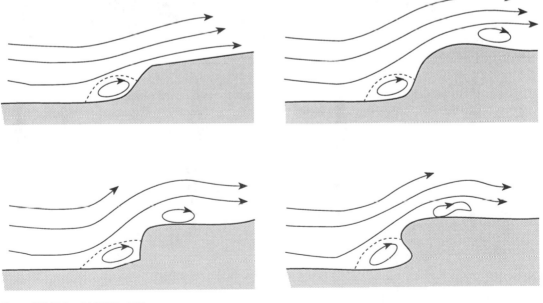

Source: J Twidell and A D Weir, 1986

Figure 7.20 *Wind flow over surfaces of different topographies*

in the path of the blades. Both kinds of machine with a capacity greater than about 50 kW are turned into the wind by an electric motor. Two or three bladed rotors are those most commonly used for generating electricity, multi-bladed rotors which have a high torque in light winds are used for pumping water and other tasks calling for low frequency mechanical power.

WECs with vertical axes have the advantage that they may, without adjustment, be driven by wind from any direction, but the torque from wind variation during each turn of the blades can produce unwanted vibations. At present most working machines have horizontal axes, but this may change as machines with vertical axes, like the Musgrove rotor (see Figure 7.22 and below), are improved.

Cup anemometers (see Figure 7.23) are used to measure wind speed or to produce power for very small rotors. They depend on drag force and the shape of the cups produces an almost exact correspondence between wind and rotational speeds.

Savonius rotors (see Figure 7.24) can be homemade for simple water pumping as they can be made from two halves of an oil drum. As in the previous WEC, the motive force is drag produced by the complicated movement of wind both through and around the curved sheet airfoils.

The Darrieus rotor (see Figure 7.25), otherwise known as the 'egg beater', has two or three thin blades with an airfoil section. The driving force is lift and maximum torque occurs when the blade is moving across the wind faster than the speed of the wind. But this rotor, which is used for generating electricity, is not, as a rule, self-starting and has to be started by the generator itself which calls either for complicated controls or constant supervision by an operator.

The Evans rotor (see Figure 7.26) is fitted with two vertical wing shaped blades, fitted on a vertical axis, which create lift when the wind blows fast enough.

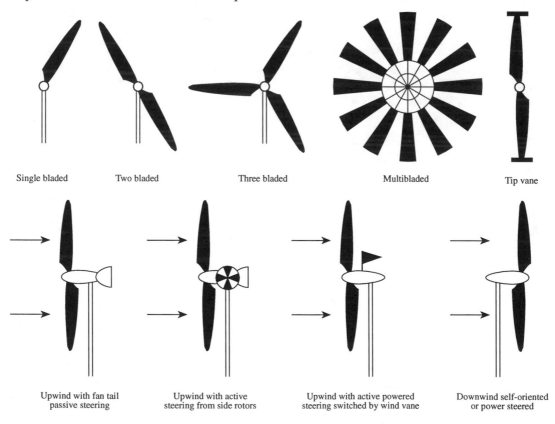

| Single bladed | Two bladed | Three bladed | Multibladed | Tip vane |

| Upwind with fan tail passive steering | Upwind with active steering from side rotors | Upwind with active powered steering switched by wind vane | Downwind self-oriented or power steered |

Source: J Twidell and A D Weir, 1986

Figure 7.21 *Horizontal axis wind machines of different types*

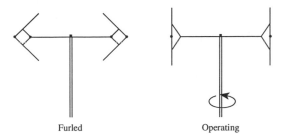

Furled   Operating

Source: J Twidell and A D Weir, 1986

Figure 7.22 *Representation of the Musgrove vertical axis machine*

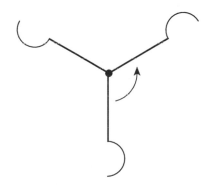

Source: J Twidell and A D Weir, 1986

Figure 7.23 *Cup anemometer*

Concentrators

As the motive force for WECs comes from inter-cepted wind, it may be an advantage to funnel, or concentrate, the wind from an area greater than the section of the rotor. Various systems for this purpose have been either designed or proposed for use on turbines with horizontal axes. It is pos-sible, for example, to tip the blades (see Figure 7.27) which are then able to drag wind in from a larger area. Neither this nor other forms of con-centrator are yet in commercial use.

Wind energy assessment

The energy in the wind is the kinetic energy of a moving mass of air.

Kinetic energy $= \frac{1}{2}mv^2$

where m = mass of the moving air and v = velocity (see Figure 7.28)

Mass of the air = volume x density

If the air is moving with velocity v ms^{-1}, the vol-

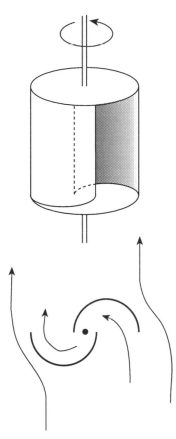

Source: J Twidell and A D Weir, 1986

Figure 7.24 *Savonius rotor*

ume of the air passing through 1m^2 of area in one second = v cubic metres.

The mass of this air = 1 x v x ρ, where ρ is the density of air.

Energy in the air which passes in one second is therefore $\frac{1}{2}mv^2 = \frac{1}{2}\rho v^3$ watts/m^2

Betz Limit

Air flowing through a turbine cannot give all its energy to the rotors, otherwise the air would pile in front of the turbine and could no longer flow through it. For a continuous stream of air passing through the turbine the maximum power the air can deliver to the rotors is 59 per cent of its kinetic energy. This figure for the ideal efficiency was first derived by Betz and is known as the Betz Limit. All real WECs are less efficient than this. When a

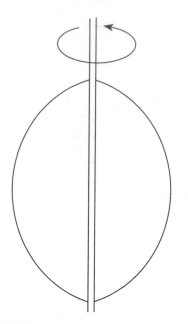

Source: J Twidell and A D Weir, 1986

Figure 7.25 *Darrieus 'egg beater'*

wind generator is rated at 70 per cent efficient this means that it converts 70 per cent x 0.59 = 41 per cent of the wind energy into rotational energy.

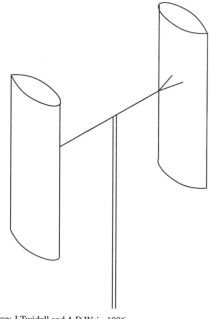

Source: J Twidell and A D Weir, 1986

Figure 7.26 *Evans vertical axis machine*

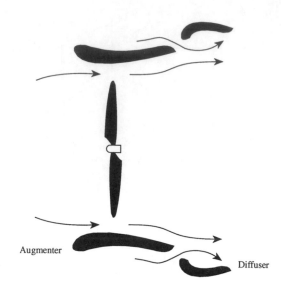

Figure 7.27 *Wind machine inside augmenter/diffuser structure*

Tip speed ratio

The efficiency with which a WEC can use the wind energy varies according to the wind speed. At very low speeds the wind will not turn the rotors, while at very high speeds the rotors become more inefficient. Once the rotors start to turn they rotate more quickly as the wind speed increases and, to maintain efficiency, the ratio of the speed of the tips of the rotor compared to the wind speed should be kept constant. This 'tip speed ratio' is an important aspect of the design of a WEC, the best value of the 'tip speed ratio' which gives maximum efficiency is different for the different types of WEC (see Figure 7.29).

Power output from wind turbines

The power output from a WEC at any given time depends on the wind speed at that time (see Figure 7.30).

There is a minimum wind speed needed before the turbine rotates and produces power. This is called the cut-in wind speed. Power output increases with the cube of the wind speed until the WEC is producing the power for which it is designed, and for which the generator, bearings and so on are designed to cope. If this power rating is exceeded then the generator can overheat and fail. If the wind gets so strong that it reaches the 'cut-out' speed then the WEC must shut down

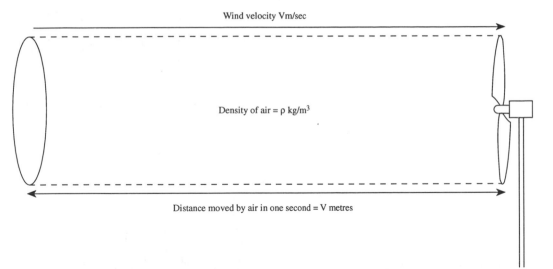

Figure 7.28 *Representation of a column of air moving past a rotor*

completely to avoid damage. So long as the wind continues to blow strongly, and the machine has reached its maximum power output, it becomes progressively less efficient and cannot make use of the extra power. The rotor blades are controlled so that as wind speed increases the WEC continues to keep within its power rating.

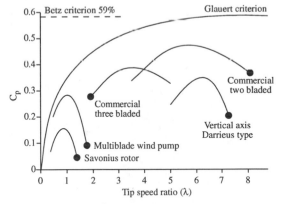

Source: J Twidell and A D Weir, 1986

Figure 7.29 *Variation of efficiency versus tip speed ratio for various types of machine*

Energy output

The energy generated by a WEC is the sum of the power it generates over a period. The watts generated in each second of the day are added up give the number of the day's joules. The outcome will depend on how often the wind blows and at what speed.

In Figure 7.31 we give a wind velocity duration chart typical of good site in the UK and it shows the number of hours in a year during which the speed is at or below a particular value.

Figures 7.32 and 7.33 show the mean wind speed around the UK averaged over the year, and it can be seen that there are large areas where wind speed exceeds 12.5 mph, and where there are calm days for less than 40 per cent of the year.

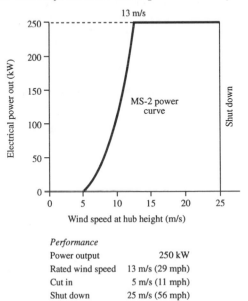

Performance

Power output	250 kW
Rated wind speed	13 m/s (29 mph)
Cut in	5 m/s (11 mph)
Shut down	25 m/s (56 mph)
Survival	60 m/s (134 mph)

Figure 7.30 *Power output versus wind speed from an MS-2 generator*

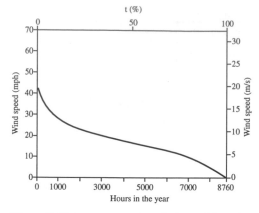

Figure 7.31 *A representative wind speed duration curve*

CALCULATION OF GENERATING COSTS

Capital cost per rated kW	C.W £750/kW
Design life expectancy n	30 years
Required real rate of return r	5%
Annual charge rate R	6.5%
Operation and maintenance M	2%
Hours in a year h	8760 h
Turbine rated wind speed (hub height) v_r	13.3 m/s
Site annual mean wind speed (hub height) v_m	9.4 m/s
Mean as fraction of rated wind speed v_m/v_r	0.71
Nominal load factor F	0.46
Machine availability A	95%
Factor for other losses a	90%
Generation costs G	2.1 p/kWh

The cost of electricity generated by WECs

Generation costs for wind energy are simply

$$G = C \ \frac{(R + M)}{E}$$

Where C is initial capital cost

R is the annual charge rate on capital

M is the annual operation and maintenance cost as a fraction of initial cost and E is the annual energy yield given by

$$E = LWF$$

Where L is the number of hours in a year (8760)

W is the rated power of the wind turbine

and F is the load factor, ie the fraction of time that the WEC is operating at rated power.

So generated costs are:

$$G = \frac{C}{W} \ \frac{(R + M)}{LF}$$

C/W is the cost per rated kilowatt and is the standard way of comparing power generation systems. For example, a coal fired power station might cost about £1000/kW, a nuclear power station about £2000–£3000/kW and a WEC £800–£1000/kW. For a modern WEC on a good wind site, the table shows figures which might

be achieved to give a generating cost of 2.1 pence/kWh.

This cost of 2.1 pence/kWh is cheaper than most estimates for the cost of electricity generated either by coal or by nuclear power stations. The introduction of the Non-Fossil Fuel

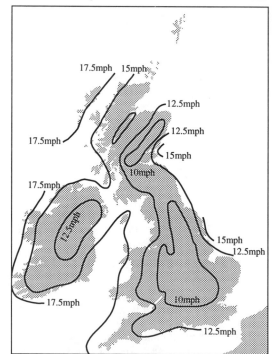

Figure 7.32 *Average wind speed data for the UK*

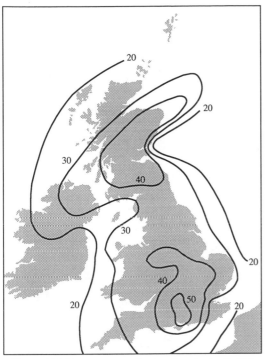

Figure 7.33 *Percentage of calm days in the British Isles*

Obligation has given rise to many windfarms in the UK. The cost of electricity from these windfarms is much higher than the 2.1 pence/kWh estimated above, because the payback time is much shorter than the 30 years assumed and the discount rate demanded is not 5 per cent pa but over 15 per cent pa in many cases. The windfarms built in the later part of the 1990s will benefit from the experience of these early farms with reduced capital costs and lower discount rates, as banks become more familiar with the technology. It is expected that energy costs will approach those of new fossil fuel plants. Windfarms have a great advantage compared to, say, nuclear power stations in that each machine takes only a short time to build and to put into operation. If a production line is set up a gigawatt of WECs can be built and installed in only about a year, whereas it takes ten years or more to build the same capacity nuclear power station. The electricity utilities in California, US, are already using over a gigawatt of wind generators.

A gigwatt of WECs can be installed on a good site in an area less than 20 km², and the access roads and the WECs themselves only take up about 2 per cent of that area. The rest could continue to be used for agricultural land etc just as the national grid pylons are sited in the middle of fields.

POWER FROM WATER

Oceans, lakes, rivers and so on evaporate as they absorb sunlight. Water vapour joins the general circulation of the atmosphere subsequently to be released as rain, much of which falls on land and runs from higher ground back to its sources. During its path to the sea, water can be intercepted by dams and channelled through turbines, or it can be used to drive the contemporary equivalent of the ancient water-wheels. Seas, and even large lakes, are not level surfaces and the differences can be used to generate power, either from waves which are caused by winds and are, effectively, stores of wind power or from tides which are caused by the gravitational pull of the moon and, to a lesser degree, the sun. The regularity of tides is useful because it makes the potential power output fairly predictable, though this is modified by the extent to which it is affected by wind.

How much energy can water produce?

Water power depends on local conditions. All streams, rivers, lakes tides or waves can be used to generate some power, but to use them cost-effectively is another matter. Cost-effectiveness is important not only to show that the resource is worth exploiting, but also to be sure that the devices used to convert water power to electricity are being used wisely. It would easily be possible to use more energy constructing the devices than they could possibly produce throughout their lifetimes if they were employed in inappropriate conditions. In Chapter 2 we explored the ways in which cost-effectiveness is critically dependent on the discount rate used in its calculation. This is particularly important in the case of water power, where the capital cost is usually high, but the lifetime of the plant is long. However, even at low discount rates water power could only be cost-effective on a limited number of sites. The price at which water power can produce electricity has also to be compared

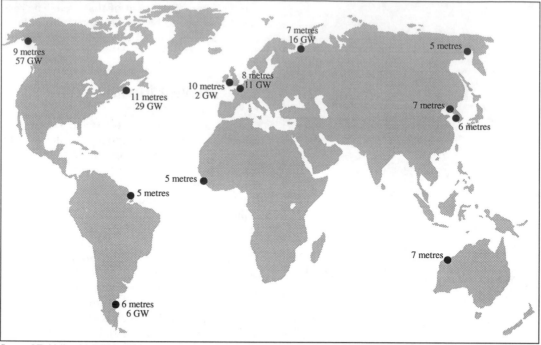

Source: J Twidell and A D Weir, 1986

Figure 7.34 *Tidal ranges at selected sites around the world and estimated power output*

with the price from other sources. Any large scheme feeding power into the national grid must compete with other large base-load power stations. Small schemes designed to provide power to a farm or a single village should be compared to the retail price of electricity. In

Region	Total maximum capacity (GW)	Total capacity (GW) in use (1983)
Asia	630	63
S America	44	75
Africa	350	18
N America (inc Mexico)	350	160
USSR (former)	240	50
Europe	150	98
Oceania	40	8
World	2200	462

World hydro-energy potential at 50 per cent capacity factor = 9700 TWh per annum

Table 7.2 *Hydro-power resources and use around the world*

developing countries the price must be compared to alternative means of supply in any given locality, whether it be by the extension of the grid, the use of diesel powered generators or the use of other renewable resources.

However, to get some idea of the total energy which might be available to us from water power, some 'broad-brush' surveys have been made. As these surveys usually ignore the smaller resources which might be of use locally, they give the lower limit of what is available, particularly in developing countries where data are more limited. Even so, as we can see in Table 7.2, the estimated total is large.

If conventional barrages are used, tidal energy is only cost-effective where there is a tidal range of about 5 m or more. The largest in the world is 11 m and is found in the Bay of Fundy on the Canadian – US border. In the UK the best-known tidal scheme is the Severn barrage, but other estuaries, particularly that of the Mersey, are also being looked at. The world's major tidal power sites have been reviewed by Sorenson (see Figure 7.34).

Sorenson has estimated (1979) that the present total world resource is potentially around an average power of 120 GW which would give an annual output of about 100 TWh.

Anyone who has been hit by a large wave knows how powerful they can be. The most powerful are those with a long period and great height, and they mainly occur in deep water because inshore waves lose much of their power through friction from the sea bed. Even so, North Sea waves can have a very considerable average energy.

Figure 7.35 shows the average annual energy per metre of wave in various parts of the world. Clearly the Scottish Atlantic coast has best of all wave conditions and the UK in general is particularly well endowed. World resources add up to 4.3 GWh/m, so, assuming an average efficiency of 60 per cent, a 500 km length of wave energy converter at each site would generate about 1300 TWh, roughly one-seventh of the world's potential hydro-power and 13 times the world's potential production of tidal power. If all the water power resources of the world were fully exploited they could generate about 11,000 TWh per annum which is about 12.5 per cent of current world energy demand (90,000 TWh).

Although water power is significant throughout the world it is not large, but in the UK it could be very large indeed (see Figure 7.36). If 500 km lengths of wave energy devices with an efficiency of 60 per cent were placed off the Atlantic Coast of Scotland, the western approaches to the English Channel and in the northern North Sea, the average power output would be around 30 GW, giving an annual energy output of 270 TWh. These figures are approximately equal to those of the present use of power and demand for electricity throughout the UK, so wave power could be very important in meeting the UK's future energy needs. However, converting this potential into actual power will demand considerable development of the currently known technologies.

Converting water power to useful energy

Hydropower technologies

Hydropower relies on the conversion of the potential energy loss of water flowing from a

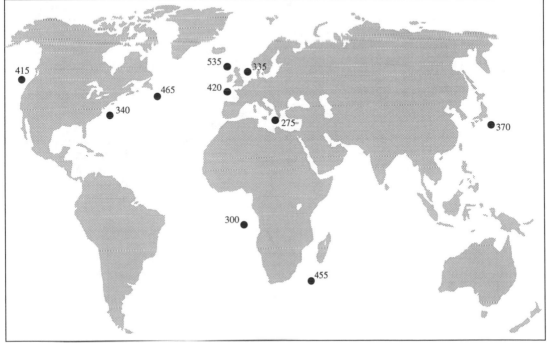

Source: J Twidell and A D Weir, 1986

Figure 7.35 *Average annual wave energy per metre stretch at selected sites (MWh)*

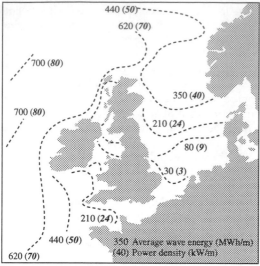

Source: J Twidell and A D Weir, 1986

Figure 7.36 *Average annual wave energy (MWh/m) and power density (kW/m) around the UK*

higher to a lower level. This loss of potential energy each second is the power available and is given by P = MgH or P = ρVgH where P is the power (watts), M is the mass flow of water (kgs⁻¹), g is the acceleration due to gravity, H is the height in metres through which the water falls, ρ is the density of water (kgm⁻³) and V is the volume flow of water (m³s⁻¹). Taking g as 10 ms⁻², the power is then P = 10MH watts or P = 10 VH kWatts, since ρ=1000 kgm⁻³.

There are two types of turbine which are used to convert this water power into socially useful power, usually electricity. These are as follows.

1   Impulse turbines, in which the flow of water hits open turbine blades in a jet and the power derives from the kinetic energy of the water.

2   Reaction turbines in which the turbine blades are fully immersed in the water and the power comes from the pressure drop across the turbine.

Pelton wheels

A Pelton wheel is an impulse turbine in which a jet of water hits a bucket attached to the wheel rim. The bucket is shaped as shown in Figure 7.37 so that the jet is divided into two equal streams and deflected from the incoming jet and out of the bucket. The direction of the water flow is reversed, giving the water a change of momentum equal to twice the momentum of the jet relative to the bucket.

The force on the bucket is $F = 2M (V_j - V_b)$, M = Mass flow rate and the power developed is $P = FV_b$, ie Power $P = 2M (V_j-V_b)V_b$.

The power, in the ideal case, is equal to the total kinetic energy per second in the jet, ie the efficiency is 100 per cent. No real Pelton wheel can achieve this because of some friction of water flowing round the bucket and the momentum of the outlet water is not quite equal to the momentum of the jet. However, efficiencies around 90 per cent are achieved in practice.

Reaction turbines can be rather more efficient than a Pelton wheel, at the cost of greater mechanical and hydraulic complexity.

Francis turbine

The Francis turbine is shown in outline in Figure 7.38. Water flows into a casing around the working parts. The water flow is guided by fixed vanes on to the rotating vanes and the water leaves via the central outlet.

To maximize the throughput of water, the machinery can be placed in a duct, of the same diameter as the rotating vanes, and the water then flows axially down the duct. The vanes are now similar to the propeller of a ship or aircraft

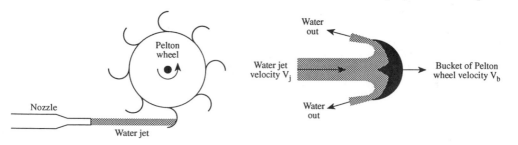

Figure 7.37 *Pelton wheel showing shape of bucket and splitting of outgoing water flow*

152

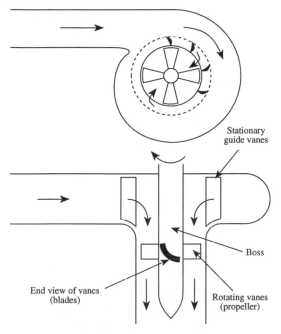

Figure 7.38 *The Francis turbine*

and they rotate because of the stream of water passing over them.

Normal propeller design will give a change of rotation if the direction of water flow is altered. This would be very inconvenient for a turbine in a tidal flow, since the electrical generator must always be driven in the same direction of rotation.

Wells turbine

A Wells turbine has propeller blades which give the same rotation regardless of flow direction, and can thus directly drive a generator from both incoming and outgoing tides.

It is possible to dispense entirely with a casing around the propeller, and use the equivalent of a wind generator, immersed in the water flow. This saves a great deal of money since the largest cost component of water turbines is usually the civil engineering work associated with dams and ducting. The simplest form of a water current turbine would be to attach a neutral buoyancy nacelle and rotor to a cable running from a sea bed anchor to a surface buoy.

In wide estuaries or rivers, many turbines could operate side by side. As with wind turbines, the power output varies with the cube of the fluid velocity, so fast moving water would give much higher output. However, unlike a wind turbine, the structure would not experience extreme speeds in gales or gusts and so would not need to be engineered to cope with excessive loads. Since water is so much denser than air, a 2 ms^{-1} water current has the same power density as a 19 ms^{-1} air current and many tidal and river sites could generate useful power. Estimates of the power available in tidal races around the UK suggest a resource of about 15 GW, so around 5 GW of electrical power could be generated. Tidal currents are variable, being zero when the tide turns twice a day so the load factor on a tidal marine turbine may only be 20 per cent, ie its annual energy output is only 20 per cent of that which it could give if it operated at full power all the time. A water turbine in a river whose flow varies little over the year might have a load factor of 80 per cent or so, giving four times the annual energy output of the same turbine in a tidal current. The economics of a river turbine would be correspondingly more attractive. The environmental impact of a submerged water turbine in a tidal estuary would be very small compared to that of a tidal barrage. There is, at present (1993), a study of the technical and economic feasibility of tidal water turbines in the UK and they may prove to be an attractive alternative to the Severn or Mersey barrages.

Wave power technologies

The energy in a wave consists of the kinetic energy of the moving water, and the potential energy associated with the peaks and troughs above and below mean sea level. For simplicity, let us consider a single wave with a wavelength λ (the distance from crest to crest) and a wave period T (the time between the passage of one crest and the following crest past a fixed point). The velocity at which the wave energy moves is given by

$$V = (g\lambda/8\pi)_{1/2}$$

and the wavelength is related to the wave period by

$$\lambda = gT^2/2\pi$$

In both these relationships, g is the acceleration due to gravity.

The total energy per unit surface area of the wave is given by

$$E = \tfrac{1}{2} \rho g a^2$$

where ρ is the density of water and a is the amplitude of the wave (the height of the crest from mean sea level, or half the height from trough to crest). The power per metre length of wavefront is

$$P = EV = (\tfrac{1}{8\pi}) \rho g^2 a^2 T \text{ or}$$

$$P = 3.8 \, a^2 T \text{ (kW) when a is in metres and } T \text{ in seconds}$$

For a wave of 1 m amplitude and wave period ten seconds, the power/metre is then 38 kW. The length of such a wave would be about 150 m, so these are the long Atlantic rollers which sweep into the west coast of Britain.

This analysis assumes that the waves are in deep water, where the sea bed has no influence on them. In shallow water, the velocity varies as the square root of the depth, so waves slow down in shallow water. This dependence of velocity on depth explains why waves usually arrive parallel to a shore and explains the breaking of waves when the trough is slowed so much that it is overtaken by the crest. Long before these effects occur, the wave is losing energy to the sea bed as it moves over the continental shelf into shallower waters, so waves close to shore are less powerful than waves in deep water.

The power per metre of a wave varies with the square of the amplitude. As waves are whipped up in a storm, the amplitude can increase manyfold, increasing the power greatly. All wave energy devices must be engineered to withstand these large destructive waves. For about 1 per cent of waves periods over 11 seconds are found. In these waves, power/metre can exceed 1 MW. The biggest waves likely to be encountered once in a hundred years have an amplitude of 30 m and powers of 20 MW m^{-1} and few structures would withstand them.

Real seas, as opposed to the ideal single wave considered earlier, consist of a mixture of waves of different lengths and amplitudes. Away from the shore, waves may approach a device from different directions, so the devices must cope with a wide variety of waves at any given time and a much wider variety from calm to storm over their lifetime.

Wave energy devices can be classified in a number of ways. The simplest classification is between active and passive devices. In active devices, some element moves with the wave and power is extracted from the relative movements of the various components. A passive device tries to capture as much energy as possible from the wave by presenting a large immovable structure in its path. At a more detailed level, wave power devices can be sub-divided into rectifiers, tuned oscillators and untuned oscillators or dampers. The rectifiers convert the energy of the wave into a head of water and the potential energy represented by this head is used to drive a water turbine. Tuned oscillators respond efficiently to a narrow range of wave periods with a fall-off in efficiency for waves of higher or lower periods. Untuned oscillators or dampers seek to absorb the energy from waves of all wavelengths efficiently, although for practical devices they absorb some wavelengths more effectively than others. The most detailed classification divides devices into ramps, floats, flaps, air bells and wave pumps.

Ramps are passive devices which allow water to run up a sloping ramp into a reservoir and water from the reservoir runs back to sea through a turbine.

Floats heave up and down on the waves, and the relative motion is used to drive a pump or generator. Flaps work by opening to allow a wave in and then closing to retain the head of water in a reservoir. Air bells usually float on the sea and have an open bottom below the water surface. The effect of a passing wave is to increase the pressure of air inside the bell as the crest passes and reduce the air pressure as the trough passes. The air escapes out of or into the air bell through a duct containing a turbine. A Wells turbine can be used to drive a generator from both the inward and outward motion of the air. Wave pumps exploit the pressure variations beneath the water surface to pump a fluid through a turbine.

The most famous wavepower device in the UK is the Salter duck, shown schematically in Figure 7.39a. It consists of a string of 'nodding ducks' on a central spline. Each duck will move more or less at random with respect to the other ducks, so the central spline will remain almost stationary. The power can then be extracted using the relative motion of the ducks and the

(a) Schematic representation

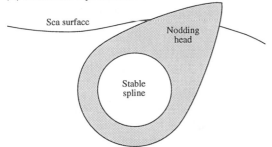

(b) Efficiency as a function of zero crossing period of the wave

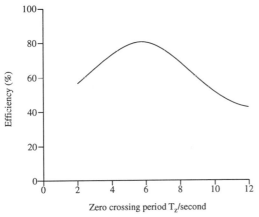

Figure 7.39 *The Salter duck*

spline. Figure 7.39b shows the efficiency of a 15 m duck as a function of the zero crossing period – effectively the wave period of the complex waves of the real sea. The device has the characteristics of a tuned oscillator, with high efficiency for waves of particular wavelength, but it does have good efficiency for a wide range of wavelengths.

A wave device under test at present in Scotland is an oscillating water column, shown schematically in Figure 7.40. It is built on a cliff face with fairly deep water at the foot. Incoming waves force water into the bell and push the air out through the Wells turbine. As the wave recedes, the water level in the bell drops, drawing air in the turbine. The chamber will respond efficiently to waves whose length is large compared to the chamber dimensions but less efficiently to short wavelengths. Since high energy waves are long, this is not a problem. The ability of the structures to withstand storms is a serious problem and a Norwegian device of

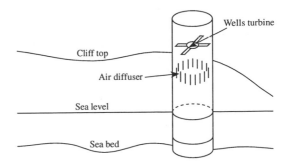

Figure 7.40 *Oscillating water column*

this sort was destroyed in a storm. Small floating air bells are used to power navigation buoys and could be useful for providing power to small island communities.

The third main type of wave device of interest in the UK is the sea clam, shown schematically in Figure 7.41. It consists of a ring of flexible bags which are squashed when a wave peak passes, driving air out of the bag. The bag springs open again in a wave trough, sucking air into the bag. The air flows past a Wells turbine attached to a generator. This device is a 'damper' type device operating as a wave pump. It responds efficiently to a wide range of wave periods and has been tested successfully on small scale on Loch Ness, but like all UK wave devices its development was almost completely abandoned in the middle 1980s. The cause of this unfortunate change in UK government policy was a belief that only very large devices were worth pursuing and conceptual designs for outputs in the order of gigawatts were studied. The leap in scale from the small devices tested to these very large conceptual designs left many engineering uncertainties and this then resulted in pessimistic cost estimates. A recent reappraisal of more sensible sizing of wave power devices has concluded that they could be cost-effective for remote and island communities.

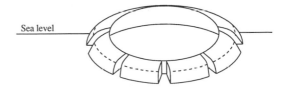

Figure 7.41 *Representation of a sea clam*

POWER FROM BIOMASS

Almost all lifeforms need sunlight for their energy (some creatures in volcanic ocean trenches use geothermal energy). Photo-synthesis by green plants converts large amounts of sunlight into biological material – grass, trees etc – which are rich in energy and form the basis of food chains for other creatures. Human society derives products such as wood or alcohol from these basic photosynthetic materials and uses them to meet various human needs. The fossil fuels which we use at the moment are products of photosynthesis many million of years ago and form an 'energy bank' on which our present society is drawing heavily.

Biomass is used extensively throughout the world today. The use of fuelwood, crop residue or cow dung for cooking is widespread in developing countries and as a free good is usually the only option for their rural poor. The use of biomass is not, however, restricted to the poor of the Third World. For instance, the US obtains as much energy from biomass as it does from nuclear power, while Sweden derives 14 per cent of its primary energy from biomass.

The biomass resource is very large, the amount stored annually world wide is equivalent to ten times the total world annual energy use. The total stored biomass in the world has an energy content equal to that of all the world's proven fossil fuel reserves.

Table 7.3 shows the potential for biomass to supply the energy demand of different regions of the world. Europe would be able to supply only half its present energy demand even if it used all of its fertile land for energy production, while North America would need over half of its fertile land to meet its present energy demand. This is due partly to the inflation of the present demand for primary fuels because of inefficient use, but also, in the case of Europe, by a population density of around 1/2 ha/person of fertile land.

South America is best placed to supply its energy needs from biomass, needing only about 3 per cent of its fertile land to supply 35 GJ/Cap pa. Central America would need one-fifth of its fertile land. Asia would need to use two-thirds of its fertile land for energy crops and would, if it did so, have severe problems of food supply. Africa would need about one-eighth of its fertile land, which could be acceptable if agricultural productivity improved.

No one really thinks that any region would rely exclusively on biomass for its energy supply, but the data in Table 7.3 do show clearly the very large potential in many areas of the world. There are four major attractions in the use of biomass: it is an indigenous resource in most parts of the world; it provides stored energy unlike most renewable sources; it is very flexible in use; and, during its growth, it captures CO_2. It also makes use of agricultural skills which are to be found throughout the world, and

Region	Population (10^6)	Total land area 10^6 ha	Croplands forests pasture 10^6 ha	Energy content of residue 10^6 GJ	Total energy consumption 10^6 GJ	Area to supply 35 GJ/Cap
N America	276	1839	968	12	93	580[1]
Europe	497	473	283	9	66	470[1]
Asia	2780	2637	1662	30.9	57.6	1091
Africa	590	2937	1641	10.2	12.1	207
C America	143	265	198	3.3	6.0	45
S America	279	1751	1541	11.6	10.8	53
World	4990	13056	8727	86.5	326	1751

1 Biomass productivity taken as 10t/ha, and the area is that needed to supply the actual 1987 energy demand (330 GJ/Cap N.A. and 133 GJ/Cap Europe) if 50 per cent of residues also used for energy supply.

For all other regions the land area needed assumes a biomass productivity of 5t/ha, with 50 per cent of existing crop residues also used for energy supply. Note that 35 GJ p.a. per capita is equivalent to 1kW per capital power demand, which could provide a European level of energy services if all conversion was at energy efficiencies equal to the present technically feasible limit.

Adapted from D Hall, 1991

Table 7.3 *The potential for the use of biomass, 1987 data*

provides rural employment, and thus, unlike most other energy technologies, does not increase the drift from rural to urban areas.

Use of biomass

The simplest use of biomass is to burn it and the most common biomass used this way is wood, but corn stalks, cow dung and many other agricultural residues are also burnt on open fires for cooking, heating and other social purposes. The fireplace is usually formed by three stones, on which the cooking pot, or whatever, is balanced. Both the fuel and the stones are gathered locally, so the only cost is in time.

The next step in sophistication is to heat the wood in an enclosed space to make charcoal which is a very convenient fuel. It is much lighter than wood and so is much more easily transported. It burns without fumes and so is favoured in urban areas, but it is a processed fuel, sold commercially to those who can afford it.

In many parts of the world, animal and sometimes human wastes are used in biogas plants. The anaerobic digestion of these wastes produces a methane rich gas and leaves behind a benign residue which makes an excellent compost. There are millions of farm or village sized biogas plants in operation around the world, particularly in China and India. But collecting waste from animals which roam freely can be so time consuming that biogas production is no longer worth while and it is only really practicable where animals are kept in pens. None the less enough gas to satisfy the family's cooking and lighting needs can be produced from the waste of the livestock owned by a typical peasant farmer. This is particularly true where fairly rapid cooking is the norm, as with the Chinese wok. In general, the richer the farmer, the more

animals the family will have, and hence the more likely it is that a biogas plant could supply the family with its cooking and lighting needs.

In the industrialized countries, and the urban conurbations of developing countries, the use of biomass would need to be on an industrial scale, far removed from farm or village sized charcoal or biogas plants. Just as farms can burn their own straw or dispose of animal waste in biogas plants, so municipalities could install waste burning and land-fill gas plants for energy production. The full potential of biomass as an energy source could, however, only be achieved by the use of energy crops and the associated processing plants.

The two major ways of processing woody biomass from energy crops are bio-conversion by a fermentation process, and thermal conversion, usually by anaerobic heating. Table 7.4 shows the products which can be derived from these processing steps.

Bio-conversion processing has been known for thousands of years, and is used to produce those important solar products beer, wine and spirits. In the Brazilian bioalcohol programme a process similar to distilling spirits is used to ferment sugar cane and distil the ethanol; in the US grain is used for the same purpose. To ferment woody biomass, produced by coppicing energy plantations, its cell structure must first be broken down by hydrolysis, acids or enzymes to allow fermentation to proceed efficiently.

There are four basic thermal conversion processes. The oldest is direct combustion in air to produce heat. This can range from the domestic wood fire to large power stations fuelled by peat, coconut fibres and other waste products.

Pyrolysis is the process of heating biomass in the absence of air and, as it reduces wood to charcoal, it produces gaseous and liquid products which, in the traditional charcoal kilns, are

Process	End products		
Bio-conversion	Electricity		
	Methane	Ethanol	Fine chemicals
	Fuel gas	Methanol	Hydrocarbons
	Bio oil		Hydrocarbons
Thermal	Charcoal		
	Slurry		
	Combustion		

Table 7.4 *Products and services from biomass conversion*

vented into the air. In fact they are valuable products and in modern pyrolysis plant they are collected and used (see Figure 7.42).

The third thermal conversion process is the liquefaction of biomass to produce bio-oil which can be burnt to produce heat and power, or can be upgraded to petrol or diesel fuel. Rape seed oil, for instance, is becoming quite widely used as a transport fuel, either on its own or as an additive to diesel.

The fourth process is gasification, which produces either, or both, medium heating value (MHV) or low heating value (LHV) gas. Each has a different chemical make-up, but they can both be burnt in air to give heat and power or they can be used as chemical feedstock. MHV gas can be synthesized into methanol and LHV gas into ammonia, both of which are important in the chemical industry.

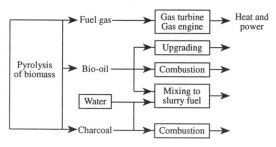

Figure 7.42 *The products and processes of pyrolysis*

Biomass programmes – experience and promise

Biomass programmes can be divided into three broad classes. There are those which are cost-effective on purely financial accounting grounds, there are those in the demonstration stage which can or could become cost-effective, and there are those which may never become cost-effective, but which bring such significant non-monetary benefits that they deserve of continuing support.

This last category is the most difficult to appraise. It includes many social forestry and agroforestry projects. If the cost/benefit analysis includes only commercial transactions then many projects seem quite unviable. However, their social and economic developmental benefits, though unquantifiable for accounting purposes, are extremely important, and often

provide justification for continuing and even expanding or replicating them.

The second category includes many programmes for the development and dissemination of improved cooking stoves, small biogas plants in many parts of the world and the production of fuels by gasification or briquetting. The viability of these schemes depends crucially on local conditions, in agriculture as well as in social and economic structures. Biomass energy or products have no general cost, only local costs determined by local conditions, and the cost/benefit analysis determined by outside agencies may be quite different from the costs and benefits perceived by local people. If these programmes are to be promoted by international agencies, an essential pre-condition for success is patience in working with and listening to local people so that the programme may be tailored to best meet their needs in their situation.

The first category, that of biomass projects judged on purely commercial grounds, is appropriate for Europe and other industrialized areas. Even so, it is not easy to produce definite cost-effectiveness judgements for them because there are so many 'spin-off' benefits. These lie in maintaining a vigorous rural economy and in improving the environment by replacing fossil fuels (whose price does not include the cost of environmental externalities) with biomass fuels.

The costs, in Sao Paulo in Brazil, of producing hydrous alcohol for mixing with petrol are shown in Table 7.5. The revenues are set at $0.18/litre and the residue (bagasse) from the process can be sold at the equivalent of $0.02/litre. The process is profitable on its operating costs, but makes a loss if the opportunity costs are included. The rate of return on investment, and hence the opportunity cost, depends on the financial circumstances of the time and changes with the economic climate. The price of alcohol is set in relation to the cost of petrol, which depends on the international price of oil, and the pricing policies of oil companies and the Brazilian government. The attractiveness of using sugar cane for alcohol rather than sugar production depends on the world price of sugar. However, if the large Brazilian producers were to switch from alcohol to sugar production there would be such a glut on the world market that prices would tumble.

It has been estimated that up to 10 GW

Item	Cost in $	
	Tonne	Litre
Total raw materials	5.832	
Cultivation	0.846	
Plant protection	1.400	
Collecting	1.771	
Transport	0.821	
Raw materials	4.837	
Distillation costs		0.125
Total direct costs	0.119	
Administrative costs	0.004	
Taxes and charges	0.003	
Opportunity costs		0.071
Break-even revenue requirement		0.196

The raw materials costs feed into the distillation costs. The opportunity costs relate to the return on investments.

Source: D Hall, 1992

Table 7.5 *Cost breakdown of production costs of hydrous alcohol in Sao Paulo, Brazil*

could be produced from the bagasse residues from alcohol production and there are proposals in Sao Paulo to use it as a solid fuel for power stations. This would transform the economics of the alcohol programme. Electricity could be produced at under $0.045 kWh and alcohol sold at $0.15/litre making it competitive even at $15/bbl for oil prices.

The biomass programme in the US is also very effective and biomass could be a major component of the US energy mix. Table 7.6 shows the energy which could be supplied annually on a commercial cost-effective basis if the target cost can be met.

It is clear that many of these potential resources are at, or close to, commercial viability. Technical developments, particularly those permitting increases in scale, are still needed but the major obstacles are structural and institutional. The exploitation of these resources requires the creation of new industries, and this takes time, even when the technical and economic conditions are favourable.

There is, however, the problem of agricultural prices. Between 1980 and 1987, maize varied from $1.41 per bushel to $3.16 per bushel. By-product prices can vary by a factor of three. These variations are caused by market

Feedstock	Biomass resource EJ/year	Cost ($/GJ) current	target
Residues	8.9		
Logging residues	0.8	> 3	< 2
Urban wood waste	1.2	2	2
Forest manufacturing residues	2.1	1	< 1
Agricultural residues	2.0	1–2	1
Municipal and food waste	2.4	2–3	< 1.5
Animal waste	0.5	4	3.5
Biomass from existing forests	9.5		
Commercial forest wood	4.5	< 2	< 2
Improved management	4.5		< 2
Shift 25% to energy forest	0.5	2	2
Biomass from energy crops	10.8		
Agricultural oil seeds	0.3	3	2
Wood energy crops	3.2	3	2
Herbaceous energy crops	5.9	4	2
Aquatic energy crops	1.4	3.5	2
Total	29.3		

1 EJ (10^8J) p a is equivalent to 32 GW continuous power.
Source: W Fulkerson et al, 1989

Table 7.6 *Net raw biomass resource in the USA, as estimated by Oak Ridge National Laboratory, before conversion to fluid fuels or electricity*

responses to world-wide supply and demand, and are thus very difficult either to control or to predict. There is thus a considerable risk that biomass industries will go through periods of unprofitable operation as world agricultural prices fluctuate, and they will need some assurance of stability through long term financing and/or guaranteed pricing.

There is a very active programme of research, development and demonstration of biomass technologies in the European Union. Contemporary European biomass resources are estimated at 455 Mt pa and could rise to 820 Mt pa in the future. The breakdown of these resources is shown in Table 7.7.

The research programme of the European

Resource	Production Mt p a (dry)	
	Now	Future
Wood	5	75
Other energy crops	–	250
Wood wastes	50	70
Agricultural wastes	250	250
Municipal wastes	60	75
Industrial/commercial wastes	90	100

Source: G Grassi, 1990

Table 7.7 *The annual production of biomass in Europe*

	Productivity dry T/ha p a		
	Present	Future	European region
Agricultural crops			
Sweet sorghum	25	35	South/Central
Miscanthus etc	20	30	South
Jerusalem artichoke	20	25	South/Central
Artichoke (tubes)	10	14	South/Central
Trees			
Eucalyptus	10/15	17	South
Poplar	12	16	North/West/Centre
Willow	10	15	North/West
Robinia	58		South
Conifers	5/6	8/10	North/West/Central

Source: G Grassi, 1990

Table 7.8 *Present and future biomass productivity in different regions of Europe*

Commission has identified a wide range of crops which could be suitable for energy cropping. These are shown in Table 7.8.

Of the species shown in Table 7.8 the front-runners for commercial energy cropping are sorghum for southern and central areas, eucalyptus for southern regions, and poplar and willow for northern Europe. The costs of these resources are expected to be about 27–30 ECU/dry tonne in production, which is low enough to ensure that the end products of the bio or thermal conversion processes are cost-competitive.

Biomass production for non-agricultural purposes could be an important part of the European Common Agricultural Policy (CAP). Unless alternative profitable non-food uses for land can be found, the CAP schemes for limiting agricultural production will mean that it is abandoned, with all the consequent social and environmental costs. About 20 million hectares of agricultural land and 10–20 million hectares of marginal land are likely to become available for biomass production by the end of the century, so using it to produce biomass could provide the employment needed to maintain rural economies. Bio-energy, in the next century, could equal the present output of the North Sea oil fields or all the nuclear power stations so far installed, and so could provide a significant fraction of the EU's demand for energy. It would also confer significant environmental benefits.

The distinctive characteristic of the European programme is its emphasis on an integrated approach to the use of biomass. The output is seen as a set of products, each of which contributes to the profitability of the enterprise, rather than focusing just on energy and treating others as by-products. The biomass industry can be targeted to meet needs in various sectors of industry, agriculture and energy in the different regions of Europe. The European programme has set target dates for demonstrating and commercializing the range of technologies needed for this integrated approach (see Table 7.9).

Biomass and the environment

Photosynthesis results in the absorption of carbon dioxide and the emission of oxygen, so the growth of plants counteracts the anthropogenic emissions of carbon dioxide from fossil fuels. The reduction in the area of high productivity plants in the tropical forests and grasslands is a cause for concern in its effect on the natural carbon cycle. The planting of trees is often regarded as a means of counteracting the increasing atmospheric concentrations of carbon dioxide. During their growth, the trees do absorb carbon dioxide, but this is re-emitted, possibly accompanied by methane, when they die and decay.

Demonstration	Year	Commercialization	Year
Short rotation forestry	1994	Advanced combustion	
Advanced combustion		for power	1996
for power	1995	Compost	1998
Advanced pyrolysis	1995	Advanced pyrolysis	1998
Pulp for paper from		Short rotation forestry	2000
sweet sorghum	1995	Sweet sorghum production	2000
Compost	1996	Ethanol for fuel	2000
Sweet sorghum production	1996	Advanced gasification	2003
Char-slurry fired		Methanol synthesis	2003
boilers, kilns etc	1997	Hydrocarbon synthesis	2005
Gas turbine fired by		Hydrogen and ammonia	
bio-oils or char-slurry	1997	production	2010
Advanced gasification	1998		
Hydrocarbon synthesis	2000		

Source: G Grassi, 1990

Table 7.9 *Target dates for completion of demonstration and commercialization of biomass technologies for Europe*

David Hall has argued powerfully (see Table 7.10) that the sustainable application of biomass within the commercial energy sector requires the substitution of biofuels for fossil fuels and has presented a scenario for the reduction in global CO_2 emissions which might be achieved by this substitution.

It is clear that biomass could offset much of the human-made emissions of CO_2 and play a very significant role in stabilizing the global climate while allowing the increase in energy use which is essential if the people of the developing nations are to have good quality of life.

The substitution of fossil fuels by biomass energy sources has a number of environmental advantages other than reducing CO_2. Biomass contains little or no sulphur, so the acid emissions of sulphur compounds is avoided. The production of nitrogen oxides can also be reduced considerably. Burning biomass as, for instance, on a garden bonfire can produce large quantities of noxious chemicals, some of which are carcinogenic, but if burning is properly controlled, in a furnace with flue gas cleaning, the overall acid emissions can be very small. The more advanced processing of raw biomass can be designed to emit very little into air, water or land.

A biomass industry would significantly benefit the rural environment. It produces compost and that, together with the improvred agronomic

practices, would help condition and stabilize the soil, and avoid the desertification and forest fires beginning to occur in Southern Europe.

Social and political benefits would also accrue from the widespread use of biomass. The creation of profitable and sustainable rural employment would reduce the drift to urban

Year	Technology	Reduction Gtc pa a
2025	Electricity and alcohol from	
	sugar cane	0.7
	Electricity from kraft pulp	
	industry residues	0.2
	Energy from other sources	0.8
	Total reduction by 2025	1.7
	Electricity and alcohol from	
	sugar cane	0.7
2050	Electricity from kraft pulp	
	industry residues	0.2
	Energy from other residues	0.9
	Energy from biomass	
	energy crops	3.6
	Total reduction by 2050	5.4

Source: D Hall, 1991

Table 7.10 *Scenario for the reduction in anthropogenic carbon dioxide emissions by the substitution of fossil fuels by bio-energy sources*

areas and to maintain the vitality of rural communities. Biomass can be produced and used locally in most parts of the world, avoiding the concentration of supply which characterizes fossil fuels. The promotion of local self-sufficiency and the geographical diversity of supply for trade will contribute to a more stable world – political environment to the benefit of all countries, but particularly to the Third World.

SOLAR HEATING

When an object absorbs sunlight it gets hot. This heat energy is usable in various ways, to provide space heating or cooling, to provide domestic or industrial hot water, to boil water or other fluids for industrial processes, or to drive engines. The solar heating or cooling of housing or working spaces can be accomplished without any machines or moving parts, but simply by the appropriate design of the buildings. Such buildings first appeared in Greece over 2000 years ago, and were common throughout the last millennium in Islamic architecture. The advent of cheap and abundant fossil fuels led to the abandonment of these traditions, but they are now being re-established on a firm scientific basis and termed passive solar technologies.

Passive solar heating

All rooms with a window facing the sun are heated when the sunlight shines in. These unplanned solar gains contribute between 10–20 per cent of the annual space heating of a typical house in the UK. Some houses have conservatories or greenhouses which are designed to make use of solar heating, and there is a growing number of houses and other buildings which are designed to minimize the total energy needed for space heating and to maximize the contribution which solar energy can make.

When the temperature inside a building is higher than that outside, heat can be lost by conduction, convection and radiation. Conduction of heat depends on temperature gradients across, and the thermal conductivity of, a given material. For a given difference, ΔT, between inside and outside temperatures the thicker the materials, for example the house walls, the lower the

Material	k
	$(Wm^{-1}K^{-1})$
Aluminium	211
Glass	1.05
Brick	0.6
Pine	0.14
Mineral wool	0.035
Polyurethane rigid form	0.025
Still air	0.026

Table 7.11 *Thermal conductivities of some common building materials*

temperature gradient and hence the lower the heat losses. Also, the lower the thermal conductivity, k, of the material, the lower the conduction. In general, the rate of energy loss through a wall of area, A, and thickness, L, is

$$P = kA\Delta T/L = UA\Delta T,$$

where U is the thermal conductance (the 'U value') of the construction. The thermal conductivities of some common building materials are shown in Table 7.11.

A window pane of 3 mm glass has a U-value of 350. A 5 cm thick layer of still air between two sheets of glass reduces this to 0.52, showing the benefits of double glazing. A brick wall 10 cm thick would have a U-value of 6, and two such walls a U-value of 3. The cavity between the walls is wide enough to allow convection currents in the air, so heat is transported readily from the inner to the outer wall. If the cavity (say 10 cm wide) is filled with polyurethane foam, the U-value of the wall is reduced to 0.25. The U-value of a typical plastered plaster board ceiling is around 20. Laying 10 cm of mineral wool over the ceiling reduces the U-value to around 0.35. A well designed and well insulated house would have an overall U-value of around 0.2 to 0.3 $Wm^{-2}K^{-1}$.

Hot air rises while cold air sinks, thus producing convection currents. These are very efficient at transporting heat and are the main mechanism by which outside walls lose heat. Inside older houses, convection currents are called draughts and result in substantial heat loss.

As we remarked in the section on solar radiation, all objects radiate energy. The rate at which they do it and the wavelength of the radiation depends on the temperature of the object.

The sun radiates mainly in the visible spectrum, while any surface at room temperature radiates in the infrared at a wavelength of around 10 μm.

Rooms with large windows present a large area through which infrared radiation from the room can escape. On sunny days a south-facing window gains more energy from the sunlight than it loses through the infrared radiation from the surfaces in the room, and the larger the window the warmer the room. If the sun is not shining, however, the larger the window the more infrared radiation escapes and the cooler the room. At night this effect can be mitigated by drawing curtains or blinds, but this is not sensible during the day. The solution is to use windows which transmit visible radiation but reflect infrared radiation back into the room. Glass itself reflects infrared more than visible light, but it is possible to enhance this effect considerably by special coatings on the glass. This then minimizes the loss of heat by infrared radiation while allowing the use of large south-facing windows to maximize the solar gain. In hot countries, other coatings can reflect much of the solar radiation while transmitting most of the infrared and so minimize the cooling needed to keep the room at a comfortable temperature.

From all this we can define the main requirements for a passive solar building. The south-facing glazed area should be large, to maximize solar gain, while the north-facing glazed area should be small to minimize radiation losses, and the construction should have a low overall U-value. To avoid claustrophobia in the rooms on the north side of the building, the windows should be tall but narrow, so that the sky and ground are both visible, while keeping the window area small. The simplest type of passive solar building is shown in outline in Figure 7.43 and such structures are said to provide 'direct solar gain'.

Additional solar gain can be provided in the morning by east-facing windows but west windows may need to be shaded to avoid unwanted solar gain on late summer afternoons. Excessive heating can be prevented by designing the roof structures which overhang the windows to provide shade against the high summer sun, while admitting the low winter sun. Alternatively, a plantation of deciduous trees in front of the south facade would provide considerable shading in the summer but little in winter when the leaves have been shed.

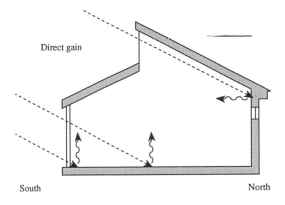

Figure 7.43 *Passive solar gain*

The solar collection area can be expanded to the entire south facade if 'indirect solar gain' techniques are used. The most common of these is a conservatory on the south wall with a means of circulating the warm air throughout the house (see Figure 7.44). A more effective, but expensive method is to glaze all or much of the south facing wall (see Figure 7.45). A black wall absorbs the sunlight, and the air between the glazing and the wall rises as it is warmed and is distributed throughout the building. This type of structure was developed by Felix Trombe in the 1950s and is often called a 'Trombe Wall'. A recent development of Trombe Walls has been to use transparent insulation as the glazing, to reduce the heat otherwise lost by conduction and radiation.

Transparent insulation was first noticed in the coats of polar bears. Each strand of fur acts like an optical fibre, transmitting sunlight to their skin. Plastic fibres laid side by side can be glued together into sheets or other shapes. Light is transmitted down the fibres, so the sheet is transparent, but if the fibres are, say, 20 cm long, the

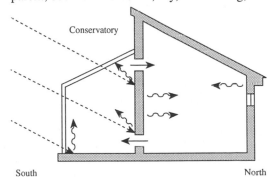
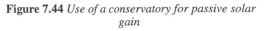

Figure 7.44 *Use of a conservatory for passive solar gain*

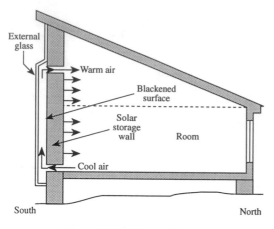

External glass

Warm air

Blackened surface

Solar storage wall

Room

Cool air

South

North

Figure 7.45 *Solar wall system*

U-value of the sheet would be about 0.5 or so. The great advantage of transparent insulation is that it can be made in standard, self-supporting shapes, like bricks, from which walls can be built.

The economics of passive solar buildings are attractive. The additional cost of passive solar and thermal insulation over and above that of a conventional new building is usually no more than 5–10 per cent. The monthly payments of mortgages plus energy costs are usually less for a passive solar building than for a similar conventional building, because the savings in energy costs are larger than the additional mortgage repayment. This fact has not yet got through to builders or mortgage lenders to the domestic market, but many commercial buildings incorporate atria and other passive solar features for the benefits that they bring to space heating and day lighting.

Passive solar cooling

Buildings can be designed so that the heat of the sun induces convection currents which draw cool air into the building and so reduce the inside temperature. Islamic architecture has used this principle for centuries and many of its buildings have a 'chimney' which draws up hot air and brings air into the building past north-facing surfaces which remain cool throughout the day. A modern variant of this uses a Trombe Wall to create the air movement. Instead of being circulated in the building, the hot air is vented to the atmosphere while the incoming air is cooled by underground, or north-facing, heavy masonry surfaces.

Active solar heating

Sunshine can be used to raise the temperature of some working fluid and the increases can vary from a few degrees to over 2000°C, depending on the type of system used.

Low temperature water heaters

If water is run through a black hose-pipe exposed to sunlight it will come out warmer than it went in. If it is filled with water and both ends are sealed, and it is then coiled flat, the water will heat up on a hot sunny day, to as much as 60°C. The water temperature will rise until the rate at which the hose loses heat to its surroundings is equal to the rate at which it gains heat from the sun. This equilibrium (also called the stagnation temperature) depends on the rate of heat loss as well as the rate of heat gain.

The rate of heat gain depends on the intensity of the sunlight and the efficiency with which it is absorbed by the surface of the hose-pipe. The rate of heat loss depends on the conduction, convection and radiation of energy from the surface of the hose. If water is flowing through the hose, the useful energy is carried away by the heated water (eg to heat a swimming pool). This useful energy is delivered at a rate equal to the difference between the rate of energy input from the sun and the rate of energy loss to the surroundings.

The rate of energy input from the sun depends on the intensity of solar radiation $I(Wm^{-2})$, the absorbance capacity (α) of the surface of the hose and a factor F (between 0 and 1), which takes account of any other influence on absorption of sunlight, such as reflections, surface roughness and surface geometry.

The rate of energy loss to the surroundings depends mainly on conduction at low water temperatures, and so varies with the difference between water temperature T_w and ambient temperature T_a. It can be written as $U(T_w - T_a)$, where U is the 'U-value' of the solar collector system.

The rate of delivery of useful energy Q (Watts) can then be written

$$Q = \alpha FI - U (T_w - T_a).$$

This is known as the Hotel-Whillier-Bliss equation, after the three people who first derived the equation and used it to study the performance of solar heat collectors.

The efficiency of a collector is the ratio of useful heat delivered to the incident solar radiation, ie Q/I, so the efficiency

$$\eta_c = \alpha F - U/I\ (T_w - T_a).$$

To produce collectors with the highest efficiency, we should increase the absorption efficiency αF, reduce the heat loss factors and operate at the highest solar intensity. Figure 7.46 shows a plot of collector efficiency against $(T_w - T_a)/I$, for different types of collectors. If the U-value of the collector was independent of temperature, the relationships would be straight lines. In fact at higher temperatures, radiation begins to play a larger role in heat loss and the efficiency falls off more rapidly. The standard solar water heater consists of a flat metal plate with a black upper surface and pipes, in good thermal contact, attached to the back. The black surface is exposed to the sunlight and so is heated. Water flowing through the pipes is warmed by heat conducted from the plate to the pipes. A great deal of heat would be lost if the plate and the pipes were exposed to winds or convection currents, so they are enclosed in a well-insulated box, with a glass or plastic front cover. For the highest efficiency, the front may be double glazed, although this adds to the cost.

The upper surface of the plate is coated with a black paint or other coating which absorbs sunlight efficiently. Most black surfaces are good absorbers of visible light and also efficient radiators of infrared. They therefore radiate heat through the glass front. Selective surfaces are good absorbers of sunlight but poor radiators of infrared and so reduce the radiation heat losses by factors of five or more. Such surfaces give rather higher efficiencies at low temperature, but, more importantly, they maintain efficiency up to much higher temperatures, as shown in curve c of Figure 7.46.

The evacuated tube collector has the lowest heat loss of any of these devices. It consists of a glass tube, sealed at both ends and evacuated of all air, with a heat collector tube running down the middle. The bottom half of the outer tube is silvered on the inside, so sunlight is focused on to the inner collector tube. The collector tube may be hollow, with water flowing through it, or it may be a heat pipe (a device which transmits heat very efficiently along its length). Since there is no air between the collector tube and the

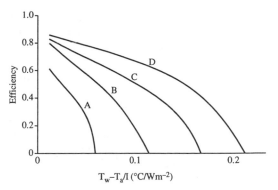

A Simple unshielded collector such as black hose-pipe.
B Standard flat-plate solar water heater.
C Highly insulated flat-plate collector with selective surface.
D Evacuated tube collector with selective surface.

Figure 7.46 *Efficiency curves for solar water heaters*

outer tube, there can be no convection or conduction loss, except at the ends where the collector tube passes through the seals. Radiation losses are reduced by using selective black surfaces on the collector tube.

A solar collector will consist of 10 to 20 of those evacuated tubes side by side in a rectangular box, having a common water inlet and outlet. Although they are more expensive than the standard flat-plate collector they are much more efficient at higher temperatures and can easily produce low pressure steam in high solar intensities, and produce very hot water even in winter sunshine in the UK.

In use the solar collector must be plumbed in to a building's water supply and heating system. The fluid in the solar collector is a mixture of water and anti-freeze, so it must be kept separate from the domestic water supply. When the fluid in the solar collector is hotter than the water in the pre-heat tank, the circulating pump is switched on. The hot fluid from the collector is sent through the heat exchanger to heat the water in the pre-heat tank, from where it is either used directly or stored in the hot water tank.

If very large areas of collector are required, it can be more cost-effective in some circumstances to use a solar pond. Any area of shallow water exposed to sunlight is heated by the solar energy absorbed by the water and the bed of the pond. Much of this heat is lost in normal ponds by convection currents which bring the hot water to the surface, where it loses heat to the atmosphere. The density of the water may be increased by adding salt. The concentration of salt is made to be higher at the bottom of the pond, and decreased gradually toward the surface. Even if the water at the bottom of the pond is hotter than at the surface, it remains more dense because it has more salt dissolved in it. In this way convection currents are suppressed. In these ponds the bottom layer of brine can become quite hot, and the upper layers of water act as a good insulator, making an efficient solar collector. The concentrated brine can be pumped through a heat exchanger to heat water or other fluids which are then often used to drive a turbine and generate electricity.

Concentrating solar collectors

If higher temperatures are required than can be achieved by flat-plate collectors, then sunlight can be concentrated by mirrors or lenses. For low concentration ratios, mirrors in the shape of a long trough whose sides form compound parabolas can be used to collect sunlight wherever the sun is in the sky without having to move the mirrors. The troughs are oriented east–west (see Figure 7.47),

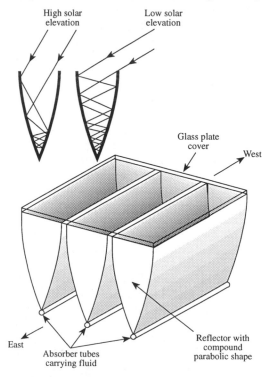

Figure 7.47 *Compound parabolic reflector concentrating sunlight*

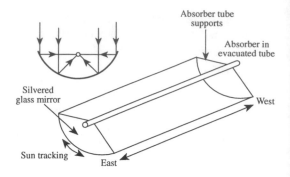

Figure 7.48 *Tracking parabolic reflector*

so that the sunlight enters the mirrors throughout the day. The mirrors can collect sunlight from both high and low solar elevations, ie in both summer and winter (see Figure 7.47). The shape of these compound parabolic reflectors is quite complex and not so easy to manufacture. Furthermore, although the mirrors accept sunlight at low solar elevations, the energy density of the solar irradiance is reduced in proportion to the cosine of the angle of the sun.

The large commercial systems use one-axis tracking of long parabolic trough-shaped mirrors (see Figure 7.48). The absorber is usually a metal tube with a 'super black' surface coating enclosed in an evacuated glass tube. The working fluid is usually an oil with good chemical stability at high temperatures. The largest of such systems is in California where the collected energy is used to drive turbine generators to supply electricity. A total of 350 MW is installed, making this the largest solar electricity generating utility in the world.

Power towers

Very high temperatures can be reached in solar furnaces, where square kilometres of mirrors are controlled to reflect sunlight on to a single absorber mounted high up on a tower – the 'power tower'. The mirrors, each around 10 m^2 in area, are mounted on a two-axis tracking system and each is controlled by computer to reflect and focus an image of the sun on to an absorber. There may be hundreds of such mirrors all focusing the sunlight on to one absorber, which can reach very high temperatures. The heat is carried away by a fluid, often a liquid metal and used to raise steam to generate electricity. These systems are extremely impressive, both technically and visually, but have not yet proved to be cost-effective.

8

ENERGY FUTURES

This study of the technical, socio-economic and environmental impacts of energy supply and demand, in both developed and developing countries, provides us with an invaluable framework within which to analyse the dynamics of present and future energy provision in all sectors of society. In particular, it deals broadly with the issues surrounding two major aspects of energy planning 'continuity' and 'change'. The former represents the continued use of present day conventional energy supplies while the latter is delivered through continued research and development into new, more efficient and environmentally benign energy resources. By articulating these oppositional concepts we can arrive at a viable technical and social understanding of the value to society of present and future energy scenarios.

Over the last 40 years, global energy use has been increasing rapidly and studies of projected trends show a large expected increase in future energy demand. In particular observed correlations between a rise in gross national product (GNP) and per capita energy use show that an increase in energy consumption is considered a prerequisite to the future progress of developing countries.

At present a number of debates have called attention to the requirement for developing countries to adopt policies and planning initiatives capable of delivering a sustainable energy future, rather than following the route taken by developed countries that has affected global environmental security.

In the preparatory sessions preceding the UN Conference on Environment and Development in June 1992, developing countries repeatedly called for an affordable and equitable transfer of environmentally benign technology that would aid economic development in line with current environmental considerations. The Global Energy Efficiency Initiative, being developed by the Economic Commission for Europe, hopes to provide developing countries with the platform from which to undertake energy efficiency reforms. In addition, the new Global Environmental Facility (GEF) established by the World Bank, UN Environment Programme (UNEP) and the UN Development Programme (UNDP) has funds of $1.3 billion, in part to facilitate the partial transfer of institutional training and equipment to develop least cost planning practices and efficient energy technologies (World Bank, 1991).

One of the most feasible energy reforms is likely to be the result of international pressure to reduce greenhouse gases (GHGs). The most important of these initiatives was the signing by 36 governments of UNCED'S Convention on Climate change. This convention, although still not internationally ratified, aims to achieve the stabilization of greenhouse gas concentrations at a level that would prevent the need for dangerous human interference. However, while this agreement is vital to long term global climatic security, a number of major shortcomings have yet to be overcome. In particular there has been a failure to do the following.

- Properly identify the 'causes' for excessive emissions and pollutants. In particular the convention, as signed under Agenda 21, appears preoccupied with acknowledging climatic 'effects'.
- Fully encourage energy efficient industries and transport policies in the developed and newly industrializing countries.
- Open up debate concerning the excessive per capita energy consumption of the developed north compared to those in low or middle income countries.
- Include other affiliated causes such as poverty as part determinant of environmental degradation.
- Identify the ownership of energy resources and technology and their inability to provide global distribution.
- To provide a practical framework within which the poor can achieve energy security without being further marginalized.

(Source: extracted from Middleton, O'Keefe and Moyo, 1993)

This example demonstrates the need for reform to embrace the problems confronting contemporary modes of energy production, consumption, distribution and their effects. The requirement is for a framework that has vision, content and commitment to sustainable energy futures, while not disregarding present day energy requirements. This is important because in order that short term energy requirements are fulfilled the 'continuity' of contemporary energy resources is vital. However, when these methods of energy production affect environmental and social security, a radical 'change' is required. This chapter is concerned with the outlining of different energy scenarios and their value to the socio-environment, while simultaneously addressing the practical, technical and political obstructions to achieving energy sustainability.

CONSUMPTION SCENARIOS

In order to assess the potential of future energy production it is vital to outline expected levels of energy demand. This is where the debate on future world energy trends becomes very tangled. The traditional response from energy planners has been to work under a number of scenarios usually termed 'high' and 'moderate' forecasts. These aim initially at determining levels of demand. However, it is equally important to incorporate future supply scenarios, trends in marginal production costs and possible geopolitical constraints. A number of scenarios have been generated from the thirteenth and fourteenth World Energy Conferences (WEC).

Those presented in Table 8.1 are composite projections from the two conferences and provide estimates of total energy demand between 1980–2050. The high scenario assumes a nominal increase in per capita energy consumption of +23 per cent between 1980 and 2050. This is an average annual increase of +0.3 per cent. The modest scenario assumes an equally modest decrease of –16 per cent between 1980 and 2050, which corresponds to an annual decrease of –9.25 per cent (P H Bourrelier et al, 1992).

There are many additional future forecasts (see J B Goldemberg et al *Energy for a Sustainable World*), although they are often contextualized within present conventional energy scenarios and take little account of possible future events such as changes in the geopolitical arena or the development of new technology. They forecast directly from historically documented trends and therefore propose scenarios that are in part a continuity of their own tradition. A reflexive forecasting project, one that offers a variety of potential directions, working towards the desired energy scenario rather than extending the present one can be implemented.

	1980	2010		2050	
		'High' Scenario (I)	'Moderate' Scenario (II)	'High' Scenario (I)	'Moderate' Scenario (II)
Population (10^9)					
Industrialized countries	0.84		1.01		1.14
Eastern Europe	0.38		0.47		0.52
Third World/rapid development	0.92		1.66		2.40
Third World/transition	2.35		3.84		5.28
World	4.45		6.98		9.34
Energy consumption by zone (Gtoe)					
Industrialized countries	4.01	6.08	4.93	7.68	6.25
Eastern Europe	1.58	2.62	2.04	3.74	2.73
Third World/rapid development	0.88	2.55	1.50	4.68	2.24
Third World/transition	1.08	1.87	1.43	3.31	2.11
World	7.54	13.12	9.90	19.41	13.33
Energy consumption by zone/per capita (toe)					
Industrialized countries	4.78	6.02	4.88	6.74	5.48
Eastern Europe	4.17	5.57	4.39	7.19	5.25
Third World/rapid development	0.95	1.54	0.91	1.95	0.93
Third World/transition	0.46	0.49	0.37	0.63	0.40
World	1.69	1.88	1.42	2.08	1.42
Consumption of renewable energies (Gtoe)	1.15	2.00	1.75	3.00	2.20
Demand for mineral energies (Gtoe)	6.39	11.12	8.15	16.41	11.10

Source: P H Bourrelier et al, 1986

Table 8.1 *World energy demand 1980–2050*

DIFFERENT ENERGY SCENARIOS

Nuclear

It has been over 50 years since the first controlled release of nuclear energy. Since then nuclear power has achieved, and sustained a high political and economic significance to both the north and, increasingly, the south. The early rise in popularity was largely due to political and military interest, however, in recent years the debate has centred on the possibility of using it to generate large amounts of 'cheap' electricity. After two decades of rapid growth in installed capacity, the falling demand for reactors, and the failure of the fast reactor programme, has meant that recent technological development in unlocking the energy potential

of ^{238}U may never be fully realized. This failure can be attributed in part to public opposition and the gradual rise of renewable energy technologies. However, the recent demand for energy technologies that do not contribute to global warming may mean that nuclear power, particularly if safe waste disposal can be achieved, has found a vital lifeline. The twenty-first century will undoubtedly be a critical period for the future of nuclear future.

In 1972, the Atomic Energy Commission estimated that by the year 2000 between 825 and 1500 GWe of installed nuclear capacity would be delivered. This was quite clearly wrong and demonstrates the futility in making predictions on present rates of uptake. The debates over energy futures consider the nature of a desired fuel mix that meets the necessary energy demand, provides cheap and efficient energy, satisfies the requirement of end users, promotes national self-reliance, and is compatible with energy strategies and other global problems.

In the next three or four decades it is anticipated that international nuclear capacity will increase, marginally, from 329 Gwe in 1990 to somewhere between 450 and 500 Gwe by 2030–40. It is not tenable to talk of a theoretical upper limit because a range of other questions still need answers. They are to do with an assessment of total uranium deposits and of a satisfactory conclusion to the nuclear fuel cycle. At present all nuclear waste is stored, awaiting 'eventual disposal'.

Nuclear energy has often been heralded as 'cheap' and reliable, but this is only so if we exclude the external costs of production and the costs of its initial development for military purposes. The conventional wisdom – that the cost of nuclear power is concentrated at the beginning of project development – is no longer valid. In particular, the environmental externalities are likely to be of considerable importance to future generations. The reliability of nuclear fuel generation is also in question after the accidents at Three Mile Island and Chernobyl.

At present, nuclear energy is the preserve of the industrialized nations, of which, in 1990, eight accounted for over 85 per cent of production. This situation is unlikely to change dramatically, largely because nuclear fuel generation is inevitably related to the production of plutonium, which can be used in the production of nuclear weapons. Most long term predictions point to a stable nuclear generating capacity in the short to medium term, with a potential decline as renewable sources of energy become more competitive.

Solar energy

In no other technology is the present gap between the potential and the actual supply of primary energy so large. It has been estimated that the continuous supply of solar energy to the earth is about 100,000 TW. This, if collected over the land surface of the earth for just two hours, would fulfil world primary energy demand for a year.

Insolation levels are estimated to be between two and four orders of magnitude above the demand for primary energy through-

out the world. This means that solar conversion technologies could contribute a plentiful supply of primary energy. However, a number of unresolved problems in the storage and instant release of this energy still remain to be solved. The two basic technologies behind collecting this power through direct solar gain are solar thermal systems and solar photovoltaics.

Even though recent technological advances make solar energy more competitive with conventional technologies, solar energy systems at present fulfil less than 0.001 per cent of world energy consumption. The possibility of collecting direct solar power is still tremendously appealing and the take-up of stand-alone units, solar pumps, lighting kits etc is expanding rapidly with about 200,000 in use around the world. These systems provide a means of bringing the benefits of electricity to the rural areas of the developing countries. However, in spite of a number of successes, solar photovolaics has failed to fulfil the expectations of its proponents and spontaneous take-up has not been exceptional.

There is no doubt that direct solar energy could, in theory, provide all future energy requirements, so long as present socio-economic and technological limitations are addressed. Solar thermal and PV stations are at present more expensive than conventional central power stations by a factor of between 4 and 30. Combined plants are known as 'solar-fossil hybrid' plants and could be attractive close to load centres. Perhaps the main limitation on the potential uptake of solar installations is the problem of matching peak energy demand with peak energy supply. At the moment peak demand in the UK is early morning and evening but the maximum supply is at noon (good weather permitting). It is also difficult to supply solar energy to certain end-users. For example, space heating by passive solar gain seems attractive, but solar power is at present of little use to public or private transport sectors or to heavy industries where 'hard' electricity is required. Solar energy technology will be most successful as part of a mixed fuel economy where its application can promote communal self-reliance. The benefits to the environment of solar technology are great, particularly in reducing CO_2 levels, however renewable energy conversion is still not a CO_2 free process as the production materials required for solar plants still involve emissions. However, despite a number of technical problems in the delivery of suitable end-use energy, the incorporation of solar power into suitable mixed fuel economies looks promising.

BIOMASS

Biomass energy is of considerable global significance and may be split into three distinct resource groups. It can be used as solid fuel in the form of wood, charcoal, forestry and crop residues, agroindustrial and municipal wastes. Then a range of liquid fuels such as ethanol, methanol and vegetable oils can be derived from biomass. The third group is biogas which is particularly common in China and India, although production plants have now been developed in California and Europe. Biogas is formed by the anaerobic respiration of biomass digesters.

Biomass currently provides about 14 per cent of the world's energy, approximately 25 million barrels of oil equivalent per day. It represents about 35 per cent of energy requirements in developing countries and, therefore, is of considerable importance to about three-quarters of the world. Estimates show that by 2050 up to 90 per cent of the world's population will live in developing countries and so one important question must be asked. If biomass energy is, and will remain, a critical resource for most of the world's population, which strategy best suits sustainable land use practice? In order to tackle this question we will use a number of case studies that will demonstrate the need for energy planning that co-ordinates socio-cultural traditions as well as technical and economic appraisals.

Different forms of biomass production deliver a variety of end-use products that should ideally be suited to the needs of specific groups of people. These different end-uses can best be delivered by changes in development strategy. We may see this in the principal differences between 'traditional' and 'social' forestry – techniques which may be thought of as competing paradigms in resource management. We may summarize their principal characteristics thus:

Traditional forestry

- High level of training and knowledge.
- Techniques for rural forestry development are same as for standard plantation forestry, eg tree nurseries, planting methods, spacing etc.
- Belief in quantities of seeds distributed rather than seed suitability.
- Strategy for rural development is to extend and decentralize existing organization and infrastructure.
- Trees seen as independent component of rural area rather than part of the fabric.

Social forestry

- Social foresters accept they know little about priorities and needs of local people, and that their knowledge is not necessarily useful on farms.
- They argue that techniques should reflect socio-cultural traditions by including small scale, multi-purpose species based on rural development practice.
- The satisfaction of end-use requirements rather than the number of seedlings is an indication of project's success.
- Active involvement of foresters and people in social forestry programmes is better than free seedling distribution.
- Accepts that trees are an integral part of land use system both in ecological and economic terms.

(Source: Gelder and O'Keefe, 1992)

By allowing the integration of cultural traditions into forestry objectives, 'social' forestry produces a land management strategy that best reflects the end-use requirements of indigenous populations. The value of woody biomass to society lies in a number of other uses for it as well as producing energy, for example, food, fodder, medicines, construction, domestic utensils, fencing, ecological protection and so on. Traditional forestry projects have not been tremendously successful in developing countries precisely because they are aimed at the uniform production of timber which means that their development programmes operate tangentially to the demands of society.

In India, a number of biogas projects have been established although they vary in their efficiency and their ability to achieve their end-use aims. There seems to be a considerable problem in enlisting support from all beneficiaries. The

Centre for Application of Science and Technology to Rural Areas (ASTRA) in Bangalore provided assistance for a biogas project in Pura village, some 200 miles west of the centre. The village has a population of 430 people with approximately half that number of cattle. The original aim was to provide enough gas for the villagers' cooking and basic lighting. However, the project faltered at first as quantities of dung differed from day to day – the result of changing human participation rather than of supply. Different households had different needs and so ASTRA finally decided to utilize biogas energy to pump water from the reservoir into six taps on the street. Each household was given a dung quota to fulfil and a roster, which increased public pressure to co-operate, was displayed in public (D O Hall et al, 1992). This example of biogas production serves to articulate the problems inherent in developing 'bottom up' energy strategies. This is particularly so where total community support is fundamental to success. However, many biomass projects are far more centralized affairs and so avoid this difficulty.

Although bioenergy is largely a southern phenomenon, various projects in developed countries now derive sizable amounts of energy from biomass. At present the US has 9000 MW of biomass electric plants and Sweden derives 14 per cent of its energy from biomass (F Rosillo-Calle, 1990)

Well-planned biomass projects can supply ample amounts of useful energy for a number of end-uses. However, one obstacle blocking the way to the wider acceptance of biomass as a source of liquid fuel, gas, heat source or electricity is the issue of land-use. There are large untapped forest and agricultural reserves where sustainable land-use projects, incorporating social forestry, could provide energy to meet indigenous demand. Nevertheless, the development of biomass resources on a sustainable level will require consistent effort and local co-operation, which makes implementation considerably harder than for centralized energy resources. The potential energy production from biomass is promising. For example, by combining the sugar cane and wood pulp industries, it is estimated that in excess of 500 TWh/yr of power could be generated. In addition to this, a further estimate suggests that the mobilization of one-third of the world's biomass could meet 10 per cent of the annual global energy demand. The environmental benefits of encouraging biomass production are also apparent at a time when atmospheric CO_2 levels need to be stabilized. However, despite these ideal scenarios, there are still economic, social, institutional and technical barriers to increasing biomass derived energy, and much research remains to be done.

MIXED ENERGY ECONOMIES

The mixed energy economy incorporates all energy technologies discussed in this book. However, 'mixed' covers a range of things in which the individual contributions of energy technologies may not be considered. It is possible, for example, to imagine a 'solar age' in which small contributions from wind, hydro and geothermal power form part of a renewable energy economy. It is equally possible to envisage a true 'nuclear age', given the adequate closure of the nuclear fuel cycle by advanced disposal and reprocessing techniques, in which renewables make only small contributions. Given the number of possible mixed energy scenarios, we must consider the effect of incentives proposed on a basis for them in Agenda 21.

The, as yet, unratified Convention on Climate, provides one of the sharpest indicators of the way that international energy policy will influence future fuel mixes. The demand that GHG emissions be stabilized by 'the end of the present decade' will create a political and economic climate in which conventional energy technologies begin to accrue their external costs. This will favour the long term development of renewables because, compared to the real costs of conventional fuels, they will become more competitive. A number of CO_2 scenarios have been offered by Krause using data from the International Institute of Applied Systems Analysis (IIASA). The first example assumes a 'best case' where GHG emissions will be insignificant by the year 2100. The second assumes a change in CO_2 emissions somewhere between the best and worst case. Krause reflects that even to achieve this small decrease in CO_2 production to these levels will require international industrial and social agreements and commitments far beyond anything proposed at present (Krause et al, 1993).

Given these scenarios, if transfers in technology from North to South are to happen, then mixed energy economies consisting of biogas, geothermal, biomass, solar, wind, nuclear power, natural gas fired heat pumps and fuel cells, methanol and ethanol along with policies for end-use conservation should be the objectives for a sustainable energy future.

PHOTOVOLTAICS

Mali Aqua Viva (an NGO) was founded in 1974 and worked primarily in the San zone of Central Mali in Africa. Its objective was to increase the amount of water available for domestic and/or agripastoral needs. By 1977 the project was running photovoltaic water pumps which had doubled the amount of available water. Its success prompted the Malian government to set up, in 1980, a project on a larger scale. A number of bilateral, multilateral, NGO and private companies financed it, and, to date, 250 photovoltaic water pumps totalling 300 kW$_p$ are in operation. However, while in many ways the project has been very successful, the main drawback to the widespread uptake of photovoltaics in Mali was the cost of installing the pumping systems. In 1987, the installation of a solar water pumping system of 1400 W$_p$ was between $35,000 and $40,000 (Y Sokona, 1992). Capital investment of this order is a major disincentive to villagers in developing countries and the need for additional national or international funding means that photovoltaic projects of this kind have been very scarce.

The largest array of thin film PVs is at Davis in California. The installation was undertaken in 1992 by Advanced Photovoltaic Systems (APS). This project incorporates 9600 PV modules and now supplies 479 kW to the grid. The modules are made from amorphous silicon deposited on a substrate of glass titanium oxide. Larger projects like this benefit from economies of scale as well as from their added attraction to investors. California also has a climate suitable for large solar array developments, thus making it economically more attractive than more boreal climates. The economic costs of production are improving. For example, in 1980, solar PVs were costed at 100–400 cents/kWh, by 1990 they were 30–100 cents/kWh and were forecasted to reduce to 4–6 cents/kWh by 2030. The primary socio-environmental impacts of PVs are land-use, and the use of solvents and other toxic materials during the manufacture of the cells.

ETHANOL

Over the last 12 years the production of ethanol has increased rapidly and in 1989 an estimated 20 billion litres was produced globally. Both large and small scale production is presently undertaken in Brazil, Zimbabwe and the US. In the US, fuel ethanol production capacity is 4.6 billion litres and there are plans to increase this by another 50 per cent. As we pointed out in Chapter 7, the US market price for maize and by-products has varied considerably, fuelling debates about the cost of US ethanol production. Apart from the price variations of maize, there are further differences between producers in the cost of ethanol, so the price varies from $0.19/litre to $0.38/litre. According to Hall, ethanol is 'cost competitive as a fuel blending agent with existing Federal excise tax exemption, with maize costs of $2.00/bushel, and with by-product recovery of 59 per cent of the cost of maize, if oil prices are $20/bbl or more' (D O Hall, 1991).

At over 90 billion litres, Brazil is the world's largest ethanol producer. Its National Alcohol Programme (ProAlcohol) was started in 1975 and since then production has increased annually. In 1989, 5 million cars ran on 12 billion litres of pure ethanol and a further 9 million ran on 20 to 22 per cent of alcohol and 78 to 80 per cent gasoline. This industry has highlighted the very real benefits of investing in renewable technologies. At present, up to 700,000 people are employed directly in the ProAlcohol programme with much additional related employment. Moreover, the national dependence on oil imports has decreased, dramatically improving Brazil's balance of payment deficit. Given that efficiency can be increased and the level of production by raised by using the remaining sugar cane residues, mainly bagasse, this renewable source of technology is likely to increase its internal market. It is also possible efficiently to convert ethanol into electricity.

Brazil and the US both illustrate the ways in which renewables can have both a considerable impact on indigenous energy production and provide end-use energy to many different consumers. They also highlight the need for government intervention in economic, industrial and agricultural policy. In addition, government incentives can provide financial encouragement for small scale production as well as research and development. Brazil's renewable programme demonstrates how decentralized developments can encourage regional equality and sustainability, promote national energy security and new production processes, and initiate employment opportunities. The fact that ethanol has achieved a market in the US and Brazil demonstrates its relative competitiveness in relation to conventional energy resources. Indeed, the technology developed in Brazil is now part of an export industry to developing countries. The ethanol project illustrates how the socio-economic limitations on diffusion must be overcome through high level political and economic intervention.

BIOGAS

Biogas, like other forms of derived energy, can benefit dramatically from drives in production and efficiency. Needless to say, a 50 per cent increase in end use conversion efficiency means only half the volume of biomass is required for the same energy output. This argument has formed the basis of much research and development into the design and efficiency of stoves and boilers which has highlighted a number of important changes needed in biogas production. These are research into the whole fuel cycle from production to conversion, the optimization of the fermentation process and the incorporation of efficient gas turbines rather than steam combustion systems.

Even though biogas technology has not yet reached its full potential, it currently provides a multiple end-use fuel to much of China. Biogas can be used for cooking, lighting, running pumps and other agricultural machinery, and electricity generation as well as internal combustion engines. Even though China has struggled to develop its biogas technology over the last 50 years, many of the 5 million household digesters were initially of poor design and are no longer used. However, it is estimated that biogas is currently used daily for cooking by 25

million people in China. In addition to this, a further 10,000 large or medium sized biogas digesters are used in light industries and farms. Many of these larger digesters transfer the gas to centralized supply stations or biogas electric power stations. The Chinese biogas programme is unique because, in addition to the digestion of animal and human dung, an estimated 2 Mt of straw is also used annually. It was estimated by Daxiong et al that even including capital and operating costs, out of 58 biogas plants the internal rate of return (IRR) varies from between 59 per cent to 114 per cent (D O Hall, 1991). Socio-economic changes in China are affecting the production levels of biogas. In particular, a decrease in central funding is leading small producers to buy coal or wood, which leaves them free to engage in alternative modes of employment. However, these changes will probably mean that China's biogas programmes will become more centralized and industrialized.

This example provides an illustration of bottom up development where individual cooperation is essential to the well being of the system. Most community biogas projects have not, however, been sustainable in the long term, usually because of maintenance costs or changing biomass supply. Biogas can supply suitable amounts of energy for household, transport and small industrial processes but it is unlikely, given present modes of development, to provide large quantities of hard energy for heavy industry. Nevertheless, drives in efficiency have increased the net energy output and new designs will bring benefits to many in the developing world. Biogas is an indigenous energy resource that can be upgraded at all stages of production and conversion, and its potential for bioenergy production, given the right investment and social structures is considerable.

It is crucial to consider the economics of production at the same time as the value to the consumer. For example, both biogas and ethanol production costs vary greatly depending on the regional location and management of the installation, whereas the value to the consumer is based on its competitive global or regional energy market.

WIND

The global environmental benefits of wind electricity generation are well documented. Once the wind generators are established they are a pollution free technology. However, with the exception of irrigation systems, wind generation uptake in developing countries has been poor. None the less, in some developed countries, wind generation is now partly supplying to the national grid.

Sixteen wind farms have been installed in the UK in projects awarded since 1991 under the Non-Fossil Fuel Obligation (NFFO). They produce 98.6 MW of renewable electricity supply. However, of the 43 contracts awarded so far under the NFFO, only half have been granted planning permission. The period over which the NFFO operates has recently been increased to 15 years, so it is now easier for wind farms to make a commercial return. It has been estimated that the development of 3000 (500 kW) wind turbine generators on land and 2000 (8 MW) offshore generators could supply up to 20 per cent of UK's energy demand.

In the US, thousands of wind generators currently supply 1.5 GW of power to the grid system and many more supply domestic users directly. Much of this development has been in California where a plentiful supply of wind as well as financial opportunities and tax incentives have encouraged both small and large investors.

Despite the socio-economic obstacles currently affecting the success of renewable energy technologies, the prospects for renewable energy are good. As conversion efficiencies improve, these technologies will quickly move into a competitive position within the energy market. In addition to this, changes in political awareness, agreements on climate regulation and increased awareness of the socio-economic impact of using fossil fuels should begin to favour renewables.

ENVIRONMENTAL IMPACT OF CONVENTIONAL AND NUCLEAR RESOURCES

This section is an overview of the various environmental effects of conventional and nuclear resources, and will highlight the technical opportunities for dealing with them.

Conventional energy resources such as coal, wood, gas etc have an increasingly large and well-documented impact on the global environment. In particular, the emission of carbon dioxide, nitrogen oxides, methane, volatile organic compounds (VOCs) and sulphur dioxide from the combustion process contribute to tropospheric ozone, global warming, acid deposition and forest decline. Global warming itself changes global temperature leading to a rise in sea level. Burning coal for energy produces the highest discharge of CO_2 and SO_2 and transport sector is the main source of NO_x and VOCs. The environmental effects of these emissions are local, regional and global, and at present CO_2 is considered to be the most threatening as it is the largest contributor to global warming. Since pre-industrial times the CO_2 content of the atmosphere has increased by 25 per cent.

At present, a number of ways of reducing CO_2 levels may be considered:

- energy conservation;
- fuel substitution;
- the use of renewable energy;
- nuclear energy;
- alternative transport fuels;
- basic materials recycling;
- CO_2 removal;
- carbon taxes.

(Source: P A Okken, 1991)

The Framework Convention on Climate is an agreement to rectify the environmental effects of conventional fuel generation and consumption. Once ratified, this convention will commit members to a number of developmental preconditions. These involve the preparation of a national strategy to deal with global warming; the development, updating and sharing of GHG inventories; the development of technical innovation to reduce GHGs; exercises in education and public awareness; the development, transfer and use of improved energy efficient technologies.

The quite specific environmental effects of the production of nuclear energy can affect us in a number of different ways. For example, periodic radioactive discharges into the local environment can have a number of biological effects depending on the dosage received:

- cancer;
- genetic effects;
- premature ageing and shortened lifespan;
- thyroid gland damage;
- weight increase;
- mutation.

(Source: Environment Committee 1985–6, p cixvii)

One of the worst modern examples of the environmental impact of nuclear resources was the explosion at Chernobyl in the former Soviet Union on 26 April 1986. It blew aside a 1000 tonne steel lid on the number four reactor and released radioactive material into the environment. Some 235,000 people were evacuated from the surrounding area, deformities are now common in the region, and so, too, are higher levels of cancer. The radiation was carried west over Europe and levels of fall-out reached as much as 200,000 bacquerels of caesium per square kilometre. Vast numbers of sheep and cattle were destroyed.

The risks of reprocessing uranium oxide and the storage of low, intermediate and high level waste are still high. Radioactive waste may be disposed of by:

- sea disposal;
- near surface disposal;
- disposal at existing deep mines;
- offshore boreholes;
- engineered near surface facilities (for example, Sellafield);
- deep geological facility on land;
- sea bed options.

(Source: Environment Committee 1985–86, p xi–xii)

All these options have very real disadvantages. To give just one example, recent ecological discoveries show that microbial activity exists 2–3 km below the earth's surface at extreme temperature and pressure. This undermines the possibility for deep repositories where the objective is to find a closed system.

FUTURE LEGISLATION AND ITS EFFECTS ON ENERGY POLICY

In 1972, member countries of the OECD agreed to base all environmental policies on a polluter pays principle (PPP). This can be thought of as an economic efficiency measure encouraging the internalization of environmental costs and incorporating them into the prices of products, goods or services.

The basic argument is that environmental resources are finite. However, because many of them have no perceived market value, their exploitation is optimal. To counter this the OECD Council recommended that public measures were necessary in the effort to reduce environmental damage by ensuring that the price paid for goods, depending on the quality and/or quantity of resources, reflected their relative scarcity. The OECD Council warned that, in a number of circumstances, the cost of remedying environmental damage may be considerable and often not worth the investment. The adoption of pollution taxes would, however, provide a suitable market based incentive for a reduction in resource misuse and in environmental damage.

Pearce et al (1989) provide a simplified example of how a more suitable system for the pricing of products and services could be constructed. The marginal cost (MC) is the cost of producing an extra unit of output. However, this cost fails, at present, to reflect the wider social and environmental costs of production. By widening the pricing arena to include these, the price (P) of a product in the market will be determined by:

$$P = MC + MEC = MSC$$

where MEC is the marginal external cost and MSC is the marginal social cost. Under the PPP pricing system the MSC will reflect the MC and the MEC. (Source: D Pearce, 1989.)

The polluter pays principal can help to reduce GHG emissions in a number of ways. However, the diversity of energy systems and sub-systems makes implementation extremely problematic. There are three principal questions to be asked. At what level of the market should these taxes be imposed? How should these policy tools be implemented? Which different taxes best suit varying pollutants? Answers are vital if environmental security is to be efficiency improved and the cost is to be minimized. Although much work has been carried out on the theoretical basis for policy intervention, its practical implications remain largely unknown.

For the sake of simplicity, we may see the

energy system as having a number of different components; primary fuel production, distribution and conversion, distribution and end-use, and the utilization of fuels or electricity in providing energy services (J D Scheraga et al, 1992). The application of taxes can be at any one of these even though at present imposing taxes at a primary level of production is favoured. In addition, taxes can be applied to carbon content, energy content or value. It is important that levels and types of tax are applied to accord with specific levels within the system. The result of inaccurate calculations would lead to misunderstanding the potential impacts of a specific tax. For example, the point at which a carbon tax of $120 per tonne at a primary level of production would mean stabilized CO_2 emissions at 1990 levels by 2030.

Implementing these policy tools is essential if cost-effectiveness and a reduction in emissions are to be adequately achieved. However, this can only be incorporated as part of the development of an effective fiscal policy package. The failure adequately to impose specific taxes and tax levels at different stages in the energy system can lead to an excessive tax burden which would be a failure in social welfare.

Polluter pays policies will increase the complexity of ascribing market prices to specific goods or services. The level of the market, suitable tax levels and appropriate taxes will have to be calculated for each specific product. As energy policy responds to these issues, it will necessarily become increasingly sophisticated.

POLICIES FOR SUSTAINABLE ENERGY FUTURES

Each specific energy source has its own particular impact upon the socio-economic, political and environmental system. Therefore, flexible sustainable energy policies that reflect this are the first need. Features of these policies are as follows.

- The satisfaction of and right to basic human needs in both the developed and developing world.
- The creation of fair economic comparisons between conventional and renewable resources (the principal demand is for externalities to be internalized).
- The correct implementation of taxes on energies to assist in reducing environmental pollution. In particular, that the range of taxes is ascribed at real prices and to all pollutants.
- The promotion of energy-efficiency improvements and improved access to environmentally benign technology.
- Increased research and development in renewables technology.
- The generation of additional financial resources and equal access to these resources.
- The promotion of national and regional self-reliance.
- The incorporation of energy strategies that reflect the nature of all socio-environmental problems at a global level.

Energy futures can reasonably be considered as environmental futures. At a time when bad energy planning and provisions can easily be seen to have cost lives and money, and to have risked the long term future of humanity, it is of paramount importance that energy policies reflect the shifting requirements of environmental and social sustainability. The world's energy industries must pay greater attention to the end-use requirements of individuals rather than to the mere provision of historically projected trends. The challenge is to create the society we want rather than to predict the society we will have.

Appendix I

UNITS AND CONVERSION FACTORS

THE BASIS OF ENERGY UNITS

Work

To a scientist work is done when a force acts upon an object, overcomes any resistance stopping it from moving and moves it for some distance. If the applied force is F and the distance is d, then work is defined by:

The work done = F x d

In the SI system of units F is measured in newtons, d in metres and the work is done in joules.

Potential and kinetic energy

In Chapter 1 it was suggested that energy could be thought of as stored work. There are two types of stored work, known as potential energy and kinetic energy.

The potential energy (PE) of an object represents its excess of energy with reference to some datum. This 'stored' energy many occur in different ways, for example:

• gravitational P E arises from the work done against the force of gravity in lifting the object a certain height;

• elastic P E arises from the work done against internal forces when compressing or stretching an object.

The most commonly discussed P E is that due to gravity and it is calculated from:

$$PE = mgh$$

where m is the mass of the object in kg, g the acceleration due to gravity ($9.8 \ ms^{-2}$) and h the height in metres through which the object has been raised.

When an object is subjected to a force it accelerates and increases in speed. At any particular speed the work done by the forces in accelerating the object to that speed is stored as its kinetic energy. The amount of kinetic energy is worked out from:

$$KE = \tfrac{1}{2}mv^2$$

where m is the mass of the object in kg and v is its speed in metres/sec.

Energy values calculated from these formulae will be expressed in joules. In principle any energy transfer can be described in terms of kinetic and potential energy changes, and so all energy values can be reduced to the common unit of the joule.

OTHER UNITS IN COMMON USE

Although the joule and watt are standard SI units of energy and power, there are many others in common use. Some of them are discussed below.

Electron-volt

In atomic and nuclear physics the electron-volt is used. This is because the basic experimental techniques involve rapidly moving particles which have their speed induced by acceleration in electric fields. The mechanism involved is summarized by the equation:

$$qV = \tfrac{1}{2}mv^2$$

where q is the charge on the particle, V the voltage used in accelerating the particle, m its mass and v its final velocity.

Because q is a constant quantity, the kinetic energy of the particle is proportional to the voltage V and this voltage is used colloquially to denote the energy of the particle. The energy of the particle in joules is equal to qV. When the particle is an electron, the value of q is e, the elementary charge and the energy of the particle is then said to be V electron-volts. The number of electron-volts, V, must be multiplied by charge (the value of e) to convert them to joules.

Calorie

In food and nutrition the Calorie is the most commonly used energy unit. This unit is derived from an old system relating energy to the amount of heat (1 calorie) required to change the temperature of 1 gramme of water by 1°C. Note that the food Calorie is written with a capital C and the heat calorie with a small c. The food Calorie is 1000 times greater than the heat calorie and is sometimes referred to as 1 kilocalorie. To convert Calories to joules use:

1 Calorie = 4200 joules

Kilowatt-hour

In the electricity industry the kilowatt-hour (kWh) is used as the unit of electrical energy and is referred to as the unit. It is the amount of energy used in an hour by an appliance which has a power rating of 1 kW. Hence:

$$1\text{kWh} = 1000 \times 60 \times 60 = 3.6 \times 10^6 \text{ joules}$$

Therm

In the gas industry the therm is the unit of energy used to describe the energy available from burning a certain volume of gas. The conversion factor is approximately:

$$1 \text{ therm} = 29 \text{ kWh} = 10^8 \text{ joules}$$

Barrel and toe

In the oil industry the barrel and tonne-of-oil (toe) equivalent are used. The approximate conversion factors are:

$$1 \text{ barrel} = 1700 \text{ kWh} = 6 \times 10^9 \text{ joules}$$

$$1 \text{ toe} = 7.5 \text{ barrels} = 4.5 \times 10^{10} \text{ joules}$$

Tonne

In the coal industry the tonne of coal is used. The approximate conversion factor is:

$$1 \text{ tcc} = 7500 \text{ kWh} = 2.7 \times 10^{10} \text{ joules}$$

Other units

In the US the foot, pound, second system of units is still in use. British thermal units (Btu) are used to measure energy, power is measured in brake horsepower (BHP). The conversion factor is:

1 Btu = 1055 joules

CONVERSION FACTORS BETWEEN UNITS

Petroleum

1 million tonnes	7.5 million barrels
	425 million therms
	1.7 million tonnes of coal
	12,500 GWh of energy

Coal

1 million tonnes	600,000 tonnes of oil
	250 million therms
	7500 GWh of energy

Natural Gas

1 million therms	100 million cubic feet
	2.75 million cubic metres
	4000 tonnes of coal
	2400 tonnes of oil
	29.3 GWh of energy

Electricity generation

If it is assumed that electricity can be generated from the fossil fuels with an efficiency of 30 per cent the list below shows the amounts of particular fuels needed to generate 1 GWh of electricity.

1GWh	500 tonnes of coal
	280 tonnes of oil
	115 therms of natural gas

Other conversions

Mass

1 kilogramme = 2.2046 lb
1 tonne = 1000 kg = 0.9842 ton
1 ton = 2.240 lb = 1.016 tonne
1 short ton = 2000 lb

Volume

$1 m^3 = 35.31 ft^3$
1 litre = 1 imperial (UK) pint = 0.264 US gallons
1 imperial gallon (UK) = 1.2 US gallons = 4.546 litres
1 barrel = 42 US gallons = 34.97 UK gallons = 159 litres

Heat and energy

1 Btu = 1.055 kJ
1 therm = 100,000 Btu = 105,506 kJ = 29.3 kWh
1 GWh = 34,121 therms
1 cal = 4.1868 J

Power

1 brake horsepower (BHP) = 745.7 W

Multipliers

kilo (k) = 10^3
mega (M) = 10^6
giga (G) = 10^9
tera (T) = 10^{12}
peta (P) = 10^{15}
exa (E) = 10^{18}

1	Mozambique	29	Ghana	63	Paraguay	93	Libya
2	Ethiopia	31	Sri Lanka	64	Tunisia	97	Saudi Arabia
3	Chad	32	Guinea	65	Turkey	98	Spain
4	Tanzania	33	Yemen, People's	66	Peru	99	Ireland
5	Bangladesh		Democratic Republic	67	Jordan	100	Israel
6	Malawi	34	Indonesia	68	Chile	101	Singapore
7	Somalia	35	Mauritania	69	Syria	102	Hong Kong
8	Zaire	43	Bolivia	70	Costa Rica	103	New Zealand
10	Lao	44	Philipines	71	Mexico	104	Australia
11	Nepal	45	Yemen, Arab	72	Mauritius	105	United Kingdom
12	Madagascar		Republic	73	Poland	106	Italy
14	Mali	46	Senegal	74	Malaysia	107	Kuwait
15	Burundi	47	Zimbabwe	75	Panama	108	Belgium
16	Uganda	48	Egypt	76	Brazil	109	The Netherlands
17	Nigeria	49	Dominican Republic	80	South Africa	110	Austria
18	Zambia	51	Papua New Guinea	81	Algeria	111	United Arab
19	Niger	52	Morocco	82	Hungary		Emirates
20	Rwanda	53	Honduras	83	Uruguay	112	France
21	China	54	Guatemala	84	Argentina	113	Canada
22	India	55	Congo	85	Yugoslavia	114	Denmark
23	Pakistan	56	El Salvador	86	Gabon	115	Germany
24	Kenya	57	Thailand	87	Venezuela	116	Finland
25	Togo	58	Botswana	88	Trinidad and Tobago	117	Sweden
26	Central African	59	Cameroon	89	Korea	118	USA
	Republic	60	Jamaica	90	Portugal	119	Norway
27	Haiti	61	Ecuador	91	Greece	120	Japan
28	Benin	62	Colombia	92	Oman	121	Switzerland

Table I.1 *Countries corresponding to the numbers in Figures 1.1, 1.2, 1.3 and 1.6*

Appendix II

BACKGROUND THEORY OF COST BENEFIT ANALYSIS

INTRODUCTION

Cost benefit analysis (CBA) is the quantitative basis for decision making in investment affairs. It is an evaluation methodology in which impacts are measured in monetary values. Here this theory will be reviewed having in mind its applications in energy projects.

DATA REQUIREMENTS

Techno-economics begins with the compilation of all expenditures and incomes connected with a particular project. The most relevant data for undertaking this task can be divided in the following classes:

- investment parameters;
- equipment;
- expenditures;
- income;
- returns; and
- depreciation.

In the following sections a detailed explanation of the significance of the different parameters used in this study is presented.

INTEREST RATE

Interest rate represents the cost of borrowing money; it is a function both of supply and demand for money, and of government policy:

$$I = (1 + i)(1 + f) - 1, \qquad (1.1)$$

where I is the market interest rate, i is the actual cost of money due to supply and demand and government policy, and f is the general inflation rate.

The relation between the present and future value of money can be given in the following equation:

$$V_t = V_0 (1 + I)^t, \qquad (1.2)$$

where V_t represents the value of money at the end of the year t, V_0 the present value of money, I the interest rate and t the time in years.

DISCOUNT RATE

In order to provide present value of money from its future value, equation (1.2) can be rearranged as:

$$V_0 = \frac{V_t}{(1+DR)^t} \qquad (1.3)$$

where DR represents the discount rate, a parameter that in essence has the same significance as that of the interest rate.

INFLATION RATE

Prices paid for goods and services may increase for different reasons. This feature is called inflation. It is, normally, expressed as an annual percentage and determined by:

$$f(t) = \frac{PI(t)}{PI(t_0)} - 1, \qquad (1.4)$$

where $PI(t)$ is the price index at year t and $PI(t_0)$ the price index at year t_0.

ENERGY ESCALATION RATE

In the analysis of projects which are heavily dependent on energy, it is recommended that separate account of the development in energy prices be taken, which may not conform to the general inflation rate. The determination of the annual energy escalation rate should be based on the price index of the particular energy source being investigated. Using the expected real increase in the cost of energy and the general inflation rate, the energy escalation rate can be determined as:

$$e(t) = [1 + \varepsilon(t)][1 + f(t) - 1 \qquad (1.5)$$

where $e(t)$ is the annual escalation rate, $e^*(t)$ is the real annual rate of increase in the cost of energy and $f(t)$ is the annual inflation rate.

SERVICE LIFE OF AN INSTALLATION

The service life of an installation is the number of years beyond which the system becomes more expensive to maintain than a new acquisition or when the efficiency of the system deteriorates such that the output product is unacceptable in quality and/or in quantity.

INVESTMENT COSTS

All costs in money and assets needed to carry out the project concerned are known as investment costs. It includes the capital costs and recurring or revenue costs.

RESIDUAL VALUE OF A PLANT

The residual value of a plant or of its individual components is determined from the possibilities of its alternative use. On the assumption that equipment or parts of a plant can be sold, the expected liquidation yield from the sale is usually taken as the residual value.

MAJOR OPERATING COSTS

The major operating costs of a project include:

- manpower;
- maintenance; and
- energy.

In utilizing solar, wind and hydro-energy, as well as geothermal energy, it can be assumed that the energy source will be directly available in the required quantity and quality, free of charge, after the installation of the necessary plant at any suitable selected site. Nevertheless, when biomass or conventional energy sources are used, it must be noted that costs will arise for their procurement, transport, processing and storage for feeding the plant, and for discharging and discarding the residues.

DEPRECIATION

Depreciation can be defined as the decrease in value of an asset due to use and/or time. A very simple operational definition of depreciation can be given as:

$$AD = \frac{CA - RV}{N} \qquad (1.6)$$

where AD represents the annual depreciation, CA is the cost of the asset, RV is the present residual value of the asset and N is its service life.

PROCEDURE OF CBA

In this section methods to undertake CBA or financial analysis will be summarized. Normally, six approaches are used in the appraisal of projects as follows:

1. net present value (NPV);
2. internal rate of return;
3. annuity;
4. cost annuity comparison;
5. calculation of pay-back period;
6. sensitivity analysis.

It is well known that a project subjected to any method of financial evaluation will have its costs and benefits spread over a number of years. In order to compare one project with another, one must reduce the time stream of costs to a single number. This is most easily done by the use of a present value function (PVF). This function can be used to determine the present value of a yearly income or expenditure which escalates at some fixed percentage each year from year 1 to year N. It is defined as

$$PVF(DR,B,N) = \frac{1+B}{DR-B}\left\{1 - \left\{\frac{1+B}{1+DR}\right\}^n\right\},$$

$$(1.7)$$

$$PVF(DR,DR,n) = 1 \text{ for } DR=B, \qquad (1.8)$$

where DR is the discount rate, B is the escalation rate (general inflation rate f or energy escalation rate e) and N is the number of years.

Any yearly expenditure that is expected to escalate at some fixed rate B, owing to inflation f or energy price escalation e, may be multiplied by PVF (DR,B,N) in order to determine its present value.

For the special case where B = 0:

$$PVF(DR,0,N) = \frac{(1+DR)^N - 1}{DR(1+DR)^N} = \frac{1}{CRF(DR,0,N)}$$

The reciprocal of the PVF with B = 0 is commonly referred to as the capital recovery factor (CRF). When multiplied by an initial sum of money, the CRF determines the periodic payment necessary to pay back that sum of money at interest DR over N periods.

Net present value

The NPV of an investment project at the point in time t = 0 is the sum of present values of all the cash inflows and outflows linked to it. In simple terms the NPV can be indicated as:

NPV = Annual Returns − Investment Costs + Liquidation Yield

$$NPV = (INC - EXP)PVF(DR,f,N) - \sum_{t=0}^{N} I_c(t)\frac{(1+f)^t}{(1+DR)^t} + RV\frac{(1+f)^N}{(1+DR)^{N'}} \quad (1.10)$$

where INC is the annual income, EXP is the annual expenditure, I_c is the investment cost, t is the period of investment, N is the service life of investment, DR is the discount rate, f is the general inflation rate, RV is the residual value of the investment project and PVF is the present value function.

An investment project is only profitable when:

NPV ≥ 0

In comparing several projects for investment, the NPV of each should be compared and investment with the highest NPV should be selected.

Internal rate of return

The internal rate of return (IRR) represents the critical discount rate, that results in a zero NPV for an investment.

An investment project is profitable if

IRR ≥ DR

Comparing different investment projects, the projects with the highest IRR is the most profitable.

Annuity method

The annuity method aims to convert all the net cash flows connected with an investment project into a series of annual payments of equal months. The conversion takes place by multiplying the NPV by CRF (DR,N):

annuity = NPV x CRF (DR,N)   (1.11)

An investment is considered profitable when

annuity≥ 0

Comparing different investment projects, the project with the highest annuity should be adopted.

Cost annuity comparison method

This method is a shortened form of the annuity method without the inclusion of income in the calculation. Cost annuity is given by:

cost annuity =

$$(1 - DR)^t \left\{ EXP \times PVF(DR,f,N) + \Sigma^N_{t=0} \frac{1}{CRF(DR,N)} \times I_c(t) \; (1+f)^t \right\}$$

(1.12)

In comparing different investment projects, the one with the lowest cost annuity should be chosen.

Pay-back period

Beginning with the year of the first payment, the present values of the annual net cash flows are summed until the total reaches a value of zero. The time from commissioning up to this point is called the pay-back period.

An investment project is favourable if the capital invested plus a minimum acceptable rate of interest is recovered by means of anticipated returns within the service life or within a maximum acceptable pay-back period, which must be shorter than the technical service life.

In evaluating the relative acceptability of alternative investment, it is assumed that the investment with the short pay-back period is the most favourable.

Sensitivity analysis

Since techno-economics deals with the future, of which one can never be certain, a single evaluation of economics with some expected values of variables seldom provides sufficient information on which to base a wise decision, due to the fact that these variables may contain uncertainties.

Sensitivity analysis is a tool for evaluating the effects of uncertainties, quantifying the economic consequence of a potential but unpredictable development in important parameters.

Generally, values of investment parameters, equipment, expenditures etc are varied by certain percentages from the expected value and the effects upon the output financial parameters are investigated.

Appendix III

ADDITIONAL INFORMATION FOR CHAPTER 4

1   Breakdown of journeys by mode of transport, region and purpose.

Main mode *Journey purpose*	*Car*	*Rail*	*Local bus*	*Other**	*Walk*	*Total*
Work and education	40.9	6.3	3.7	3.8	0.8	55.5
Personal business	27.8	1.4	3.3	2.6	1.4	36.5
Leisure	54.6	3.7	2.3	6.3	1.2	68.1
All purposes	123.3	11.4	9.3	12.7	3.4	160.1

* Includes other buses (eg works, school, express or tour buses), cycles, motorcycles, taxis, internal flights.

Table III.1 *Distance (km)/person/week by journey, purpose and main mode of transport for journeys over 1.6 km, 1985/6*

Main mode	*London*	Urban areas		*Rural areas*	*All areas*
		Other urban	*Small towns*		
Cars	109.5	106.6	143.5	181.9	123.3
Rail	26.2	9.2	8.1	10.9	11.4
Local bus	9.7	10.8	7.1	5.8	9.3
Other	10.5	12.6	14.2	13.7	12.7
Walk (>1.6km)	2.9	4.0	3.2	1.9	3.4
All modes	158.8	143.2	176.6	214.2	160.1

Table III.2 *Distance (km)/person/week by type of area and main mode of transport, 1985/6*

Journey purpose	London	Urban areas Other urban areas	Small areas	Rural areas	All areas
Work and education	59.9	48.1	58.9	79.7	55.5
Personal business	31.9	31.9	41.2	55.2	36.5
Leisure	66.8	63.1	75.8	79.4	68.1
All purposes	158.6	143.1	176.1	214.3	160.1

Source for these tables: Department of Transport, 1988

Table III.3 *Distance (km)/person/week by type of area and journey purpose, 1985/6*

2 The specific energy consumption (SEC) is calculated for these two sets of data using the following definitions:

For passenger transport:

$$SEC = \frac{\text{Fuel consumption/unit distance travelled} \times \text{Gross calorific value of fuel used}}{\text{Passengers carried} + \text{driver}}$$

and is measured in MJ/passenger-kilometre
For freight transport:

$$SEC = \frac{\text{Fuel consumption/unit distance travelled} \times \text{Gross calorific value of fuel used}}{\text{Weight of freight (tonnes)}}$$

and is measured in MJ/tonne-kilometre.

3 Public service vehicles in the UK

Vehicle type	Population	% diesel	Average km/year	Energy use PJ/year
Minibus	56,610	53	25,000	7.2
Single deck	43,142	94	50,000	23.7
Double deck	28,220	95	50,000	19.7
Taxis*	26,183	100	30,000	3.6
Total	154,155	81	–	54.2

* Does not include Private Hire cars
Source: Department of Transport

Table III.4 *Passenger transport vehicles, Great Britain, 1986*

Vehicle and journey type	Seats	Vehicle occupancy %	SEC MJ/ passenger-km
Suburban minibus	15	25–50	1.6–0.8
Suburban single-decker	33	25–50	1.2–0.6
Motorway single decker	50	25–50	1.0–0.5
City Centre double-decker	75	50–75	0.4–0.3
Suburban double-decker	75	25–50	0.9–0.5

Source: Department of Transport 1988

Table III.5 *Specific energy consumption for public passenger transport, Great Britain, 1986*

4   Passenger rail transport in the UK

Mode of traction	Loaded train-km (10^6 km)	Energy consumption (GJ/100 train-km)	Energy use (PJ)
British Rail			
High speed train	34.3	19.7	6.7
Diesel locomotive	54.1	18.6	10.0
Electric locomotive	30.1	23.9	7.2
Diesel multiple unit	82.5	10.0	8.3
Electric multiple unit	126.7	8.8	11.1
London Underground			
Electric train	48.0	12.2	5.9
auxiliaries	–	–	1.0
Other urban railways			
Electric train	7.0	12.5	0.9
Totals	382.7	–	51.1

Source: Department of Transport, 1988

Table III.6 *Passenger transport by rail, Great Britain, 1986*

Operator/Service	Passenger-km (10^6)
British Rail	
Inter-City services	12500
Network Southeast	13300
Local provincial	4800
Urban services	
London Underground	6200
Strathclyde PTE	38
Tyne and Wear PTE	296
Total	37134

Source: Department of Transport, 1988

Table III.7 *Passenger traffic, Great Britain, 1986*

Mode of traction and journey	MJ/seat-km	Assumed train occupancy (%)	Average SEC (MJ/ pass.km)
Intercity trip (high speed train)	0.46	39	1.2
Intercity trip (electric locomotive)	0.53	40	1.3
Provincial/sub-urban trip by diesel multiple unit	0.30	22	1.4
Provincial/sub-urban trip by electric multiple unit	0.26	22	1.2
Underground train journey	0.22	15	1.4

Source: Department of Transport, 1988

Table III.8 *Specific energy consumption for rail passenger transport, Great Britain, 1986*

5 Details of freight transport in the UK by road and rail

Vehicle type	Number licensed	10^9 vehicle-km			
		Built-up roads	Non built-up roads	Motorways	Total
Vans: up to 1 ton	838,528		No data		
Light utility vehicles	204,668		No data		
Vans: 1 ton to 1.5 ton	795,240		No data		
Vans: over 1.5 ton ⎫	197,084	4.40	5.83	2.88	13.11
2-axle trucks ⎭	350,499				
3-axle trucks	30,176	0.28	0.61	0.24	1.13
4-axle trucks	21,938	0.19	0.56	0.27	1.01
Articulated:					
up to 25 ton	11,423	0.10	0.34	0.20	0.64
25–32.5 ton	50,573	0.47	1.51	1.93	3.91
over 32.5 ton	31,941	0.16	0.97	1.20	2.32

Source: Department of Transport, 1988

Table III.9 *Road transport of freight, Great Britain, 1986*

Train type		Loaded train-km (million)	Energy consumption (GJ/100 train-km)
Freight:	*diesel locomotive*	43.9	19.9
	electric locomotive	6.1	18.3
Parcels:	*diesel locomotive*	16.0	11.2
Total		66.0	

Source: Department of Transport, 1988

Table III.10 *Freight train operations, Great Britain, 1986*

6 Effect of Technical Changes on Fuel Consumption in PSVs

	Vehicle type	Built-up roads	Non built-up roads	Motorways
Overall-current emissions regulations	Minibus/taxi	–4%	–4%	–5%
	Single/half deck buses	–6%	–6%	–7%
	Double deck buses	–6%	–6%	–7%
Overall-stringent emissions regulations	Minibus/taxi	–2%	–2%	–3%
	Single/half deck buses	+2%	+2%	+1%
	Double deck buses	+3%	+3%	+2%

NB + indicates an increase and – a decrease in fuel consumption
Source: Department of Transport, 1988

Table III.11 *Changes to PSV fuel consumption due to rapid technical change*

7 The possible energy savings resulting from changes to buildings and their appliances.

Insulation of roof and walls and double glazing	20–40
Draughtproofing, door seals etc	5–10
New boiler	30–40
Control systems	10–20
Reducing distribution losses and heat recovery	5–10
Overall for boiler systems	55–75
* for electrical systems*	30–55

Source: Department of Energy, 1989

Table III.12 *Possible cost-effective energy savings in space heating (%)*

Reduction in water temperature from 70°C to 60°C	20
Reduction in water use from taps and showers	10
Heat recovery	5–10
Point of use heating	10–20
Overall	35–50

Source: Department of Energy, 1989

Table III.13 *Possible cost-effective energy savings in water heating (%)*

In the commercial sector	50
In the domestic sector	35

Table III.14 *Possible cost-effective energy savings in lighting (%)*

Washing machines	20
Dishwashers	10
Refrigerators	25
Fridge-freezers	25
Freezers	25
Television	25

Source: Watt Committee Report No 23

Table III.15 *Possible cost-effective energy savings in appliances in domestic dwellings (%)*

BIBLIOGRAPHY

CHAPTER 1

Devins, D W *Energy – Its Physical Impact on the Environment*, J Wiley, Chichester, 1982.

Department of Energy, *Development of Oil and Gas Reserves in the UK*, HMSO, London, 1990.

DGXVI, *Energy in Europe. Annual Energy Review*, p 9, 1993.

Digest of UK Energy Statistics, HMSO London, (annually).

Energy for Planet Earth. Readings from *Scientific American*, Freeman, San Francisco, 1991.

Energy and Power: A Scientific American Book, Freeman, San Francisco, 1971.

FAO, *Tropical Forest Resources*, Forestry Paper No 30, 1986.

Foley, G, *The Energy Question*, fourth edn, Penguin, Harmondsworth, 1992.

Fowler, J H *Energy and the Environment*, second edn, McGraw-Hill, London, 1984.

Humphrey, W S and Stanislaw, J, Economic Growth and Energy Consumption in the UK 1700–1975, *Energy Policy*, March 1979, 29–42.

Leach, G et al *Energy and Growth: A Comparison of 13 Industrial and Developing Countries*, Butterworth, London, 1986

Kraushaar, J J and Ristinen, R A, *Energy and Problems of a Technical Society*, second edn, J Wiley, Chichester, 1993.

Oppenheim, D, *Small Solar Buildings in Cool Northern Climates*, Architectural Press, London, 1981.

Simmons, I G, *Changing the Face of the Earth: Culture, Environment, History*, Basil Blackwell, Oxford 1989.

Slesser, M, *Energy in the Economy*, Macmillan Press, London, 1978.

Smith, K, The Biofuel Transition *Energy Policy*, No 12, 1992.

Thomas, J A G, *Energy Analysis*, IPC Technology Press, Guildford, 1977

World Bank, *World Development Report*, OUP, Oxford, 1990.

CHAPTER 2

Hohmeyer, O, *Social Costs of Energy Consumption*, Springer Verlag, 1988.

Hubbard, H M, *The Economics of Safety and Physical Risk*, Basil Blackwell, Oxford 1989.

Jones-Lee, H and van Ierland, E (eds), *Valuation*

190

Methods and Policy Making in Environmental Economics, Elsevier Science Publishers, Oxford, 1989.

Pearce, D W, and Markandya, A, *Environmental Policy, Benefits: Monetary Evaluation*, OECD, Paris, 1989.

Pearce, D W, Markandya, A and Barbier, E B, *Blueprint for a Green Economy*, Earthscan, London, 1989.

CHAPTER 3

African Development Fund. *Terms of Reference for the African Energy Programme*

Bradley, P et al 1985 Development Research and Energy Planning in Kenya. *Ambio* 14: 228–36

O'Keefe, P *Energy – People's Power*, 1992.

O'Keefe, P and Soussan, J *Power to Some People.* ROAPPE,1991.

Soussan, J, *Primary Resources and Energy in the Third World*. Routledge, London, 1988.

Soussan, J and Mercer, E, *Fuelwood: An Analysis of Problems and Solutions*. World Bank, 1990.

Soussan, J O'Keefe, P and Mercer, E, Finding local answers to fuelwood problems: a typological approach. *Natural Resources Forum*. Butterworth Heinemann. London, 1990.

Van gelder, B and O'Keefe, P, *The New Forester,* 1992.

CHAPTER 4

Anderson, V, *Energy Efficiency Policies*, Routledge, London, 1993.

Digest of UK Energy Statistics, HMSO, London, (annually).

Energy for Planet Earth. Readings from *Scientific American,* Freeman, San Francisco, 1991.

Evans, R D and Herring, H P J *Energy Use and Energy Efficiency in the UK Domestic Sector up to the Year 2000*, Department of Energy, HMSO, London, 1990.

Herring, H, Hardcastle, R and Phillipson, R, *Energy Use and Energy Efficiency in UK Commercial and Public Buildings up to the Year 2000*, Department of Energy, HMSO, London, 1988.

Johansson, B, Bodlund, B and Williams, R H (eds), *Electricity: Efficient End-Use and New Generation Technologies and their Planning Implications*, Lund University Press, Lund, 1989.

Leach, G et al, A Low Energy Strategy for the UK, *Science Reviews*, 1979.

Leach, G and Gowen, M, *Household Energy Handbook: An Interim Guide and Reference Manual*, World Bank, Washington DC, 1987.

Martin, D J and Shock, R A W, *Energy Use and Energy Efficiency in UK Transport up to the Year 2000*, Department of Energy, HMSO, London, 1989.

Thurlow, G G (ed), *Technological Responses to the Greenhouse Effect*, Elsevier Applied Science, Oxford, 1990.

Transport Statistics of Great Britain 1979–1989, Department of Transport, HMSO, London, 1991.

CHAPTER 5

Bending, R and Eden, R, *UK Energy*, OUP, Oxford, 1984.

BP Statistical Review of World Energy, BP, London, 1990.

Brown, G C and Skipsey, E, *Energy Resources: Geology, Supply and Demand*, Open University Press, Milton Keynes, 1986.

Cochrane, R, *Power to the People*, Newnes, 1985

Department of Trade and Industry, *The Energy Report 2: Oil and Gas resources of the United Kingdom*, HMSO, London, 1994.

Eden, R and Evans, E, *Electricity Supply in the UK*, Gower, Aldershot, 1986.

Greenhalgh, G, *The Necessity for Nuclear Power*, Graham and Trotman, London, 1980.

King Hubbert, M, *Resources and Man*, W H Freeman, 1969.

King, S Y and Halfter, S Y, *Underground Power Cables*, Longman, Harlow, 1982.

McMullan, J T, Morgan, R and Murray, R B, *Energy Resources*, second edn, Edward Arnold, London, 1982.

Riva, J P, *World Petroleum Resources and Reserves*, Westview Press, Colorado, 1983.

Roberts, L E J, Liss, P S and Saunders, P A H, *Power Generation and the Environment*, OUP, Oxford, 1990.

Schumacher, D, *Energy: Crisis or Opportunity?* Macmillan, London, 1985.

Tiratsoo, E N, *Natural Gas*, third edn, Scientific Press, 1979.

CHAPTER 6

Bennet, D J and Thomson, J R, *The Elements of Nuclear Power*, Longman Scientifical and Technical, Harlow, 1989.

BMA, *The BMA Guide to Living With Risk*, Penguin Books, Harmondsworth, 1990.

British Nuclear Energy Society, *The Environmental Impact of Nuclear Power*, 1981.

Cheshire, J, Why Nuclear Power Failed the Market Test in the UK, *Energy Policy*, Vol 20, No 8, pp 744, 1992.

Fremlin, J H, *Power Production: What are the Risks?* OUP, Oxford, 1987.

Kraushaar, J J and Ristinen, R A, *Energy and Problems of a Technical Society*, second edn, J Wiley, Chichester, 1993.

MacKerron, G, Nuclear Costs: Why Do they Keep Rising?, *Energy Policy*, Vol 20, No 7, pp 641, 1992.

Martin, A and Harbison, S A, *An Introduction to Radiation Protection*, third edn, Chapman and Hall, London, 1986.

Mosey, D, *Reactor Accidents*, Nuclear Engineering International Special Publication, 1990.

Paterson, W C, *Nuclear Power*, second edn, Penguin Books, Harmondsworth, 1983.

Sutcliffe, C, *The Dangers of Low Level Radiation*, Avebury, London, 1987.

NRPB, *Radiation Exposure of the UK Population – 1988 Review*, 1989.

Rippon, S, *Nuclear Energy*, Heinemann, London, 1984.

'World Reactor Survey', *Nuclear Engineering International*, June 1990.

CHAPTER 7

Baker, A C, *Tidal Power*, Peter Peregrinus for IEE, 1991.

Review of Renewable Energies, *Energy Policy* Vol 19, No 8, 1991.

Flood, M, *Solar Prospects: The Potential for Renewable Energy*, Wildwood House (in association with FOE), 1982.

Hislop, D (Ed) *Energy Options*. Intermediate Technology Publications, London, 1992.

Johansson, T B, Kelly, H, Reddy A, K, Williams, R H, *Renewable Energy*, Island Press, Washington DC, 1992.

Sorenson, B, *Renewable Energy*, Academic Press, London, 1979.

Taylor, R H, *Alternative Energy Sources: for the generation of electricity*, Adam Hilger, Bristol, 1983.

Twidell, J W and Weir, A D, *Renewable Energy Sources*, E and F Spon, London, 1986.

CHAPTER 8

Bourrelier, P H, de la Tour, X and Lacour, J J, Energy in the Long Term, *Energy Policy*, p 311, 1992.

First Report from the Environment Committee, *Radioactive Waste*, HMSO, London, Vol 1, pp 35–44, Session 1985–1986.

Hall, D O, Biomass Energy, *Energy Policy*, Vol 19, No 8, pp 711–20.

Hall, D O, Rosillo-Calle, F and de Groot, P Biomass Energy, Lessons from Case Studies in the Developing Countries, *Energy Policy*, January 1992.

Krause, et al, *Energy Policy in the Greenhouse* pp 1.2–10–12, Earthscan, London, 1991

Middleton, N, O'Keefe, P and Moyo, S, *Tears of the Crocodile*. Pluto Press, London, 1993.

Okken, P A, *CO_2 Reduction Consensus: A Conceptual Framework for Global CO_2 Reduction Targets, the Importance of Energy Technology Development*, The Netherlands Energy Research Foundation (ECN).

Pearce, D, Markandya, A and Barbier, A, *Blueprint for a Green Economy*, Earthscan, London, 1989.

Scheraga, J D and Cristofara, A, *A Comprehensive Strategy to Curb Global Warming*, Forum for Applied Research and Improving the Efficiency of CO_2 Emissions, *Energy Policy*, pp 394–404, May 1992.

Sokona, Y, *Energy and Rural Development in West Africa in International Experience in Energy Policy Research and Planning*, Elan Press, pp 120–2, 1992.

World Bank, *Funding for the Global Environment: The Global Environment Facility*, Discussion Paper, World Bank, Washington DC, 1990.

INDEX